P9-EGN-745

SHOCKING TRUE STORY

SHOCKING TRUE STORY

The Rise and Fall of *Confidential*,
"America's Most Scandalous
Scandal Magazine"

HENRY E. SCOTT

Pantheon Books
New York

Copyright © 2010 by Henry E. Scott

All rights reserved. Published in the United States by Pantheon Books,
a division of Random House, Inc., New York, and in Canada by
Random House of Canada Limited, Toronto.

Pantheon Books and colophon are registered trademarks of Random House, Inc.

Library of Congress Cataloging-in-Publication Data
Scott, Henry, E., [date]
Shocking true story: the rise and fall of Confidential, "America's most
scandalous scandal magazine" / Henry E. Scott.
p. cm.
Includes bibliographical references and index.
ISBN 978-0-375-42139-6 (alk. Paper)
1. Confidential (New York, N.Y.)   2. Tabloid newspapers—
United States—History—20th century.   I. Title.
PN4900.C65S36 2010
051—1dc22   2009023648

www.pantheonbooks.com
Printed in the United States of America
First Edition
2 4 6 8 9 7 5 3 1

To Les Strong, Susan Obrecht, and Philip Claus,
whose willingness to listen helped me learn

Contents

List of Illustrations　　　　ix

1. "Why Joe DiMaggio Is Striking Out with Marilyn Monroe!" *(August 1953)*　　　3

2. "They Started in Their Birthday Suits!" *(November 1953)*　　　11

3. "Winchell Was Right About Josephine Baker" *(April 1953)*　　　19

4. "Exclusive Photos! How Rita Hayworth's Children Were Neglected" *(September 1954)*　　　30

5. "The Strange Death of J. Robert Oppenheimer's RED Sweetheart" *(November 1954)*　　　43

6. "Does Desi Really Love Lucy?" *(January 1955)*　　　54

7. "A Tale of Two Chippies . . . the Day Hollywood Trembled!" *(May 1955)*　　　61

8. "What Makes Ava Gardner Run for Sammy Davis, Jr.?" *(March 1955)*　　　66

9. "Have You Heard the Latest About Sammy Davis, Jr.?" *(March 1956)*　　　72

10. "The Untold Story of Van Johnson" *(September 1954)*　　　79

11. "Lizabeth Scott in the Call Girls' Call Book" *(September 1955)*　　　95

12. "The Big Lie About Filter Cigarettes" *(March 1955)*　　　101

13. "The Wife Clark Gable Forgot!" *(July 1955)*　　　110

14. "Robert Mitchum . . . the Nude Who Came to Dinner!" *(July 1955)*　　　120

15. "How Long Can Dick Powell Take It?" *(July 1955)*　　　127

Contents

16. "The Real Reason for Marilyn Monroe's Divorce"
    (September 1955)   136

17. "What They 'Forgot' to Say About . . . Kim Novak"
    (January 1956)   141

18. "The Left Hook That Unhooked Lana Turner from
    Bob Topping" *(September 1956)*   147

19. "Joan Crawford's Back Street Romance with a
    Bartender" *(January 1957)*   151

20. "Here's Why Frank Sinatra Is the Tarzan of the
    Boudoir" *(May 1956)*   156

21. "It Was the Hottest Show in Town When Maureen O'Hara
    Cuddled in Row 35" *(March 1957)*   159

22. "Why Liberace's Theme Song Should Be, 'Mad About
    the Boy!'" *(July 1957)*   164

23. "Hollywood vs. *Confidential*" *(September 1957)*   169

24. "Believe It or Not, There Are Ten Near-Crashes in the
    Air Every Day" *(November 1957)*   179

25. "*Confidential*'s New Policy" *(April 1958)*   186

Acknowledgments   193

Notes   195

Bibliography   207

Index   211

Illustrations

8 Marilyn Monroe and "Joltin' Joe" DiMaggio (Photofest)

9 "Why Joe DiMaggio Is Striking Out with Marilyn Monroe!" story on *Confidential*'s August 1953 cover

21 Josephine Baker, 1920s (Photofest)

24 Walter Winchell (Photofest)

27 Robert Harrison with girlfriend June Frew, 1956 (*New York Daily News*)

33 Rita Hayworth, Dick Haymes, and Hayworth's daughters Rebecca and Yasmin, 1952 (Photofest)

38 Francesca de Scaffa with Ken Carlton in *Edge of Hell*, 1956 (Photofest)

39 Francesca de Scaffa, 1951 (*New York Daily News*)

41 Fred Otash, *Confidential*'s primary investigator, Los Angeles, 1957 (Photofest)

46 J. Robert Oppenheimer (Photofest)

49 Howard Rushmore, 1939 (International News Photo)

56 Lucille Ball and husband, Desi Arnaz, 1955 (Getty Images)

57 Lucille Ball, Desi Arnaz, and their children, Lucie and Desi Jr., 1953 (Photofest)

69 Ava Gardner, 1954 (Photofest)

70 Ava Gardner, 1950s (Photofest)

75 Sammy Davis Jr. and Meg Myles on the magazine's cover in 1956 (Photofest)

76 Doris Duke and Porfirio Rubirosa, 1947 (Photofest)

77 Doris Duke and her African prince on *Confidential*'s May 1955 cover (Photofest)

84 Rock Hudson on the cover of *Life*, 1955 (Photofest)

85 "Movie Star Rory Calhoun . . . a Convict" on *Confidential*'s May 1955 cover (Photofest)

Illustrations

86 Rock Hudson and wife, Phyllis Gates, 1956 (Photofest)

88 Tab Hunter, with starlet Venetia Stevenson, 1957 (Photofest)

89 Roddy McDowell and Tab Hunter, 1955 (Photofest)

91 Van Johnson and Keenan Wynn, 1945 (Photofest)

92 Van Johnson and Eve Wynn (Photofest)

93 Van Johnson, Eve, and daughter Schuyler, 1948 (Photofest)

97 Marlene Dietrich and daughter Maria Riva (Photofest)

99 Lizabeth Scott, with Michèle Morgan, 1954 (Getty Images)

106 Robert Harrison hospitalized, 1956 (*New York Daily News*)

113 Clark Gable's first wife, Josephine Dillon, coaching Bruce Cabot, 1930s (Photofest)

115 Clark Gable and his second wife, Ria Langham Gable, 1933 (Photofest)

117 Josephine Dillon, 1960 (Photofest)

123 Robert Mitchum, 1953 (Photofest)

124 Jerry Geisler, 1958 (Getty Images)

130 June Allyson, 1949 (Photofest)

131 June Allyson, Dick Powell, and children (Photofest)

132 Howard Rushmore, 1958 (International News Photo)

133 Robert Harrison, 1957 (*New York Daily News*)

138 Marilyn Monroe on *Confidential*'s cover, September 1955 (Photofest)

143 Kim Novak article in *Confidential*, January 1956

145 Kim Novak (Photofest)

149 Lana Turner and Bob Topping, with her daughter, Cheryl Crane, 1950 (Photofest)

153 Joan Crawford on the cover of *Confidential*, January 1957

162 Maureen O'Hara, 1955 (Photofest)

166 Liberace, 1955 (Photofest)

167 Liberace and his mother, 1954 (Photofest)

177 Robert Harrison's niece, Marjorie, and her husband, Fred Meade (Photofest)

190 Howard Rushmore and wife, Frances, found in a New York City cab, January 3, 1958 (*New York Daily News*)

SHOCKING
TRUE STORY

1

"Why Joe DiMaggio Is Striking Out with Marilyn Monroe!"

He put the wood to the best fastballs ever served up in the American League, but "Joltin' Joe" DiMaggio kept swinging at and missing those lovely curves in his world series of the heart—that gallant attempt to make Marilyn Monroe his wife.

The "pitcher" in this case had the male half of the North American continent sighing in frustration when gossip columnists said she'd jiggle down the aisle with the famed Yankee slugger. Marilyn and the headline-conscious publicity department of Twentieth Century–Fox made a six-month riddle out of the question: "Will or won't the wedding bells ring?" For months on end, the bosomy beauty made much of the fact that she hadn't even been asked for her hand and what came with it. Many a baffled male thought this was bedrock proof that DiMaggio was cracking up.

DiMaggio Isn't Talking

From his place in the matrimonial batter's box, Joe said practically nothing. It wasn't unusual. DiMaggio's always been the kind of man who let his actions speak for themselves and his devoted attention to Marilyn spoke volumes. He even prompted the wrath of his ex-wife, Dorothy Arnold, who sued for complete custody of their nine-year-old son, on grounds that DiMaggio was taking Joe, Jr., along on his dates with the chesty blonde.

3

It was as obvious as a line drive into Yankee Stadium bleachers that Joe was wearing his heart on his sleeve for Marilyn. But he, too, knew he was fanning out like a bush leaguer with Marilyn. He couldn't figure out, for some time, who the opposition manager was.

Fans of Joe's and Marilyn's, who are still scratching their heads over this puzzle, can relax. The answer is Joe Schenck, an old artist at the fade-away pitch in the Hollywood league. Genial Joe (Schenck, that is) said "No dice," when Marilyn went to him to confess palpitations of the heart over one of the best ball players since Babe Ruth. In effect, he told her, "Have fun, kid, but don't get serious." That was enough to change a four-bagger into an easy out.

Sultry Marilyn Listens to "Daddy"

The uninitiated may well inquire how a balding, squat little gnome old enough to be her grandfather could exert such a strong influence over the beauteous Miss Monroe. Insiders will confess they, too, are often a little baffled over Joe's Rasputin-like powers. But none deny his abilities.

Schenck, they point out, occupies the role of a "father" in Miss Monroe's life. He guides the luscious blonde's career, inspires her ambitions, lauds her triumphs and lulls her fears. He's always there with a paternal hug or a strong shoulder to cry on.

It was he who assigned top designers to create a wardrobe that beautifully just misses clothing Miss Monroe. To him go the honors for putting witty writers to work spinning those headline-catching remarks she makes (sample comment against sun-bathing: "I like to be blonde all over"). To others, Joe Schenck might be a bald-headed old man. To Marilyn, he was, and is, the kind of guy every little girl wants—the man who snaps his fingers and gets results.

If Marilyn was ripe for such a relationship, there can be no argument that Schenck is a cum laude graduate of the university for "Daddies, De Luxe." This stubby Galahad has been a knight in a cream-colored convertible for years to gals from six to 36 (beyond that age bracket, a girl isn't supposed to need a pop).

Excerpt from "Why Joe DiMaggio Is Striking Out
with Marilyn Monroe!"
(August 1953)

On this summer afternoon the businessmen in the gray flannel suits and the secretaries who assisted them were at their desks. Outside, it was amateur hour on the streets of New York City as aimless tourists, their heads bobbing down to look at maps and up to look at tall buildings, meandered along Broadway. Robert Harrison, forty-eight, blue-eyed, deeply tanned, and dapper as always in his white suit and white fedora, glided through this crowd like a broken-field runner, the ever-present cigarette dangling from his lip and a copy of *Confidential* magazine in his hands. It was August 1953, and Harrison smiled the smile of a man who knew he was at the top of his game in the greatest city in the greatest country in the world. On almost every corner he passed in the five blocks between his home at the Parc Vendôme on West Fifty-seventh Street and his Broadway office, there was a newsstand. And on each newsstand only Harrison's magazine promised the answer to the question that was on every American's mind: "Why Joe DiMaggio Is Striking Out with Marilyn Monroe!"

Harrison had launched his semimonthly *Confidential* nine months earlier with a press run of 150,000 and a racy mix of stories that included a feature on a homosexual wedding, a portfolio of pictures of women in their underwear, an exposé entitled "I Was Tortured on a Chain Gang," and a "science" story by a Manhattan psychiatrist that revealed that athletes are lousy lovers. No matter that the gay wedding, purportedly set in Paris, was staged and photographed in Harrison's New York City apartment, that the chain gang story was utter fiction, and that the underwear pics were retreads from Harrison's stable of girlie magazines—*Beauty Parade, Whisper, Eyeful, Titter, Wink,* and *Flirt.* Readers loved the pulp paper magazine with the lurid red and yellow covers that used exclamation marks as often as other magazines used periods. Now, by issue number 3, Harrison knew that Hollywood was the country's richest source of sensational stories. And with the August issue of *Confidential* he was to learn for sure what Twentieth Century–Fox already knew—Monroe sells.

In 1953 her three films—*Niagara, Gentlemen Prefer Blondes,* and *How to Marry a Millionaire*—grossed more than $25 million, making

Marilyn the studio's most valuable property. With its promise of "the story behind the story" on the Monroe-DiMaggio romance, Harrison discovered Marilyn was equally valuable to *Confidential*, whose circulation for the August 1953 issue would climb to a stunning 800,000 copies, far surpassing tame movie industry favorites such as *Photoplay*. Harrison himself had written the story, using the pseudonym Harrison Roberts. It said that Joe Schenck, co-founder and chairman of Twentieth Century–Fox and one of Hollywood's richest and most powerful men, opposed the Monroe-DiMaggio marriage. Heavy with innuendo, the *Confidential* story said Schenck was Monroe's "daddy," a role it averred he had played with a number of other young actresses. Indeed, Hollywood insiders knew Monroe as one of Schenck's "girls," invited to sit in on the high-stakes card games at his Holmby Hills estate where aspiring actresses met, and slept with, studio executives and producers. *Confidential* offered titillating details, reporting, for example, an IRS investigation into Schenck's attempt to deduct as business expenses the new car and furniture he supplied to a young woman he met in Miami and brought to Los Angeles as a "secretary."

In some ways, the swipe at Schenck was a foolhardy move for a publication in business less than a year. After all, Schenck wasn't a public figure whose foibles would interest the average reader. He was, however, a powerful Hollywood aristocrat so concerned about his image and reputation that he was rumored to have backed *Hollywood Reporter*, then as now one of the film industry's major trade organs, to assure a steady flow of good news, or at least forestall any bad publicity.

To Hollywood insiders, the Monroe story was a clear sign that *Confidential* wasn't going to play by the unwritten rules that governed timid fan magazines such as *Photoplay*, *Film Pictorial*, *Modern Screen*, *Motion Picture Classic*, and *Silver Screen*, and docile trade publications such as *Variety* and *Hollywood Reporter*, all financially dependent on or easily intimidated by the studios. The very existence of so obstreperous a publication was another in a growing number of signs, albeit initially a small and easily overlooked one, that the studios were losing their tight grip on the film industry, its stars, its theaters, its public, and even its sense of magic.

Hollywood in the Golden Age of the thirties and forties had become the funhouse mirror in which the country checked its reflection. And America had become accustomed to a reassuring, if remarkably distorted, image. The mirror showed America's men in the image of John Wayne and Jimmy Stewart—strong, solid, exemplifying the integrity and rightness of America herself. And America's women? In Hollywood, they ran the narrow gamut from Doris Day to Betty Grable, from beauty, integrity, and wholesomeness on one end of the spectrum to beauty, integrity, and sexiness on the other. Thanks to legions of publicists and an inept and sometimes corrupt press, magazines and newspapers propounded the myth that the real Hollywood, spread across affluent neighborhoods in central and west Los Angeles, was every bit as wholesome as the cinematic one.

The Motion Picture Production Code was partially responsible for Hollywood's image of America and America's image of Hollywood. "No picture shall be produced which will lower the moral standards of those who see it," the code stipulated. In the service of that principle, it stipulated that "passion should be treated in such manner as not to stimulate the lower and baser emotions." Its earliest versions demanded moral retribution for every sin, including sex out of wedlock. Thanks to its strictures, abortions and illicit drug use were as rare on the screen as were homosexuality and miscegenation.

The code was a way to gild with legitimacy an industry born in the nickelodeons of America's crime-ridden immigrant slums. It was a great device for deflecting attacks from the Catholic National Legion of Decency and various state censorship boards. It appeased federal legislators, who moved on to regulate the television industry instead. And it reassured good people everywhere who had been alarmed by the movie colony's drug and sex scandals in the 1920s and by the revolutionary fervor of films during the Great Depression.

Morals clauses in the contracts of all movie stars helped ensure that their private lives mirrored their wholesome movie images. What the code and the morals clauses didn't dictate was assured by the upper-middle-class mores of the affluent Jewish immigrants who owned the studios and were largely responsible for creating Hollywood as Shangri-La. As in their own private worlds, so in the movies, black people, if evident at all, knew their place. Communism was the devil's own work.

Confidential claimed in its August 1953 issue that Joe Schenck, chairman of Twentieth Century–Fox, stood in the way of Marilyn Monroe's marriage to "Joltin' Joe" DiMaggio. Attacking the powerful Schenck was a bold move for a magazine less than a year old and a sign that it wouldn't be intimidated by the Hollywood studios.

And on the silver screen the prosperity and social stability that blessed America in the war years stretched unending into the future.

Certainly the men who ran Hollywood knew life was more complicated than that. Thanks partly to the success of television, theater attendance by 1950 had declined by nearly half from its postwar peak in 1946. Yet Hollywood still hadn't decided how to come to terms with that little box. Antitrust rulings and other forces had conspired to break up the studio system that had oppressed and nurtured a generation of stars. Backlots that had hummed with the production of as many as one hundred movies a year in the 1940s were being sold and subdivided for commercial use by the 1950s. Leading ladies and men reveled in the

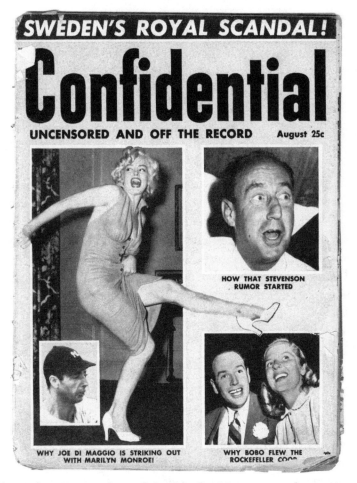

Publisher Robert Harrison learned that Marilyn Monroe moved magazines when he put the "Why Joe DiMaggio Is Striking Out with Marilyn Monroe!" story on *Confidential*'s August 1953 cover. Circulation jumped from 150,000 copies for the magazine's first issue to 800,000 copies for this issue, its fourth.

growing freedom to pursue vastly more profitable futures outside the constraints of exclusive contracts with a particular studio. But they also were nervous without the protection of the studios, which had provided regular salaries and legions of publicists. Thousands of other workers were even less sure of their employment prospects.

On the political front, life also was complicated. Hollywood largely had been "cleansed" of Communists and fellow travelers in the late 1940s. But in the decade that followed the blacklist remained in effect. Congressmen Francis Walter and J. Parnell Thomas continued to summon actors and directors to testify before the House Committee on Un-American Activities in the persistent belief that some elements of Hollywood wanted to tint America Red. There also were signs that young Americans who had left the farms and towns of Middle America to fight overseas in World War II had come home with a more cynical and sophisticated view of the world than what Hollywood was offering.

Against all these threats and uncertainties there was something reassuring to studio executives about the image of a right and innocent America and a moral and proper Hollywood that they had worked so hard to construct and now struggled so hard to maintain. Thus there was a lot at stake in December 1952 when the trucks of Publishers Distributing Corporation rolled out across America to deliver the first issue of *Confidential*, proudly subtitled "Uncensored and Off the Record." Not five years later, in a nasty courtroom battle whose excited news coverage made it the O. J. Simpson trial of its time, Hollywood seemingly vanquished *Confidential*. But its damage had been done. The magazine, in stripping away layer upon layer of Hollywood puffery, left a legacy of skepticism and cynicism that was quickly embraced by Americans who had come to doubt the oh-so-wholesome image of life they saw projected endlessly on the silver screen.

Although *Confidential* eventually fell, it spawned dozens of imitators, some of which continue to prosper. In many ways, *Confidential* was father to the *National Enquirer*, the *Star, E! True Hollywood Story, Access Hollywood,* TMZ.com, and for that matter, today's *Vanity Fair. Confidential* was, in a sense, inevitable. "Half-fictionalized as they are," said Camille Paglia, the feminist social critic who grew up reading *Confidential*, "the tabloids, with their twin themes of sex and violence, tell the lurid pagan truth about life." As Robert Harrison put it, "I sincerely believe the basic vehicle of the story-behind-the-story will be here long after we are all dead."

2

"They Started in Their Birthday Suits!"

During those dismal months of 1930 when America was engulfed in the Great Depression, a young movie actress still in her teens was setting the stage—some 4,000 miles away in Vienna—to give Americans the biggest lift they'd had since Otis developed the elevator. On location in a woodland dell, this young nymph, scarcely over 15 but with a beautifully matured body, slid sinuously into a brook and showed America—as well as the rest of the world—the shape it should be in.

For the tawny dryad frisking about in the ole swimmin' hole unencumbered by anything so prosaic as a bathing suit was Hedy Lamarr, making her bow in her birthday suit. The movie, of course, was the daring and now famous *Ecstasy*, and after the bathing sequence nobody bothered to find out whether Hedy could act, too. Nor did they care.

Almost before she could get her clothes back on, Hedy was signed for Hollywood by Louis B. Mayer, who put her in *Algiers* opposite Charles Boyer, where she made history. In the process she shed one husband, Fritz Mandl (who spent a fortune unsuccessfully trying to suppress *Ecstasy*), and acquired three others, producer Gene Markey, actor John Loder, and hotelman Ted Stauffer.

When a Gal Makes a Rep in the Raw

While it's undoubtedly true that there's nothing so chaste as nudity, a girl who makes a rep in the raw is certain to be chased—especially by

Hollywood. This season's case in point is a blonde whose appearance in the altogether caused her to zoom from obscurity to the cover of just about every magazine except the *Harvard Law Review.*

The gal's name is Norma Jean Mortenson, a monicker hung on her at birth in Los Angeles, but when she grew up and turned to modeling for a living, and had her pelt photographed in four colors, she attracted a following as enthusiastic as an American Legion convention.

. . . Actually, there are many other Hollywood stars today who . . . figuratively and literally speaking . . . have been caught with their panties down. And in sharp focus, yet.

Excerpt from "They Started in Their Birthday Suits!"
(November 1953)

It would be a few months after publication of the Monroe-DiMaggio story before Harrison learned from his distributors the extent of that issue's success. But there were clear signs it would be a big one. One night after it first hit the newsstands, a copy of the magazine had surfaced while Harrison was at the Colony, the former mob hangout turned society enclave on East Sixty-first Street that attracted the likes of Angier Biddle Duke, the Duke and Duchess of Windsor, and Mrs. William K. Vanderbilt. To Harrison's amusement and amazement, owner Gene Cavallaro had rented the twenty-five-cent magazine out at a dollar a read to his curious and enthusiastic patrons, donating the money to charity. Harrison also had spotted café society reading *Confidential* at El Morocco and '21.'

So Harrison decided to feature Monroe (née Mortenson) in his next issue. This time she shared billing with other stars in a fluffy piece of reporting that revealed little, save for a grainy photo of young Hedy Lamarr and Yvonne De Carlo ("who did more for cheesecake than Leo Lindy of restaurant fame"), who had appeared in the buff early in her career. Cheesecake photos, chorus girls, birthday suits—it was the type of story that Harrison knew well.

One of his first forays into writing, which can't help but have influ-

12

enced his approach to *Confidential,* was a story he had written as a young man during an eight-month stint as a writer for the *New York Evening Graphic.* It was about a dancer Harrison fancied in Florenz Ziegfeld's *Frolics,* a midnight revue that featured girls clad in balloons. The *Graphic* was to newspapers and Broadway what *Confidential* would become to magazines and Hollywood. The afternoon paper was launched in 1924 by Bernarr Adolphus Macfadden, a health faddist known as much for walking to work barefoot as for his role as publisher of *True Story* and other magazines. Macfadden's concept was a newspaper by and for "the people," an idea that extended to inviting ordinary citizens to write about the fires, burglaries, and other incidents that enlivened and plagued their lives—a foreshadowing of today's Internet fad of "citizen journalism."

But what really distinguished the *Graphic* was its coverage of society divorces and murders and the use of composographs—doctored photos that purported to show everything from Rudolph Valentino's arrival in heaven to a society party that featured a naked girl in a bathtub. The *Graphic* failed in 1932, but not before it launched the careers of a young sportswriter named Ed Sullivan and a Broadway columnist named Walter Winchell and helped mold the journalistic sensibilities of young Robert Harrison.

When the *Graphic* went out of business, Harrison did a variety of jobs, from writing copy for Cook's tour brochures to selling song lyrics. In 1935, he finally landed work with Quigley Publishing Co., which gave him six years of stability and an introduction to the industry that would become the focus of Harrison's own publishing empire. Although based in New York City, Martin J. Quigley, Harrison's boss, was a real Hollywood insider. He fell in love with Hollywood after reviewing D. W. Griffith's *The Birth of a Nation* in 1915 for a Chicago newspaper. He quit his newspaper job and started publishing the weekly *Exhibitors Herald,* a movie trade journal. By 1930 he had purchased two other weeklies and merged them into *Motion Picture Herald.*

Quigley became a confidant of movie industry titans such as Cecil B. DeMille, Howard Hughes, Samuel Goldwyn, Darryl F. Zanuck, Walt Disney, Louis B. Mayer, Irving Thalberg, Harry Cohn, and Jack and Harry Warner. He also, oddly enough, helped write the very Motion Pic-

13

ture Production Code that enforced the mythic view of Hollywood that Harrison and *Confidential* helped destroy. Quigley, a Catholic layman, teamed with Daniel A. Lord, a Jesuit priest, who professed himself shocked at the language of talking pictures. "Silent smut had been bad," he wrote in *Played by Ear*, his autobiography. "Vocal smut cried to the censors for vengeance."

Will H. Hays, president of the Motion Picture Association of America (MPAA), accepted Quigley and Lord's draft of the code. It was a "deeply Catholic text," wrote Thomas Doherty, a professor of American Studies at Brandeis University who has studied the impact of such censorship on Hollywood. "The Code was no mere list of Thou-Shalt-Nots but a homily that sought to yoke Catholic doctrine to Hollywood formula: The guilty are punished, the virtuous are rewarded, the authority of church and state is legitimate, and the bonds of matrimony are sacred."

The result, says Doherty, was "a Jewish-owned business selling Roman Catholic theology to Protestant America."

To prod the MPAA and the studios into actually enforcing the code, Catholics formed the National Legion of Decency. The Legion's pledge called on good Catholics, and Protestants and Jews, to "condemn absolutely those debauching motion pictures which, with other degrading agencies, are corrupting public morals and promoting a sex mania in our land. Considering these evils," the pledger proclaimed, "I hereby promise to remain away from all motion pictures except those which do not offend decency and Christian morality." Joseph I. Breen, himself a Catholic, was named to head the Production Code Administration, which checked film scripts for code violations and issued a Production Code Seal of Approval that became essential if a studio wanted its film screened.

Harrison took to advertising but, unlike Quigley, not to Hollywood. Quigley sent him to the film capital in 1935 as a reward for his hard work. "I hated it," Harrison remembered. "It was a dull town. I knew nobody there. There was no night life, and I like night life." Nor was Harrison, ever the entrepreneur, satisfied working at seventy dollars a week for Quigley. In addition to providing passes to musical revues where Harrison could indulge his taste for showgirls, Harrison's contacts at Quigley Publishing were a rich source of cheesecake photos. So Harrison started collecting them. Before long he had enough to mock up a concept for the sort of magazine he wanted to read and publish.

Harrison's publishing venture took on some urgency on Christmas Eve of 1941, when Quigley heard about it and fired him. Harrison's sisters Helen and Edith rallied around their baby brother. Helen passed the hat and turned over five hundred dollars, four hundred of it borrowed from Edith's young daughter, Marjorie. Now, Bob Harrison was in business for himself with a magazine he called *Beauty Parade*, which carried the subtitle "Girls, Gags & Giggles." In short order he launched three new titles—*Eyeful, Titter,* and *Wink*—and hired his sisters to help manage his growing magazine empire. In 1946 he rounded out the collection with *Whisper*, a magazine that in many ways foreshadowed *Confidential* with consumer stories such as "Gas Stations Rip-Off!" along with more lurid tales of crime and sex.

It was a family enterprise, published from a two-room apartment that Harrison shared with sister Helen and later, when he began to make money, from a nine-room apartment in Manhattan's Parc Vendôme that he shared with Helen and her husband, Dan Studin. Harrison's success allowed him all sorts of luxuries. Over his bed he mounted an enormous oil of a nude man and woman that had been commissioned as art for one of his magazines. He turned one room of the apartment into a miniature nightclub, complete with tables with checkered cloths, a bar, and zebra stripes that recalled El Morocco. Harrison also began to indulge his taste for the custom-made white Cadillac Eldorados, expensive white suits, and white fedoras that distinguished him from the other swells who drifted from the *Follies* to the nightclubs most nights in Manhattan. He brooked no criticism about his indulgences. "It so happens I have three white polo coats," he told an interviewer. "What the hell's wrong with that? I love them! Any guy with a little showmanship would go for that."

Harrison took the girlie magazine business to new heights, or new lows, depending on one's perspective, by intuiting and exploiting passions and curiosities that were off limits to more conventional publishers. One innovation was credited to Edythe Farrell, an editor he hired from *Police Gazette*, a newspaper launched in the early 1800s that professed to educate its readers about crime while titillating them with all the most gruesome details. It was Farrell, described by a contemporary as "a high-tension number who could swear like a fishwife," who introduced her new boss to Krafft-Ebing's *Psychopathia Sexualis* and the idea that whips and chains and spike heels would sell.

"Edythe was a Hunter graduate who had majored in psychology," recalled someone who witnessed her meeting Harrison for the first time at a cocktail party. "She told him that the average fetishist is completely disinterested in nudes but the most innocuous things could arouse them. She told him all about sadism and masochism. When he said: 'I don't dig that stuff,' she told him: 'But it has appeal.' "

Soon Harrison's magazines became known for girls in bondage, girls wrestling, and girls chained by their evil slave masters, who likely as not were portrayed by Harrison himself, as much to save a buck on modeling fees as for the fun of it. He posed as everything from a white slaver to an irate husband spanking his wife in set-up photos in his magazines. It made the office a wacky and entertaining place. "The place was just nuts," remembered Larry Sanders, who edited the girlie magazines for a time. "You'd be trying to write a caption and you'd look up and this gal would be walking through pulling 20 yards of chain, and Bob would come out in his bathrobe needing a shave after just have gotten up at 11 a.m., yelling 'Let's do a fanetta (posterior) shot' or: 'Let's do a buz-zoom (bosom) shot,' and the photographers would be crawling up a ladder to shoot down the girl's cleavage."

Truth be told, his innovative photo stories hardly deserved to be called stories. A typical one was "Trunk and Disorderly," published in *Eyeful*, that offered four pages of photos of a blond clad in fishnet hose and a chain-mesh-and-rubber bra struggling to open and then close a trunk. For his covers, Harrison hired talented artists such as Earl Moran, Billy De Vorss, and Peter Driben—all recognized today by collectors of this exotic art form as being at the top of the craft. Driben had studied at the Sorbonne and worked for the film studios, doing the original posters and publicity materials for *The Maltese Falcon*. His approach was typical of the Harrison magazine cover, with a girl posed to show as much leg as possible against a bold background of red, yellow, blue, or green.

Models weren't hard to find. Harrison had his pick from among the thousands of strippers and showgirls who flocked to New York in search of fame. One of his most popular models was Bettie Page. The Tennessee girl with the ice blue eyes and coal black hair was named "Miss Pinup Girl of the World" in 1955, in no small part because of her poses in Harrison's magazines in bondage gear and lingerie.

But for all his success, Harrison fretted that his wasn't a "respectable" business. As a girlie magazine publisher, he had his first brushes with the law, ranging from a relatively minor arrest for photographing half-naked models posing as Ku Klux Klan members on a New Jersey golf course to a damaging decision by the U.S. Post Office to bar his magazines from the mail, later modified to require its prior review. Worse, by early 1952 the group of girlie magazines, beset by competitors, was in financial trouble. Casting about for a new idea, Harrison noticed that everyone in his office was transfixed by the televised Kefauver hearings on the inner workings of organized crime. Estes Kefauver, chairman of the U.S. Senate's Special Committee on Organized Crime in Interstate Commerce, convened the hearings in May 1950, giving ordinary Americans an inside look at what investigators called a secret "government within a government."

The Kefauver hearings featured testimony from the likes of Virginia Hill, the glamorous mistress of Las Vegas mob boss Bugsy Siegel, who was said to have named his famous Flamingo Club casino in tribute to her long legs. Especially gripping were eight days of testimony in March 1951 about the inner workings of the Costello crime family. It was a week, said *Life* magazine, that "will occupy a special place in history . . . People had suddenly gone indoors into living rooms, taverns, and clubrooms, auditoriums and back-offices. There, in eerie half-light, looking at millions of small frosty screens, people sat as if charmed. Never before had the attention of the nation been riveted so completely on a single matter."

In 1947, Harrison had mocked up a "fact" magazine called *Eyewitness.* Now, with the Kefauver hearings before him, the idea jelled. "It was then that I believe people suddenly awakened to the excitement in learning of the inside about other people with whom they were familiar because they may have seen their pictures in the paper, or in the newsreels," Harrison recalled in an interview years later. "There was excitement and interest in the lives of people in the headlines and getting behind the story. That's when we started *Confidential*." Thus was born the magazine that Tom Wolfe, decades later, would call "the most scandalous scandal magazine in the history of the world."

3

"Winchell Was Right About Josephine Baker"

Walter Winchell was virtually the only newspaperman in America who had the guts to stick his chin out and tell the world what a phony Josephine Baker was when she provoked the now-famous "Stork Club Incident" last winter. For his pains, Winchell became an international target for charges of discrimination.

Time and the lady herself have proved how right the columnist was about Josephine Baker.

France made an unofficial countess of Josie when she was a lanky, frizzle-haired dancer of 20. Ever since, she has detested the United States because the title wasn't transferable. For well over a quarter century this continental crank has alternated between tossing her torso around stages and hurling insults at the land which gave her birth and her first shove up the ladder of fame. Josie's major complaint has been that we treat the Negro shamefully, a point many a wiser and more dignified spokesman for her people has adequately covered from time to time.

Even Walter White, that patient and gentlemanly executive of the National Association for the Advancement of Colored People, winced in pain when la Josephine scuttled off to Argentina late in 1952 and there, having tossed bouquets at iron-fisted dictator Juan Perón, proceeded to picture the United States as a nation drenched in the blood of lynched Negroes. Her own best friends in this country finally had to finger Josie as an outright liar.

19

What About Her Own Bias?

What they didn't say, but what you'll learn in these pages, is that Josephine Baker has always used the honest fight against discrimination for her own cynical ends. Anyone who didn't drop to their knees for her, personally, was lashed and vilified as being obviously biased against the color of her skin. Just how much bias she had on this subject herself, has never been satisfactorily aired.

For example, Jo-Jo flares like a Fourth of July rocket when you recall that she studiously avoids social contact with any but the most prosperous and successful colored people in France. She made no secret of her preference for dating white men and proved it conclusively by marching to the altar with three of them.

Excerpt from "Winchell Was Right About Josephine Baker"
(April 1953)

Josephine Baker walked into the Stork Club at 11:15 p.m. on October 16, 1951, causing an audible stir among patrons and staff usually inured to the presence of celebrities. Nearly three decades earlier, Baker's appearance onstage in Paris garbed in only three bracelets and a skirt fashioned from sixteen bananas had won her an enthusiastic reception from the French. Her work for the French Resistance and marriage to a Frenchman earned their enduring affection. Now, weighing a move back to the United States, she was in New York for a two-week engagement at the Roxy, Samuel "Roxy" Rothafel's palatial show palace on West Fiftieth Street. Nothing could be more natural than an evening out at the nearby Stork Club, the home away from home of New York's café society, thanks in no small part to endless plugs from Walter Winchell, a regular. Winchell, whose column in the *New York Mirror* and whose regular radio appearances made him America's most powerful and best-paid journalist, called the Stork Club "New York's New Yorkiest place."

The glamorous and exotic Baker and her fourth husband, French orchestra leader Jo Bouillon, and three friends were quickly seated in the club's exclusive Cub Room. Soon a waiter appeared to take their

Josephine Baker blamed celebrated columnist and broadcaster Walter Winchell for not coming to her defense when she allegedly was discriminated against at New York City's Stork Club because of her race. *Confidential* responded by attacking Baker as a hypocrite who married only white men. The story led Winchell to promote *Confidential* as his "pet mag."

orders. In time, each of Baker's companions was served. Conspicuous by its absence was the steak and crab salad ordered by Baker, the only black person at the table and indeed the only black person in the club. After an exchange of angry words with the club's staff, Baker and her companions stormed out of the Stork and into a meeting the next morning with the NAACP and the then-liberal *New York Post*. The story got lots of press. Despite *Confidential's* assertion that Baker's fight against discrimination was self-serving, she was known as one of the only black performers who refused to perform before a segregated audience, which had cost her a number of engagements. She was so esteemed by the NAACP that in 1951 it had named May 20 "Josephine Baker Day."

It was no surprise that Baker and her supporters focused their anger on Sherman Billingsley, the Oklahoma-born owner of the Stork Club and a confirmed bigot. But also caught up in the controversy was Winchell. Baker complained that the columnist had been present during the incident at the Stork Club and hadn't taken Billingsley, his old friend, to task. Winchell's many enemies, including columnist Ed Sullivan, and *New York Post* editor James Wechsler, gleefully exploited the charge. Barry Gray, whose show on New York City's WMCA radio won him fame as "the Father of Talk Radio," earned Winchell's eternal enmity for putting Baker on the air for two days running to talk about the incident, followed by two days of criticism by Ed Sullivan.

The incident couldn't have come at a worse time for Winchell. It provided a rallying point for a group of "journalists, celebrities, politicians, artists, socialites—[who] were terrified of Walter's power but despaired of ever having the means of fighting it," explained Neal Gabler in his authoritative biography of Winchell. Whether opposed to Winchell because of his perceived megalomania, his power to destroy reputations, or the view that he had become a voice for "irresponsible anticommunism," this group coalesced around the Baker affair. "Though Winchell had had premonitions of his demise ever since the war's end, the long, torturous descent actually began precisely at 11:15 p.m. on October 16, 1951, in the Cub Room of the Stork Club when Josephine Baker arrived," Gabler wrote.

Winchell was furious. He treasured his reputation for racial tolerance, and indeed had actively campaigned for justice for a black machine gunner denied the Congressional Medal of Honor, a black prisoner sentenced to death, and on behalf of many black readers who wrote to complain of more minor acts of discrimination. He maintained that he hadn't been aware of what was going on the night Baker was at the Stork Club. Although more than a year had passed since the incident, Winchell was delighted in April 1953 when *Confidential* published a story that portrayed Baker as a liar, attacked her for alleged Communist sympathies, and focused on her decision years earlier to become a French citizen.

For *Confidential,* the story wasn't about politics, one of many subjects about which Harrison was amazingly ignorant. Asked once about his political position, he responded: "I don't like to get into these political things." Asked about Joe McCarthy and his campaign against Communism, Harrison replied: "That stuff is as foreign to me as Europe is." A friend of Harrison's, alluding to his lack of sophistication about the world, once remarked: "Bob Harrison's mind has been broadened by travel—between the Harwyn Club and El Morocco." To Harrison, the Baker story not only wasn't about politics, it also wasn't really about Baker. It was all about Walter Winchell. While it took until issue number 3 for Harrison to figure out that revelations about Marilyn Monroe and other celebrities would attract the masses whose quarters to buy the magazine added up to millions of dollars, he had bet from the start that Winchell's support would sell magazines. "Harrison gave us orders to write a short Winchell profile in the first issue of *Confidential*—butter the old boy up," an early magazine contributor recalled. "We wrote a five-paragraph piece. Harrison read it, heaved it out. Said it smelled. Too obvious."

Confidential tried again in November 1953 with a story entitled "Red Murder, Inc." "In America this very minute 1,000 Benedict Arnolds, trained secretly in Moscow, await word to paralyze industry and liquidate top anti-Reds," the story proclaimed, listing key targets such as Catholic bishop and television personality Fulton J. Sheen, Red-hunting U.S. senator Joseph R. McCarthy, FBI chief J. Edgar Hoover, and . . . Walter Winchell. "America's top reporter enjoys the distinction of having been hated by both Communists and Nazis alike as a result of his fearless exposes of Anti-American elements on the international scene," said the lightly sourced story, written by Howard Rushmore, a crusading journalist who would come to play a major role at *Confidential.*

But the Baker article was the ticket. "Harrison saw the story and a light lit up in his head," the *Confidential* contributor said. "Man, he's

Walter Winchell's influence was ebbing in the early fifties, but his broadcasts and columns still reached millions of listeners and readers, making him an important promoter of *Confidential.* "Butter the old boy up," Robert Harrison ordered his editors, who proceeded to churn out stories attacking Winchell's enemies.

quick to spot an angle. He says, 'Rewrite the head, make it read, "Winchell Was Right About Josephine Baker." Make it a praise-Winchell piece . . .' Out comes the magazine. That Sunday night we all sat around the television at Harrison's apartment, watching Winchell. We were sweatin'. All of a sudden, there it was. Winchell was waving the magazine, shouting how good it was to all the ships at sea."

Harrison confirmed the strategy. *Confidential* "started running a Winchell piece every issue," Harrison told an interviewer many years later. "We'd try to figure out who Winchell didn't like and run a piece about them. One of them was 'Broadway's Biggest Double Cross.' It was a piece about all the ingrates who Winchell had helped to start their careers who turned their backs on him . . . And he kept on plugging *Confidential*. It got to the point where we would sit down and rack our brains trying to think of somebody else Winchell didn't like. We were running out of people, for Christ's sake!"

Winchell delivered no fewer than sixteen plugs for *Confidential* over six months to his millions of readers and listeners. *Confidential*, he said, was his "pet mag." His support for *Confidential* even fostered rumors that he was an owner of the magazine.

As 1953 drew to a close, *Confidential*'s stunning circulation figures and the adulation of Walter Winchell convinced Harrison that his new enterprise was a business success. Thanks to the magazine, he also was a social success, at least in certain circles. That Harrison was welcomed at the Colony and El Morocco and '21' was a clear measure of how far this son of poor Jewish immigrants had traveled. Add that Sherman Billingsley had granted him access to the vaunted Cub Room at the Stork Club, perhaps New York's most famous celebrity haunt. And consider the two large Utrillos, the sketch by Matisse, and the brunette babe of a receptionist in a low-cut dress who greeted visitors when they stepped off the elevator and into the lobby of Harrison Publications Inc. In the circles that mattered to him, Bob Harrison certainly had arrived.

Even the journalistic establishment showed signs of coming around. Early on, many prominent journalists had refused Harrison's entreaties to write for the magazine. But with Winchell's help, he had been able to convince one of them, Howard Rushmore, to write for *Confidential* and, in December 1953, come on board as a contributing editor.

Rushmore, a leading anti-Communist, was a columnist for William Randolph Hearst's *New York Journal-American* and, with such as William F. Buckley Jr. and J. B. Matthews, a contributor to the prestigious *American Mercury* magazine. Harrison wanted him to round out *Confidential*'s editorial mix with a focus on politics. Harrison saw Rushmore's willingness to join *Confidential* as important evidence that he was a player. Little did he know it was to be the most important and fateful hire he would ever make. Now Harrison, whose sense of such things was relative, could proudly tell an interviewer: "With *Confidential*, I have finally gone respectable."

Some of his friends and associates saw Harrison's ambition and insecurity as a response to the doubts of his father, Benjamin, a coppersmith born in Russia, who died in 1933, well before Harrison achieved the "respectability" he craved.

"His father always pooh-poohed his aspirations," a former *Confidential* editor recalled. "He always wished the old man were around so he could sort of rub his nose in what he had achieved . . . He would continuously say, 'My father wouldn't believe I'd ever be this important.' This is what makes Bob sweet and pathetic, because his entire drive was to show his father he would be one of the rulers of the world. When you hear a mature man express this as often as Bob has, you realize the significance. He always wanted to tell his father, 'Look at me, I can go anywhere and be accepted anywhere.' "

Harrison disputed that. "Na-a-ah! I'm not trying to prove nothing to anybody," he once told a reporter. "My father and I never saw eye to eye. He was religious, and he was from the Old World. He used to say what I did was all 'air business.' He felt one should have a trade and stick to it, one should keep the station in life to which he was born. I had a flair for writing and I enjoyed it. My father felt I should be a carpenter—but I couldn't drive a nail straight. There was a lack of understanding."

Harrison said his attraction to publishing rather than to more prosaic trades was "a natural urge . . . I know very well that I would be in it today if I could not make money at it, because this is the sort of thing I enjoy," he told an interviewer.

Benjamin Harrison, thirty-three, and his wife, Paula, made their way to America from what is now Joniškis, Lithuania, and landed at Castle Garden on Manhattan's southern tip in August 1890. The family's original name was lost to history. In all probability, the new anglicized name was meant to honor U.S. president Benjamin Harrison, who had spoken out against the Russian pogroms, although more for fear of what immigration would do to the United States than out of concern for the persecuted Russian Jews.

The Harrisons left behind a life of poverty and brutal oppression that had grown worse with the assassination of Czar Alexander II in

1881. While Alexander II had been relatively liberal, his successor introduced in May 1882 a series of repressive measures that came to be known as the May Laws. They barred Jews from rural areas and from towns of fewer than ten thousand people, including those in the Pale of Settlement, a region encompassing much of present-day Belarus, Lithuania, Moldova, Poland, Ukraine, and parts of western Russia where Jews were permitted to settle. Alexander III also established quotas that limited access by Jews to schools and work. His government

Robert Harrison said that by abandoning girlie magazines to publish *Confidential* he had "finally gone respectable." He didn't offer the respectability of marriage to girlfriend June Frew, seen here, who nevertheless frequently identified herself as his wife.

refused to intervene as rioters murdered thousands of Jews in fierce pogroms. In response, more than two million Jews emigrated between 1881 and 1914, with most headed to the United States, a land about which they knew little save for its reputation for equality and opportunity. The earliest waves, of which the Harrisons were a part, generally were uneducated, young, and poor.

It was a difficult journey. Emigrants from Russia's western border typically made their way first to Berlin by foot, wagon, or train, and from there to one of Germany's northern ports. Then, perhaps in Hamburg or Bremen, young Benjamin and Paula would have been steered like cattle into sheds where, stripped, they were disinfected. By then penniless (the passage in steerage from Bremen to New York was about $30 a person, equivalent to $650 in today's dollars), Benjamin and Paula were herded into the lowest level of the ship where they would spend the next fourteen days in the near dark, with limited rations, little access to a toilet, and no opportunity to wash, breathing fetid air filled with the thick odors of garlic, tobacco, and sweat.

After passing through Castle Garden, the Harrisons initially settled, like most Russian Jews, in the tenements of the Lower East Side, where Paula gave birth to Helen four years later. While less dangerous, life there wasn't much easier than it had been in Russia. For one thing, their new neighborhood was crowded, with 522 inhabitants per acre in 1890, making it the city's most densely populated area and reputedly more crowded than the worst slums of Bombay. By 1897, with the opening of mass transit through the Upper East Side, the Harrisons decided to leave, joining nearly 100,000 other Russian Jews in settling East Harlem, to that point largely an Irish-German neighborhood. The family moved to East Ninety-sixth Street, where in 1898 Paula gave birth to a second daughter, Gertrude, who died in her early forties. Ida, who came to be known as Edith, was born in 1899. By 1900, Benjamin's sister Freda had joined the family. Thus little Max Harrison, who later adopted the name Robert, was surrounded by five doting women when he came into the world on April 14, 1904.

By all accounts Harrison's was an ordinary childhood, with the family moving from block to block in East Harlem before finally settling in the Bronx, a working-class neighborhood whose spacious apartments had became accessible to immigrants from Manhattan's tenements with the opening of the first subway line in 1904 and the construction of the Third Avenue elevated train. There young Bob showed an early entrepreneurial flair. At one point he set up shop at a subway exit to rent umbrellas during a rainstorm. Around the age of twelve, he hit on the idea for his first magazine, *Harrison's Weekend Guide,* a guide to roadside inns and other services for the new motoring public, which quickly was appropriated by an unscrupulous printer. What Harrison didn't show was an aptitude for education. He lasted only two years at Stuyvesant High School, which he entered before the Board of Education imposed the entrance exams that gave it its reputation for educational excellence. He took a few night courses at Columbia, and then worked at a series of jobs over the next two decades in one form or another of journalism and advertising—the "air businesses" his father decried.

4

"Exclusive Photos! How Rita Hayworth's Children Were Neglected"

It was a shocked and disbelieving nation that picked up its newspapers late this spring to read the incredible story of Rita Hayworth's children. The new Mrs. Haymes immediately cried "foul," and set off a nationwide debate as to whether she was being persecuted or whether the little girls had, in fact, been neglected.

Spread before you on these pages are authentic pictures which settle that argument for all time. They tell, better than words, exactly how Yasmin—four-year-old daughter of a Moslem prince and heir to a $500,000,000 fortune—was living in White Plains, New York, with nine-year-old Rebecca. These are pictures a whole world who discussed the case never got to see and this is a report never before put in print . . .

Tipped off by angry neighbors, I went to White Plains to investigate this modern Cinderella story last March 18th. Perhaps they were the same neighbors who later protested to the Westchester Children's Society; I do not know. But there was no doubt that I had found a million-dollar baby—literally—among the ash cans of White Plains.

Asked Lensman Not to Photograph Yasmin

Little Yasmin and her half-sister Rebecca had been living—off and on—in the seedy, rundown home of an antiques and second-hand-furniture dealer ever since Rita, Dick and the two children were tossed out of a Greenwich, Conn., mansion Haymes had rented. Newspaper reports at the time quoted Dick's landlord as claiming he was owed $675 in back rent, plus another $4,000 for damage to his property while the four had lived there.

Rita, Dick and the little girls swept off to the swank Madison Hotel, one of Manhattan's best hostelries, and Mrs. Haymes maternally told the press "the children are going to stay with us from now on." She emphasized her mother's role by asking photographers not to snap pictures of Yasmin, explaining that she was still nervous over letters she had received threatening the child's life.

Less than 48 hours later, however, the little girls were dumped in the custody of an aging matron whose strongest claim to her right to care for the youngsters was the fact that she'd known Dick for five years.

I arrived at the combination shop-and-home of Mrs. Dorothy Chambers, to find Yasmin in a trash-littered backyard, playing among an assortment of loaded ash cans.

What added to the irony of the picture she presented was that afternoon newspapers of that very day were headlining a statement to the effect that Prince Aly Khan was on the verge of settling $1,000,000 on the little girl, plus a maintenance income of $7,000 per year. As I watched her play and talked to her, she looked like she'd have traded the whole thing for a cup of hot soup and a friendly lap to sit on.

Excerpt from "Exclusive Photos! How
Rita Hayworth's Children Were Neglected"
(September 1954)

In April 1954, Rita Hayworth appeared before a New York judge to answer allegations that she had neglected her children. The following September, *Confidential* enraged Hayworth with a portfolio of pictures showing her and husband Dick Haymes dining at El Morocco while her children, Rebecca, daughter of Orson Welles, and Yasmin, daughter of Prince Aly Khan, played in a basket of garbage and sat on the dingy porch of the rooming house to which they'd been exiled by their mother.

31

Confidential editor Jay Breen, posing as a prospective lodger, described the filth and poverty in which the children lived. At the same time, he reminded readers that Haymes had recently tipped a Manhattan restaurant doorman five dollars to watch his dog. This sort of Hollywood scandal was becoming increasingly important to *Confidential*. And Hayworth became as frequent a subject as Marilyn Monroe. In January 1956, for example, the magazine reported in the article "Why Rita Hayworth Walked Out on Dick" that Haymes brutally beat her on many occasions. "The facts are that not just one night but the entire two years of their marriage were a non-stop nightmare for Rita, during which the best-loved pinup girl of World War II *was subjected to countless cruel beatings!*" *Confidential* reported, with italics and exclamation point for emphasis. "Haymes' favorite form of assault was to grab Rita by her world-famed tresses and slam her head against a wall until her senses reeled."

Of Romani ancestry, Hayworth had restyled her hairline with electrolysis, her nose with surgery, and her lush dark hair with a red dye job to join Betty Grable, Dorothy Lamour, Hedy Lamarr, and Lana Turner as one of World War II's most popular pinup girls. Her success in *You'll Never Get Rich* and *The Strawberry Blonde* in 1941, *Tales of Manhattan* in 1942, and *Gilda* in 1946 made her one of Columbia's biggest stars of the 1940s. While her acting career was on hiatus during her marriage to Haymes, *Confidential's* attack on her didn't endear the magazine to Columbia studio chief Harry Cohn, who so treasured Hayworth he had refused to loan her to other studios. By Hollywood standards, perhaps even more foolhardy than attacking Joe Schenck was *Confidential's* giving offense to Cohn.

"Harry Cohn, as absolute a monarch as Hollywood ever knew, ran Columbia like a private police state," recalled Jesse Lasky Jr., a Columbia contract writer. "He was tough, feared, ruthless and courageous, unbearably crude, profane, quirky, a hammer-headed power-machine who held total financial and physical control over his self-made empire. He chewed cigars and relatives. It was said that he would fire and blacklist a man for mentioning verboten subjects like death or disease in his private studio dining room, where a coterie of privileged henchmen vied for his favors. It was said he had listening devices on all sound stages and could tune in any conversation on the set, then boom in over a loud-

Rita Hayworth had suffered negative publicity from her April 1954 appearance before a New York City judge to answer allegations that she had neglected her children, Rebecca and Yasmin. *Confidential*, which operated under the theory that celebrity scandal was always newsworthy, published a story five months later with photographs showing her children playing in garbage at the dingy rooming house where she had left them. It reminded readers that while Hayworth's children lived in poverty, her husband, Dick Haymes, had tipped a restaurant doorman five dollars to watch his dog.

speaker if he heard anything that displeased him. It was said that every evening he personally toured his big studio, trying to catch anyone who might have left on a light."

Yet, because of the risks Harrison took with stories like the Hayworth piece, *Confidential*'s circulation grew with every issue. By the summer of 1954 it exceeded a million copies. It was clear how important Holly-wood stories were to *Confidential*'s success. Harrison worried that the magazine no longer could depend on over-the-transom tips. In September 1954 he went to Hollywood for only the second time in his life to set up a network of informants that was to become as critical to the magazine's success as to its eventual demise.

The Hollywood that Harrison visited had changed a lot since his previous tour, courtesy of Martin Quigley, nineteen years earlier. Hollywood in 1954 looked more prosperous than it had in 1935, twenty-five years after the filming of D. W. Griffith's *In Old California* had made it America's film capital. The streets were lined with faux Spanish haciendas and Art Moderne buildings and rumbled with expensive automobiles. There also was nightlife. Mocambo, with its walls lined with glass cages holding parrots and macaws, had opened on Sunset Boulevard and offered dancing until dawn. Chasen's, on Beverly Boulevard in nearby Beverly Hills, drew Dean Martin, Sammy Davis Jr., and Frank Sinatra, among other celebrities. The Hollywood Chamber of Commerce had even stepped in to fix one blight from the 1930s—a crumbling sign that read "Hollywoodland," erected in 1923 on Mount Lee to promote a real estate development in the Hollywood Hills. The chamber stripped the last four letters off the sign and repaired the rest.

But there was trouble under that gloss of prosperity and fun. In 1935, Hollywood had been well into its so-called Golden Age. Five major studios (MGM, Paramount Pictures, RKO, Twentieth Century–Fox, and Warner Bros.) dominated the industry. They were distinguished from the "Little Three" (Columbia Pictures, United Artists, and Universal Pictures) by their ownership of production facilities, distributors, and theaters. Thus vertically integrated, they produced, marketed, distributed, and exhibited the films they made.

In the years that followed Harrison's first visit, and particularly since the end of World War II, Hollywood's fortunes had undergone a sharp reversal. For one thing, stars began rebelling against the contracts that kept them in thrall to one studio for a seven-year period. While a desire to manage one's own career was a major impetus, so was the marginal federal income tax rate of 90 percent that had been instituted to help fund the wartime military effort. Well-paid stars found it more profitable to establish their own companies rather than work for wages for a studio. While a downturn in box-office revenues late in the forties dampened that push to independence, the trend was set when Olivia de Havilland won a 1945 suit against Warner Bros. The studio had suspended her after she refused to be loaned to other studios for insignificant roles following her appearance in *Gone With the Wind.* The courts ruled that contracts could not be extended as a disciplinary measure beyond their seven-year term. The California legislature soon passed a law codifying the court decision. The studios had lost an important tool for controlling their talent.

A much bigger issue was the U.S. Supreme Court's 1948 ruling against Paramount in a federal antitrust case that challenged the studio system of forcing movie theaters to accept less attractive films if they wanted to screen more-popular ones. The court sent the case back to a lower court, suggesting that busting up the vertically integrated operations would cure what it saw as monopolistic behavior. Before the lower court could rule, Howard Hughes, who controlled RKO, agreed to separate his production business from his distribution business and sell one or the other. That agreement, on November 8, 1948, put pressure on the other major studios to do likewise. It took a while to unwind, but by 1954 the all-powerful studio system, with its tight control of talent, production, marketing, and distribution, was no more.

Add to that the anti-Communist witch hunters, who had turned their attention to Hollywood. In May 1947, Congressman Parnell Thomas, Republican of New Jersey, met with studio executives to express his concerns about Reds among their screenwriters. In October of that year, Thomas's House Committee on Un-American Activities held hearings in Washington that led to the imprisonment for contempt of the "Hollywood Ten," a group of screenwriters and directors who had

35

refused to testify before the committee, citing their Fifth Amendment right against self-incrimination. The hearings, as planned by Thomas, attracted enormous publicity. One of the star witnesses for the Red hunters was Howard Rushmore.

All of this couldn't have come at a worse time for the studios. Where box-office grosses totaled $1.7 billion in 1946, by 1950 they were at $1.4 billion. Profits of $121 million in 1946 had fallen to $48 million in 1948. The advent of television, the suburbanization of America (and resulting decline of neighborhood theaters), the development of other forms of entertainment such as bowling and night baseball, and an absence of blockbuster hits were all blamed for the decline.

Hollywood paid little attention to Robert Harrison's second foray into the heart of Filmland. But he got plenty of attention from cops, private detectives, prostitutes, and B actors delighted to find a market for the information they picked up in the course of their various lines of work. "*Confidential* . . . would get tips from starlets, party girls, night-club hatcheck girls, cynical press agents with a meat cleaver to grind and any one of that great army of disgruntled movie people who hate somebody or other for once doing them wrong," wrote Ezra Goodman, *Time* magazine's Hollywood correspondent. "Some of the tipsters were even among the press."

Among the magazine's most important tipsters was Veronica "Ronnie" Quillan, a beautiful redheaded prostitute and madam, then in her late thirties, who was known to tabloid writers as the "soiled dove." Quillan had briefly been married to screenwriter Joseph Quillan, perhaps best known for *Our Miss Brooks* (1956), before becoming what magazines called "Hollywood's number-one madam." Quillan had emerged from Hollywood's darker shadows in 1949, when newspapers reported that her ear almost was severed by a razor in a fight with French singer Roland Gerbeau. In December 1950, she was in the headlines again when she was arrested for cutting up singer Billy Daniels with a butcher knife while he was at her apartment. She later made news by using a razor to slash Herb Jeffries, an actor known as the Bronze Buckaroo for his role in several all-black Westerns and her husband at the time. She agreed to gather information from her network of "girls" and to inform on former lovers such as Jeffries and Desi Arnaz.

There also was the exotic Countess Francesca de Bourbon y de Scaffa, twenty-four, a blond Venezuelan beauty who also claimed at various times to be of Italian, Chinese, Hindu, French, and Egyptian ancestry. De Scaffa, whose slight film career included minor appearances in *On the Riviera* (1951) and *Captain John Smith and Pocahontas* (1953), tooled around Hollywood in a white Jaguar. She was the former wife of actor Bruce Cabot and the paramour of Clark Gable, Orson Welles, and the Shah of Iran, whose indiscreet cables to her were to be lavishly displayed in a *Confidential* story. Another consort was Jaime Bravo, perhaps Mexico's most famous bullfighter at the time. In Hollywood, rumor had it that the mysterious and beautiful de Scaffa was the illegitimate daughter of the king of Spain. She offered to have an affair with any man if it got a story for *Confidential*.

And there was Fred Otash, a former L.A. vice squad cop with a lust for celebrity and a skill at wiretapping. While still a cop, Otash managed to sell Louis B. Mayer an idea for a movie, appear on a television program extolling his success in curbing shoplifting at Los Angeles's Farmer's Market, and bed more than a few actresses. "Good looking actresses and show girls . . . have a yen for strong, protective men," Otash explained. His passion for publicity and his rebellious personality had put him at odds with Police Chief William Parker, who fired him. Otash promptly opened a private-investigation agency. He became an FBI informant on the L.A. mob and sold Harrison information on his clients and on girlfriends such as Kim Novak and Anita Ekberg. For Otash and others of *Confidential*'s more productive informants, the work was lucrative. By 1955, Otash was making $35,000 a year from the magazine, a sum equivalent to $250,000 today.

Their work was facilitated, according to *Time* magazine correspondent Ezra Goodman, by Hollywood's infatuation with new technology. Hollywood in the fifties was a "beehive of 'private eyes' [who] tapped telephones and recording machines. It sometimes seemed as if every telephone had a tape recorder attached to it—you never knew whether your conversation was being recorded or not. Miniature recording machines that could be concealed on one's person were big sellers at the

Paid *Confidential* informant Francesca de Scaffa claimed at various times to have been of Egyptian, Chinese, French, Hindu, Italian, and Venezuelan ancestry. Her brief film career included minor appearances in *On the Riviera* (1951) and *Captain John Smith and Pocahontas* (1953) and ended with a featured role in *Edge of Hell* (1956, shown here with Ken Carlton).

leading recording concerns to everyone from members of the vice squad to vice presidents in charge of production, and from agents to secret agents." Even Ronnie Quillan was said to have equipped her girls with wristwatches with embedded microphones.

Recordings and other documentation were important to Harrison. From the very beginning, he had been worried about lawsuits. In addition to hiring informants to provide a regular flow of story tips, *Confidential* paid to check out tips that others brought forward. That was an important part of the magazine's fact-checking process, one for which

Francesca de Scaffa said she was the paramour of Orson Welles, Clark Gable, and the Shah of Iran, on whom she informed for *Confidential*. She said she would have an affair with any man if it helped her get a story for the magazine.

Harrison engaged investigators around the world. One of the most colorful, Michael Mordaunt-Smith, an Englishman, was a direct descendant of Mary Tudor, a former subaltern in the Black Watch, and later the mastermind of an "only in England" effort to raise pigs in the drawing rooms and boudoirs of the castle on his uncle's three-thousand-acre Irish estate. Mordaunt-Smith claims to have vetted eight hundred stories for Harrison and was kept on a retainer of $350 a week as *Confidential's* London source. He was assigned to interview Uruguayan Esteban Larraura for a *Confidential* story alleging that Ava Gardner had attempted to seduce the thirty-two-year-old bandleader during a London visit. Among the more explosive stories that he vetted was a piece that claimed Maureen O'Hara had "taken the darndest position to watch a movie" with a Mexican man in a back row at Grauman's Chinese Theatre.

Harrison also retained a lawyer, Albert DeStefano, who obtained sworn affidavits that provided further legal protection. DeStefano, a Fordham graduate who took his law degree at night school and was a happily married homebody, became one of Harrison's closest confidants. He taught *Confidential* that another way to ward off legal attacks was to print slightly less than it knew. DeStefano explained that if the magazine published a story accusing a celebrity of having sex with a woman not his wife, it might choose to withhold the detail that the lover was an underage girl. The threat that the whole story would come out in court was sufficient to deter most libel suits. Otash concurred. What *Confidential* actually published was "pretty thin stuff" compared to what he and others turned up, the detective said.

Harrison's concern about accuracy didn't stem solely from a fear of lawsuits. He believed that accuracy was one of *Confidential*'s strongest selling points. Indeed, over the years, most of the stories in *Confidential* proved to be true. In 1954, trumpeting that selling point, the magazine changed its cover line from "Uncensored and Off the Record" to "Tells the Facts and Names the Names."

It was an important distinction. The traditional fan magazines, desperate for advertising revenue and access to stars, were more than willing to yield to studio pressure. "We controlled the fan magazines," said MGM publicist Esme Chandlee. "When a star did an interview, the story was submitted to us, and we took out whatever we wanted."

"Right at the beginning, one of the things I told Harrison is we should never print a retraction," DeStefano recalled years later. "It would hurt our credibility. Even if we had to take a licking in court, we wouldn't retract. So we had to make sure our stories were accurate." It was a rule Harrison broke only once. In a story published in its second issue, entitled "The Mob Moves In on Show Business," *Confidential* claimed Ray Muscarella, Tony Bennett's manager, was a mobster. Only a week after the issue hit the stands, Harrison was visited by Muscarella and an associate who, as some stories have it, dangled Harrison upside down from his office window until he promised a retraction. "Harrison

Fred Otash, a former vice-squad cop, was *Confidential*'s primary investigator in Los Angeles. His involvement in Joe DiMaggio's infamous "Wrong Door Raid" on Marilyn Monroe's supposed love nest led to a California legislative inquiry into improper behavior by private eyes. Otash sold the magazine information on former girlfriends such as Kim Novak and Anita Ekberg.

proceeded to apologize personally and forward a letter of apology, and then publish a full retraction." The headline: "When We Make a Mistake, It's a Beaut!"

"The . . . problem was that Muscarella was not the person *Confidential* thought he was," reported the *Chicago Sun-Times*. "The story was a horrible mistake." But Harrison's apology, no doubt prompted in large measure by the threat of defenestration, was too hasty. Bennett later described Muscarella, whom he hired in the 1940s, as an "unsavory character" and explained that in those days his line of work usually was connected with the underworld. In 1955, he said, he paid Muscarella off and parted company with him.

With his back covered in Hollywood, Harrison further strengthened his relationship with Walter Winchell on his return to New York. He appointed Howard Rushmore, whom he'd named a *Confidential* contributing editor on Winchell's recommendation, as associate editor to provide a steady flow of stories on political scandal and hidden Communists. Rushmore, a newspaper journalist and Red hunter, was to become the most famous of a string of *Confidential* editors. They included the *Police Gazette*'s Edythe Farrell; A. P. "Al" Govoni, another *Police Gazette* editor, who had helped Harrison mock up the earliest dummies of the magazine; and Jay Breen, a former United Press writer whom Harrison later credited with writing "half the magazine" and who was to die of alcoholism. Harrison attributed Breen's drinking problems to his inability to cope with the success he found at *Confidential*.

5

"The Strange Death of J. Robert Oppenheimer's RED Sweetheart"

Police found her nude body in the bathroom of her San Francisco apartment. There was a grim touch of neatness, even comfort, in the way she had met death. After filling the tub with water, she had arranged a stack of pillows around the edge and drowned herself.

But in the fireplace in the living room, a wisp of smoke still curled from a half-burned stack of documents and her father was explaining to the bewildered cops that he had been burning her "private correspondence."

The California newspaper shrugged off the story as a routine suicide, describing the girl as "Dr. Jean S. Tatlock, 29, a psychiatrist, and daughter of Dr. John S. Tatlock, University of California English professor." The date was January 6, 1944.

This May Be Key to the Mystery

The full details behind the Ophelia-like death in the pillow-lined bathtub have never been disclosed until now. For the pretty doctor who left a note saying she was "disgusted with everything" had a few months before been a vivacious, happy person with that inward glow that comes only to a woman in love.

And in the same apartment where tragedy was to strike, she had entertained for the entire night a married man whose name has been on Page One of the nation's newspapers for the past year. Jean Tatlock's self-confessed lover was J. Robert Oppenheimer, the "Father of the Atom Bomb."

What made this sad-eyed scientist with the crew haircut and the almost-posed look of a wistful Ivy Leaguer leave at a critical state in the development of the world's most dangerous weapon to keep a tryst at Jean's apartment at 1405 Montgomery Street?

Only recently, the Atomic Energy Commission denied Oppenheimer security clearance and publicly announced that it had found "fundamental defects" in his character.

The key to the mystery may revolve around the statement Oppenheimer made under oath to the AEC: "She [Miss Tatlock] was, as it turned out later, a friend of many fellow travelers and Communists, a number of whom I later was to become acquainted with."

Why did Jean Tatlock introduce her circle of Red friends to the man who, in 1941, was one of the few persons in the world who knew about the planned construction of the A-bomb—a secret that Soviet spies were spending millions to discover?

> *Excerpt from "The Strange Death of*
> *J. Robert Oppenheimer's RED Sweetheart!"*
> *(November 1954)*

Jean Tatlock introduced Robert Oppenheimer to her circle of friends not to pry atomic secrets from him, but because she and Oppenheimer were, in some sense of the word, in love.

Before he met Tatlock in the spring of 1936, Oppenheimer was as naïve about politics as he was sophisticated about nuclear physics. "My friends, both in Pasadena and in Berkeley, were mostly faculty people, scientists, classicists and artists," he wrote in a 1954 letter responding to his notorious suspension that June from the Atomic Energy Commission as a security risk.

"I was not interested in and did not read about economics or politics. I was almost wholly divorced from the contemporary scene in this country. I never read a newspaper or a current magazine like *Time* or like *Harper's*; I had no radio, no telephone; I learned of the stock-market crash in the fall of '29 only long after the event . . . To many of my friends, my indifference to contemporary affairs seemed bizarre, and they often chided me with being too much of a highbrow."

All that changed by the fall of 1936, when Oppenheimer fell in love with Tatlock, who was universally described as warmhearted and beautiful, although prone to periodic bouts of depression. Tatlock, a medical student at the University of California at Berkeley, introduced him to her friends, and for the first time he became aware of what was going on in the wider world.

Those friends included many members of the Communist Party, with which Tatlock had flirted for years. Others were so-called fellow travelers, committed to fighting Fascists in Spain or Nazis in Germany. Oppenheimer, who inherited the equivalent of $4 million in today's money on the death of his father in 1937, began supporting his friends' causes.

"Beginning in late 1936, my interests began to change," Oppenheimer said in his 1954 letter. "These changes did not alter my earlier friendships, my relations to my students or my devotion to physics; but they added something new. I can discern in retrospect more than one reason for these changes. I had a continuing, smoldering fury about the treatment of Jews in Germany. I had relatives there, and was later to help in extracting them and bringing them to this country. I saw what the Depression was doing to my students. Often they could get no jobs, or jobs which were wholly inadequate. And through them I began to understand how deeply political and economic events could affect men's lives. I began to feel the need to participate more fully in the life of the community. But I had no framework of political conviction or experience to give me perspective in these matters."

Oppenheimer and Tatlock broke up in the fall of 1939 when she refused his proposal of marriage. Perhaps one reason Tatlock turned him down was that she was lesbian, a detail that surely would have been trumpeted in *Confidential*'s story if Harrison had known it. Oppenheimer went on to marry Katherine Puening Harrison, herself a former Communist Party member.

Oppenheimer's affair with Tatlock played only a minor role in the Atomic Energy Commission's decision to revoke his security clearance.

J. Robert Oppenheimer's affair with Jean Tatlock, a leftist medical student who later committed suicide, left the nuclear scientist open to questions about his patriotism that were leveled in a November 1954 story by Howard Rushmore.

More important was his failure to promptly tell authorities that Haakon Chevalier, an assistant professor of French literature at Berkeley who had been introduced to him by Tatlock, had pressed members of his staff to leak information to the Communist Party. Oppenheimer also had hired his brother, Frank, a former Communist Party member, to work with him on his atomic bomb projects. Perhaps most damning, at least in the eyes of the military establishment, Oppenheimer lobbied for international control of atomic weapons after seeing the destruction his creation had wreaked at Hiroshima and Nagasaki.

While not central to Oppenheimer's loss of his security clearance, the Tatlock affair provided salacious copy for *Confidential*. "Oppenheimer, when asked about his girlfriend, admitted he had seen her at least 10 times after he was married to Katherine Harrison in 1940," the magazine reported.

"Questioned by counsel for a government loyalty board, Oppenheimer said flatly when asked why the Tatlock girl had to see him:

" 'Because she was still in love with me.'

". . . After his marriage in 1940, the meetings with Jean continued and the scientist said:

" 'I do not think it would be right to say that our acquaintance was casual. We had been very much involved with one another, and there was still very deep feeling when we saw each other.' "

The story, written by Howard Rushmore, was relatively old news by the time the magazine hit the newsstands in October 1954. At that point, Oppenheimer had lived three months with the disgrace of losing his membership on the Atomic Energy Commission. He had put Los Alamos and Washington behind him and returned to Princeton. But the story did cement the magazine's, and Rushmore's, relationship with FBI director J. Edgar Hoover, who was convinced that Oppenheimer was a Soviet agent.

The Red Menace was yet another insecurity in American life that Harrison used to *Confidential*'s advantage, both as a circulation builder and to craft an aura of social purpose in what was, after all, a gossip magazine. It was the main focus of Rushmore's work, when he wasn't writing attacks on enemies of *Confidential* patron Walter Winchell, who helped him get his magazine job. He was ideal for the task. He had earned a living and a reputation for much of his adult life by exploiting the fear of Communism. Appearing as an expert witness in 1947 before a House Committee on Un-American Activities hearing on communism in Hollywood, he had identified screenwriters Alvah Bessie, John Howard Lawson, Clifford Odets, and Dalton Trumbo, and actor John Garfield as party members. That, and further hearings in the spring of 1952, in which director Elia Kazan had named other entertainment industry figures who once had belonged to the Communist Party, kept Hollywood on edge.

Ironically, Rushmore had joined the Communist Party himself at the age of twenty-one. That didn't surprise friends in Mexico, Missouri, the small town near his mother's family home to which the Rushmores had retreated in 1925 after his father had lost his job on the railroad and failed at farming in South Dakota. Howard always had been the obstinate one—the boy who marched left when everyone else marched right, and vice versa.

There was that time, for example, at Mexico High School, when Howard and two fellow students had been hauled before the principal for publishing articles critical of the faculty in the *Yellow Yap*, their unauthorized student newspaper. The principal agreed to let the boys go unpunished if they'd fold the *Yap* and apologize to everyone before a school-wide assembly. Classmates Jim Sterner and Bill Taft dutifully offered their apologies. But when Rushmore stood up before his classmates and teachers, he announced that he was apologizing only because he was being forced to. Days later he was expelled and enrolled in St. Brendan's Catholic school, where his Southern Methodist upbringing, if not his cantankerous disposition, assured him outsider status. Rushmore quit without ever earning a high school diploma. Cantankerous. Awkward. Ill at ease. Different. These were the words Rushmore's friends used to describe him.

Rushmore maintained it was his search for "true democracy"—not a desire to be difficult or different—that took him to the Communist Party in the first place. A truly egalitarian society would have helped his father and mother survive on their South Dakota farm, where George Rushmore worked from dawn to dusk seven days a week without irrigation or modern machinery. "My mother helped with the chores, milking the cows, slopping the hogs, tending the huge garden and canning the vegetables that would be our winter food . . . They grew old before my eyes," Rushmore later recalled. The problem, he decided, was the form of democracy practiced in the United States. In the Mexico Public Library he read about Fascism and discarded it as an answer. Then, the summer of his freshman year in high school, he took a job picking fruit in Washington State and became convinced of the unfairness of the laws of supply and demand.

"The pay was ten cents an hour; the peaches sold back home for five cents each," Rushmore wrote in the *American Mercury*. "One day in the library I picked up a book on the Russian experiment and was overpow-

Howard Rushmore joined the Communist Party as a youth and worked his way to a job as movie critic for the party's *Daily Worker*. In December 1939 the newspaper fired Rushmore for writing a glowing review of *Gone With the Wind*, which the party viewed as racist. The firing convinced Rushmore that he had a more promising future as an anti-Communist.

ered by a flood of new ideas from a new world. My mind was receptive then, and had this been a book on democracy in action, explaining that gradually democracy was doing things to help jobless youth, the aged and the sick, I would have clung to democracy with renewed conviction. But there was no such book . . . So, weary of poverty, bewildered by selfishness and ignorance, I grasped this new utopia."

The article, like many he wrote about his youthful flirtation with Communism, smacks of historical revisionism. It was typical of Rushmore to exploit his impoverished beginnings, as if he felt they somehow ennobled him. But in truth his family was desperately poor. Jim Sterner recalled a visit to his high school friend's house for dinner. "Another friend and I, invited by Howard's mother to a meal, couldn't help but note that the coffee apparently had been made with minimal grains, and we wondered if perhaps that had been a cupful borrowed from a neighbor," Sterner said. "And that meal, we learned, somehow, later, had been a rooster, last survivor of the flock. To repeat, in those Hoover years, nobody had any money. But in my family, and in most, there was food to eat and there were some niceties, if minimal. But the Rushmores were poorer than poor."

In his library search for a world beyond Mexico, Missouri, Rushmore discovered Jack Conroy, a novelist who lived in nearby Moberly, Missouri. Conroy was founder of the *Anvil*, which billed itself "the Proletarian Fiction Magazine" and published the early works of writers such as Langston Hughes, Richard Wright, and William Carlos Williams. Conroy made Rushmore an associate editor of the *Anvil*. He also introduced Rushmore to Stanley Ferguson, editor of *Forge*, a leftist journal published in St. Louis, who convinced Rushmore to join the Communist Party in 1933. In the Depression era of the thirties, the party wasn't seen as an evil force the way it was in the 1940s and 1950s. With about eighteen thousand members, and perhaps five times as many followers, the Communist Party of the Great Depression drew support for its focus on the rights of blacks and its efforts to help workers organize. The party's support of Franklin Roosevelt's presidential candidacy in 1936, and its decision in 1935 to make common cause with Socialists and others to its right, helped it win acceptance from a broad range of American intellectuals.

In addition to writing for the *Anvil*, Rushmore had a brief sojourn as editor of the Young Communist League's newspaper and then as an organizer of farmers in the Dakotas. Rushmore also served as the party's assistant state organizer in Iowa.

He moved to New York City in 1937 to write for Tass, the Communist Party wire service, at a salary of $100 a week. In a matter of weeks, he took a pay cut to move to the *Daily Worker*, the party's newspaper, where he soon was named film critic and had a U.S. audience that Tass couldn't provide.

While in many ways Rushmore was the passionate ideologue, in others he was a typical young bachelor in the big city. He settled into an apartment on Barrow Street in Greenwich Village, at the time the most

bohemian of American neighborhoods ("It is in the Village and surrounded by fairies and fruits of all kinds and descriptions," he wrote to
Jim Sterner of his apartment.) In letters home he boasted about how
hard he was working and about his love life in jocular terms that would
have surprised those who came to know him later as stern and dour.
"Have a little girl trouble now," he wrote one friend in December 1935.
"Had a nice dame for a while here—she moved to Chicago. Then my
old girlfriend from Tucson and St. Louis looks me up but she drops out
of the picture and I find another nice one. This week: the bitch comes
back from Chicago, Miss Tucson becomes active . . . No Don Juan. Just
a lack of social planning."

Rushmore struggled to pay his bills, writing friends back home for
the occasional loan of two dollars here and ten dollars there. His pay put
cocktails out of reach, he complained, although he wrote that he could
afford the occasional beer. Things got tighter when, in a cost-cutting
move, the *Daily Worker* cut his full-time job and made him a freelance
reviewer. Money became even more of an issue in December 1936,
when Rushmore married Ruth Garvin, who wrote a women's column
for the *Sunday Worker Progressive Weekly*, and they began talking about
starting a family.

Ever cantankerous, Rushmore found himself in fights from time to
time with his *Daily Worker* editors. He got into an argument with David
Ingram, a senior editor, over Ingram's view that the *Daily Worker's* sports
pages were a "bourgeois influence." Rushmore also found suspect his
editor's orders to soft pedal certain stories (the decision by England and
France to declare war on Germany, then in a nonaggression pact with
Russia, was given only a one-column headline).

However, what forced Rushmore out of the *Daily Worker* and the
Communist Party, onto the front pages of the nation's newspapers, and
eventually to *Confidential*, was his review of *Gone With the Wind*. Rushmore loved the movie, as did the rest of America (it eventually sold more
tickets than any other film in history and won ten Academy Awards).
GWTW, as the headline writers called it, at that point the most expensive movie ever made, was itself front-page news when the *Daily Worker*
ordered Rushmore to rewrite the glowing review he had submitted. He
refused and was fired.

"Our decision to drop Rushmore as a contributor followed his submitting of a review of *Gone With the Wind* which was a shameless glorification of white chauvinism and an affront to the Negro people," the *Daily Worker* announced on its front page. "Because of Rushmore's youth and inexperience, the *Daily Worker* sought in the past patiently to clarify him on various fundamental issues. But when he was released from his regular duties on the *Daily Worker* several months ago, Rushmore's previously concealed careeristic, mercenary, and anti–working class tendencies came out more and more into the open. Their expression in a most blatant form was climaxed in his shameful review of *Gone With the Wind*. His previous anti–working class tendencies, culminating in the review, definitely placed him in the camp of reaction, as an enemy of the working class."

"Reds Fire Film Critic For Enjoying GWTW," screamed the *New York Journal-American* on its front page. "Red Paper Critic Gone With Wind," reported the *New York Post*. "*Daily Worker* Critic Forced Out of Job On Refusal to Attack *Gone With the Wind*," wrote the *New York Times*.

Rushmore took quick advantage of the furor, writing a lengthy article on the front page of Hearst's stridently anti-Communist *Journal-American* the next day (for which he received $400) that was titled "Red Paper's Lies Bared by Ex-Critic." "Thanks to David Selznick and Margaret Mitchell my last illusions about 'Communism being the Americanism of the Twentieth Century' have gone with the wind," Rushmore wrote, quoting a slogan of U.S. Communist Party boss Earl Browder. "The refusal of the *Daily Worker* to print my review of the $4,000,000 film epic marked the last episode in my six years of activity in the Communist Party. For three years, as a member of their staff in a number of editorial positions, I saw the lie elevated to an art in a paper that boasts a slogan 'The Truth in the News.' Our copy desk rule was: There is no God but Stalin, and the *Daily Worker* is his American prophet."

Rushmore disputed the *Daily Worker's* charges that he was racist, anti-Semitic, and anti–working class. "My ancestors, since 1650—on both sides of the family—have been farmers, miners and sailors. I was raised on a Wyoming homestead and was pushing a plow through the sagebrush when [*Daily Worker* managing editor] Sam Don and the *Daily Worker* editors were learning their Marx in Moscow."

Rushmore mailed the story to his hometown friend Jim Sterner on the day it appeared. "For once in my life I didn't care about making page 1," he wrote, somewhat disingenuously. "I just wanted to get things off my chest, and lo and behold, my ugly mug and name were above the fold in every Friday edition. Am wondering Dave Selznick's reaction." A week later, Rushmore wrote again, with more good news. "Got all the god-damned publicity in the world," he told Sterner. "*Newsweek* had about the best spread. Did you see it? And right now I'm trying to convert all those words into a bank account, something I've never had and am going to have. At the same time I'm keeping a few ideals so I won't become an utter sonofabitch. One of Broadway's best publicity men has me under his wing and has a lot of plans which now are being hatched."

Rushmore's new life offered greater fame and financial rewards than his job as the *Daily Worker*'s film critic. But it also put him in opposition to old friends such as Jack Conroy and Nelson Algren, another writer who, in the working-class neighborhoods of Chicago, had been a fellow traveler in the Depression-era search for social justice. Conroy never forgave Rushmore. "Just for a handful of silver he left us," he said, quoting Browning's "The Lost Leader," "Just for a riband to stick in his coat."

It wasn't just ideology and friends that Rushmore abandoned in his new life as a minor celebrity. He also left behind his wife, and their daughter Barbara. In 1945, he married Frances Everitt McCoy, a writer and editor on the women's pages of the *Journal-American* who had two daughters from her first marriage. McCoy was a former Powers model whose image had graced a number of magazine covers.

Soon Rushmore found himself sitting at the right hand of Senator Joseph McCarthy, who hired him as research director for his Red-hunting Sub-Committee on Investigations. To nervous witnesses, Rushmore was an imposing figure because of both his six-foot-five-inch height and his well-known friendship with Walter Winchell. Rushmore became a star writer for the rabidly anti-Communist *Journal-American*. He joined the editorial board of the influential *American Mercury*. And he began to dine at the Stork Club, although his guests were more likely to be Roy Cohn or William F. Buckley Jr. than the starlets and chorus girls who decorated Harrison's table.

6

"Does Desi Really Love Lucy?"

Exactly what makes a husband leave home is something that has been baffling wives since Adam and Eve. For an outstanding example, let's take one of the nation's most famous pops, Desi Arnaz, co-star of television's top show, *I Love Lucy*, and legal partner of luscious Lucille Ball. The jackpot question is: With a curvy, red-haired tid-bit like Lucy waiting for him at home, would Desi be foolish enough to prowl Hollywood like a bachelor wolf and, if so, why?

Just Wait Till Lucy Finds Out

Part of the answer is going to jolt the 45,000,000 fans of the show right out of their TV hammocks. For Desi is most certainly a duck-out daddy.

Why he does it is something you'd have to ask Arnaz. Close friends of his have been holding their breaths for years in fear that his scarlet-tressed wife may bring the discussion up any moment, possibly with a flat-iron in her hand. Lucy, they point out, is a lass with a temper to match her flaming hair, and not one to shrug off a misbehaving Mister.

Desi has, in fact, proved himself an artist at philandering as well as acting, because Lucille is a clock-watching mama, the kind that checks her hubby's collar for lipstick when he comes home. And the couple have such a back-breaking work schedule to produce their weekly TV drama that Desi's had to sandwich in his sin.

Under the circumstances, he's done pretty well. Because behind the scenes, Arnaz is a Latin Lothario who loves Lucy most of the time but by no means all the time. He has, in fact, sprinkled his affections all over Los Angeles for a number of years. And quite a bit of it has been bestowed on vice dollies who were paid handsomely for loving Desi briefly but, presumably, as effectively as Lucy.

> *Excerpt from "Does Desi Really Love Lucy?"*
> *(January 1955)*

An illicit assignation in August 1954 at a bungalow at the Beverly Hills Hotel, a rendezvous at a prostitute's home on Hollywood's North Cherokee Boulevard in the winter of 1951, and a weekend affair in Palm Springs in 1944. Unlike many of its stories, in which *Confidential* merely hinted at the possibility of scandal, here it named dates and places. But the call girls it quoted were as pseudonymous as Brad Shortell, identified as the writer of the story, who actually was Howard Rushmore.

The major source was none other than Ronnie Quillan, blessed with an incredible memory for detail, who had spent the 1944 weekend with Arnaz while he briefly was estranged from Lucille Ball. Quillan was later to say she received $1,500 for information regarding the Arnaz affair and another involving her ex-husband, Herb Jeffries. The magazine hit the newsstands almost simultaneously with the December 1954 issue of *Look*, whose main story, "Lucy and Desi, TV's Favorite Family," was promoted by a cover photo showing Lucy, Desi, little Lucie, and little Desi Jr., as the ideal American family.

"Desi met our dark-eyed temptress, Sally [Quillan's pseudonym], in the cocktail lounge of the Ambassador Hotel and asked both her and her girl friend to join his table . . . Before the excitement-hunting babes knew what happened, they found themselves at a party in the home of an army officer stationed in Palm Springs," *Confidential* reported. "The girl recalls she spent the next five or six hours smooching and drinking with Desi . . . Long after dawn had risen, she accepted Arnaz' invitation for a nightcap at his hotel . . . 'I knew Desi was inviting me for more than a drink,' said the babe."

In 1955, Lucille Ball was forty-four and insecure about her looks and her relationship with her husband, Desi Arnaz. *Confidential*'s story in January of that year about Desi's rendezvous ten years earlier with prostitute Veronica Quillan didn't help matters, even though the encounter apparently had taken place during the couple's short-lived mid-1940s divorce proceedings.

Arnaz quickly denied the story. Ball attempted to make light of it. "I remember Lucy wanted to get a copy," recalled Arnaz assistant Johny Aitchison. "She said, Christ, I can't go out and buy that *myself*. Someone go out and get one for me."

The story came at an uncomfortable time for the couple. At forty-four, Ball, six years older than her husband, was more insecure than ever about her looks. She was aware that her husband had a thing for young blondes, and apparently redheads. Arnaz had started drinking heavily, and his philandering had become more outrageous. All of which made Lucy worry about the security of her marriage.

Confidential's story about Desi Arnaz's affair with a prostitute hit the newsstands just as the cover of *Look* magazine promoted Arnaz and Lucille Ball and their children, Lucie and Desi Jr., as the ideal American family.

It was the sort of story Rushmore hated writing. He told old newspaper colleagues that he had nothing to do with flamboyant stories like the Lucy-Desi piece, and others such as "Batista's Eight Million Dollar Divorce," "A Cop Tried to Blackmail Marilyn Monroe," and "The Rory Calhoun Story." In each case, a pseudonym provided him cover. But his family knew the truth, and it was a source of friction. "What he does in his private life is none of your business," one of his stepdaughters had told Rushmore after he wrote a story about one of her favorite stars. "You're no better than a Peeping Tom."

Rushmore later claimed to have been particularly upset when Harrison asked him to write a story about Joan Crawford and her adopted children, one of whom famously accused her of abuse in a 1978 book entitled *Mommie Dearest*. "Our information is that she's mean to the kids," Harrison had told him. "Dig up everything."

"I talked to Miss Crawford for two hours," Rushmore wrote of a meeting that had been arranged by Mike Connolly, the influential gossip columnist for the *Hollywood Reporter*, who was attempting to dissuade *Confidential* from doing the story. "When she had finished, I was convinced of three things: she believed in family discipline; she was a wonderful, understanding and generous foster-parent; I was the lowest creature on earth, digging into the private life of her family.

" 'Thank you for the time,' I said when I left. 'As long as I'm editor of *Confidential*, your children will never be mentioned.' I notified the publisher that the 'facts' he wanted could not be proved."

Rushmore also claimed he was uncomfortable with *Confidential*'s Hollywood sources. He especially objected to Ronnie Quillan, "the soiled dove," saying her work as a madam repulsed him. "She was a woman whose occupation had been halted several times by the Los Angeles vice squad," he wrote. "After ten minutes talking to her I said, 'As long as I'm editor, I'll never use a word of your information.' "

If the flamboyant and gregarious Harrison saw *Confidential* and the hiring of Rushmore as a big step toward respectability, the serious and moody Rushmore worried that the magazine would take his reputation in the opposite direction. "Bob is rude, crude, unlettered and totally unprincipled in the ordinary sense," Rushmore said some years later. "He would print scandal about his mother if he thought it would sell, and then would be indignant if you criticized him for it."

Rushmore had turned Harrison down when he first called in early 1953 at Senator Joe McCarthy's offices in Washington, D.C., where Rushmore was working on leave from the *Journal-American* as a special investigator. Rushmore was invited to work for America's leading anti-

Communist after a series of appearances before investigatory committees around the country. In 1941 he testified at the San Francisco deportation hearing of Harry Bridges, director of the Congress of Industrial Organizations, that Bridges had been accorded special editorial treatment by the *Daily Worker.* In 1947 he testified before the House Committee on Un-American Activities that screenwriter John Howard Lawson was head of Communist Party activities in Hollywood and that the party viewed Charlie Chaplin and Edgar G. Robinson as "sacred cows." In July 1948 he told the Washington state legislature's Committee on Un-American Activities that 150 U.S. government employees were Communists and that Reds had infiltrated the staff of former vice president Henry Wallace, then running for president on the Progressive Party ticket. In 1949, he told the Illinois Seditious Activities Investigation Commission that thirteen University of Chicago educators belonged to Communist-front groups. That same year, he testified before U.S. Senator McCarthy's Judiciary subcommittee that Eleanor Roosevelt and former Secretary of State Cordell Hull had intervened in 1944 to help Raissa Browder, the Russian-born wife of the general secretary of the U.S. Communist Party, obtain a U.S. visa.

Rushmore's testimony, and his writing for the *Journal-American,* attracted the attention of J. Edgar Hoover, director of the FBI, which had placed a wiretap on his Huntington, Long Island, home in 1945, an odd testament to his importance. Hoover, after reading an internal memo in June 1952 about an upcoming Rushmore story about the Communist leadership in America, wrote on the margin: "This makes me a little sick—to know so little about so many top Commies. Certainly not very complimentary! H."

Harrison, wanting to broaden the coverage of *Confidential* to include politics, and please Winchell, kept after Rushmore, offering him a chance to write an exposé of liberal *New York Post* editor James Wechsler, who'd been a member of the Young Communist League as a young man. That got Rushmore's attention—how could he turn down an assignment like that? After all, Wechsler and Dorothy Schiff, the liberal owner of the *Post,* were high on the list of Commie-coddlers that Joe McCarthy and J. Edgar Hoover were trying to expunge from American political life. That was what Howard Rushmore was all about.

Originally, Rushmore signed on only as a freelance "associate editor" to write about communism and politics. Admittedly those were strange elements in a magazine dominated by headlines such as "Sex Styles Change in New York" (about the increasing sophistication of the Big Apple's call girls). With Winchell's prodding Harrison eventually promoted Rushmore from associate editor to *Confidential*'s president and top editor in 1954.

It was harder for Rushmore to carry the title "editor in chief" and disavow most of the magazine's content. But when Harrison offered him the top job, he needed the money. In October 1954 the *Journal-American* had fired him in what it billed as a cost-saving move. Rushmore said his firing was retaliation for "criticism of Roy Cohn . . . plus my persistent exposures of the crackpots calling themselves McCarthyites." Rushmore had helped Cohn land a job on Joe McCarthy's Senate Sub-Committee on Investigations. But in a *Journal-American* column in June 1954, Rushmore turned on Cohn, now the McCarthy committee's powerful chief counsel, claiming he was "self-seeking and publicity grabbing."

In addition to the paycheck, Rushmore was attracted by *Confidential*'s circulation, now approaching four million copies for some issues. He reasoned that it was a great platform for him and his campaign to expose America's hidden Communists. For his part, Harrison saw naming Rushmore *Confidential*'s president and editor in chief as another opportunity to curry favor with his patron Winchell.

7

"A Tale of Two Chippies . . . the Day Hollywood Trembled!"

Scandal, exposure and economic ruin has been, and always will be, a big threat to Hollywood's he-men matinee idols. The mere linking of a star's name with an unsavory person or incident can and has shattered many a promising career, regardless of the circumstances. So it is readily understandable that probably the greatest threat of this kind that ever menaced the film colony has been kept a secret for more than five years.

What could have been screenland's Waterloo was met and squashed in 42 fantastic days that held many of the town's top-flight actors, producers, directors, writers and composers—even the industry itself—on the brink of disaster.

Together they represented more than $100,000,000 worth of talent. Yet their brilliant futures were literally in the hands of two $100-a-night call girls!

It's an incredible tale, one that even movieland's best gossips have hesitated to whisper about. Beyond the distinguished males involved, scarcely two dozen Hollywoodites ever heard this tale of two chippies—until now.

And those who had heard rumors grimly sealed their lips on a sizzling scoop that would have set the nation's presses roaring.

The strange story began on a night in September, 1949, when a short, dumpy operator of a Los Angeles radio school marched into the District Attorney's office and detailed a complaint of extortion he leveled at two of the city's best-known Jezebels.

*Excerpt from "A Tale of Two Chippies . . .
the Day Hollywood Trembled!"
(May 1955)*

"Short, dumpy" Ben Klekner had a problem. He had fallen for two prostitutes, Helen Keller, twenty-three, and her friend Toni Hughes, twenty-eight. As *Confidential* put it: "Ben might have continued his pay-as-you-go romance indefinitely, had not something more ominous crept in."

Helen and Toni wanted cash, and lots of it, to keep their assignations with Ben a secret from his wife. By the time he visited the Los Angeles district attorney, he already had paid out $3,000, and they were looking for another $11,000.

The district attorney indicted Keller and Hughes on charges of prostitution and extortion. "But even the D.A. had no idea he was only a few steps away from a vice trial which would have rocked Hollywood to its foundations," *Confidential* reported.

The women hired Hollywood lawyer Glenn Lane, who hit on the idea of calling to the stand other customers whom they'd never intended to extort. Soon both found their bail posted. "Not long after taking the case, Lane began getting 'anonymous' contributions to the defense running into the thousands of dollars, enough to hire squads of private eyes to round up evidence buttressing the not guilty plea.

"Careers were at stake, in some cases even homes and families," *Confidential* reported breathlessly, before going on to reveal the very names whose concealment it argued had been so vital. "There wasn't a man in the lot who could afford to have his name involved in such a scandalous suit. More than a few decided they were long overdue for a vacation and the airlines did a record business in celebrated passengers."

Luckily, *Confidential* confided, the women won their case without having to reveal the names of their clients. Now, the magazine said, Bing Crosby, Bob Hope, Walter Pidgeon, Orson Welles, Montgomery Clift, Jimmy Cagney, George Raft, and George Jessel could rest easy. And so could others, "less known to the movie-going public [who] were even bigger Hollywood luminaries." They included S. P. Eagle (a pseudonym of Sam Spiegel), producer of *On the Waterfront*, and directors Otto Preminger and Edmund Goulding.

With tales like that, it was clear that *Confidential*, a minor irritant when it launched in 1952, couldn't be ignored by 1955, when its average circulation of two million copies made it one of the best-selling newsstand publications in the nation. Yet, actors complained, the studios acted as if they were impotent against *Confidential*'s power.

"They [the studios] say it's up to the individual [to take action]," said Humphrey Bogart. "What do they mean by that double-talk? Actors belong to the movie industry; they're products of the industry, and they should be backed up by the industry.

"If somebody kept writing that Cadillacs had lousy brakes, wouldn't the Cadillac company take some action? The industry needs some guts."

Joan Bennett, profiled in a *Confidential* competitor, called for government action. "I believe in freedom of the press but the law should be changed to protect individuals . . . from this type of journalism," she said. "In the meantime, no responsible news agency . . . should handle this type of material."

The studios knew that if they didn't act, their publicity problems would only get worse. It was an open secret that *Confidential* had sent Howard Rushmore to Hollywood in January 1955 to meet with its network of tipsters. In fact, Universal Studios had provided Rushmore with a limousine and driver during his stay, only to have *Confidential* publish several negative stories about its stars in subsequent issues. On Rushmore's list were Ronnie Quillan and Francesca de Scaffa, whom Harrison had met earlier. Rushmore also approached journalists about writing for *Confidential*, as always under a pseudonym. Among them was Aline Mosby, a young Hollywood correspondent for United Press International and the longtime mistress of *Time* correspondent Ezra Goodman. She already had achieved a measure of fame for going native in a 1953 story about a nudist colony. Also on the list were Mike Connolly, the closeted gay writer of *Hollywood Reporter*'s "Rambling Reporter," an influential gossip column, and Agnes Underwood of the *Los Angeles Herald Express*, who was celebrated as the only female city editor of a metropolitan daily.

Money was the lure for most of *Confidential*'s contributors. But Connolly's biographer, Val Holley, suggests a bigger payoff may have been *Confidential*'s agreement not to reveal that Connolly was gay. Connolly, who lived with a male lover and frequented gay bars, was made nervous by hints about his sexuality dropped by Ezra Goodman.

Connolly was careful to slam *Confidential* and its accomplices in print from time to time, Holley said. "You'd upchuck over the names of the well-known writers making a fast, lousy buck writing for *Confidential*," was one such comment. But despite that, Holley said, "Connolly always noted Harrison's arrivals in Hollywood in his column . . . The attention Connolly paid to Harrison's entrances and exits was nothing short of avid. In an extremely interesting development, he disclosed that Frederick Fell and Company, who had already published Connolly's book, *I'll Cry Tomorrow*, was planning to publish a biography of Harrison. That scheme must have fallen through, because later Connolly said Simon and Schuster was gearing up to bring out the story of Harrison's life. This book never materialized either."

Eventually the studios concocted a scheme to embarrass *Confidential* and perhaps lay the ground for a bankrupting libel suit. The effort reportedly was coordinated by Mervyn LeRoy, a cousin of producer Jesse Lasky who was famous in his own right as head of production at MGM, where he was responsible for *The Wizard of Oz*, and for directing such films as *Mister Roberts* and *Little Women*. At his direction, the studios put together a secret fund, revealed two years later by the *Los Angeles Mirror-News* and variously estimated to total $150,000 or $350,000, equivalent to $1 million to $2.5 million today.

They also enlisted an unnamed star—"one of the all time favorites of filmland . . . whose reputation was beyond reproach"—in an effort to trap the magazine into publishing a costly libel. "Bogus affidavits, trumped-up witnesses, wire-recorded conversations, bugged phone calls, all the props were prepared—by experts," the newspaper reported. "The story was planted through the usual circuitous route of tipsters and go-betweens. It got to Harrison. He liked it. It was slated for publication."

By one account, it was Harrison's niece, Marjorie Meade, who now worked for him, who smelled a rat. She hired eight detectives to check the story out and persuaded Harrison to let it go. The studios then approached Fred Otash, the former cop turned private eye who was a well-paid *Confidential* operative. Otash said he was offered $50,000 for his help, a figure later boosted to $150,000 (roughly $1 million today). He declined. "I laughed at them," he recalled. "If I'd made that deal, I'd have been through. Besides I make pretty good dough as it is." Another private detective, William Lewis, who claimed to have been approached by LeRoy on the matter on three occasions, said the studios dropped their plan "for fear that it might boomerang," apparently by generating its own negative publicity.

When guerrilla war failed, the studios tried diplomacy. Eight publicity chiefs, meeting at the Beverly Hills Hotel in the spring of 1955, agreed to approach Harrison directly. They dispatched Sam Israel, publicity director for Universal-International Studios, to New York to reason with Harrison and the editors of several of his imitators. Israel asked them to focus on politicians, socialites, and athletes and leave Hollywood alone. Harrison told the publicist that he was ignoring two realities—magazines that attacked politicians risked losing their second-class postal permits (which allowed them to be mailed at discounted rates), and people wanted to read about Hollywood.

Finally, the trade journal *Hollywood Reporter* announced that an industry group was planning to release to the movie studios "a list of individuals who have received payment from those magazines for writing articles about Hollywood's personalities . . . It is hardly necessary to point out that every writer on this list automatically will be persona non grata both socially and professionally in the industry."

The list never materialized. The industry beat a retreat. Some continued to argue that stars should file libel suits. But many actors feared that the magazine, known for publishing only a fraction of what it knew, would respond with more damaging disclosures in open court. And then there was the problem that *Confidential*'s stories were, for the most part, true.

8

"What Makes Ava Gardner Run for Sammy Davis, Jr.?"

Having shown up barefoot over Europe and half of Latin America, luscious Ava Gardner even topped herself last month when she popped up on the cover of a national Negro magazine with an article, under her personal byline, titled "Sammy Sends Me." On the inside, Ava declared herself at the top of her handsome lungs.

"Don't ask me why," she gurgled, "I just know that Sammy Davis, Jr., just sends me, as a performer."

It would be highly inappropriate to ask the lovely lady why. But a question more in order would be: How do you mean, "as a performer?" Because the evidence is that Sammy sends Ava, period.

Nor is he the first bronze boyfriend to rate high in the Gardner date book, as you will soon discover. For now, let's see how far Sammy sends her.

There is, for instance, a windswept night last fall when the telephone tinkled softly in Ava's 16th-floor suite at New York's elegant Drake Hotel. When the spiciest dish on the silver screen answered it, she got a message she couldn't resist.

"I'm calling for Sammy," said a rich, deep baritone. "He wants you to come uptown and have some kicks."

The sultry Miss Gardner needed no further identification, or a road map. She reacted as though she'd been given orders for a command performance. Throwing a mink wrap around her million-dollar shoulders, she darted out into the night and headed straight for Harlem, the home of happy feet.

She Made an Unscheduled "Guest Appearance"

She was bound for the famed Apollo Theater, headquarters for the world's top colored entertainers, where Sammy was closing a record-breaking week featuring his songs, dances and comic routines. The last show turned out to be the best when, to the pop-eyed amazement of a howling, cheering crowd that packed the theater to the rafters, Ava came slinking into the spotlight for an unscheduled "guest appearance."

Hand in hand with Sammy, she "goofed it up" for a few minutes, then the pair pranced off into the wings and, after a couple of curtain calls, strolled out of the place for a date more sensational than anything advertised on the theater's marquee.

Slowly, Sammy and Ava elbowed their way through the dense crowds swarming around them. Even those who didn't immediately recognize Hollywood's "Queen of Sex" needed no glasses to determine that Davis had on his arm a choice item of "ofay," Harlem's slang term for a white chick.

In a desperate effort to escape the mob at their heels, the pair ducked quickly into the Shalimar, one of the plushiest upholstered cellars on uptown Seventh Avenue. Moving to a table, Ava and Sammy ordered up a few rounds of Scotch and milk, currently her favorite drink because, as Ava likes to explain to friends, it's wise to get your vitamins with your tippling.

Excerpt from "What Makes Ava Gardner Run
for Sammy Davis, Jr.?"
(March 1955)

America's simmering nervousness about race came to a boil in December 1955, when Rosa Parks's refusal to move to the back of a Montgomery, Alabama, bus sparked a broad attack on institutional segregation in the South. But Robert Harrison began adding race and miscegenation to *Confidential*'s story mix well before such conflict became a front-page newspaper staple. One of the most controversial stories, at least in the eyes of MGM executives, featured Ava Gardner, daughter of a tobacco farmer in rural Johnston County, North Carolina, for whom the studio publicity department coined a label that stuck: "the most beautiful woman in the world."

"Some girls go for gold, but it's bronze that 'sends' sultry Ava Gardner," *Confidential* wrote in March 1955. "Here's why high-flying music-makers like Dizzy Gillespie and Herb Jeffries call her 'the greatest.' "

Linking Gardner with black bandleader Gillespie, black crooner Jeffries, and Davis added heat to some moviegoers' already simmering resentment of Gardner because of her marriage to Frank Sinatra. Many Catholic moviegoers were upset because she was named as the "other woman" in the decision of Sinatra, a Catholic father of three, to divorce his wife, Nancy. Gossip columnist Hedda Hopper, with her widely syndicated newspaper column and NBC radio show, and her archrival, Louella Parsons, who wrote for the Hearst newspapers, attacked the Sinatra-Gardner marriage, doing serious damage to Sinatra's career.

The Gardner-Davis story wasn't *Confidential*'s first piece on mixed-race affairs. In 1953 it had explored the romance between Denise Darcel, the French singer turned actress who starred with Lex Barker in the 1950 film *Tarzan and the Slave Girl*, and Billy Daniels, the black big-band singer famed for his rendition of "That Old Black Magic." That same year it also carried a first-person piece by Martha Braun Daniels, who claimed "nymphomaniac" white women broke up her marriage to Billy Daniels.

Mixed-race relationships were an explosive issue for the studios. The Motion Picture Code had dropped its ban on depictions of love and sex between the races in 1954, but it wasn't until 1965 that Hollywood had the courage to meet the issue head-on with Stanley Kramer's *Guess Who's Coming to Dinner*." Movie distributors in the South were a particular concern. Even after the code permitted depictions of interracial romance "within the bounds of good taste," there were local censors such as Lloyd T. Binford, of the Memphis Board of Censors, who banned positive depictions of blacks from Memphis theaters. In 1947, for example, Binford rejected *Curley*, a Hal Roach comedy about a multiracial group of schoolchildren. "I am sorry to have to inform you that the Memphis Board of Censors was unable to approve your *Curley* picture with the little Negroes as the South does not permit Negroes in

MGM's publicists called Ava Gardner "the most beautiful woman in the world." The label stuck. The daughter of a North Carolina tobacco farmer, she was celebrated for her performances in films such as *Show Boat*, *Mogambo*, and *The Barefoot Contessa*. But she upset Catholic moviegoers when Frank Sinatra, a Catholic, left his wife for her, and she upset Southerners when she was romantically linked with various black performers.

white schools nor recognize equality between the races, even children," he said in a letter to United Artists.

MGM, where Gardner was under contract, received thousands of letters complaining about her relationship with Davis. Many Southern movie exhibitors resisted showing Gardner's films because of the *Confidential* story. The mayor of Shreveport, Louisiana, announced his intention to ban future Ava Gardner movies in his town. The chamber of commerce in Gardner's hometown of Smithfield, North Carolina,

In a March 1955 story, *Confidential* all but said Ava Gardner was having an affair with Sammy Davis Jr. Some Southern movie exhibitors responded by refusing to show Gardner's films, and the chamber of commerce in her North Carolina hometown dropped her name from its promotional materials.

dropped her name from its promotional brochure. "Even my own family criticized me," Gardner said. "And there wasn't any use in telling them how it happened. They wouldn't understand. Hell, they wouldn't even believe it."

For all the trouble its insinuations caused, the *Confidential* story about Gardner didn't actually say that she was having an affair with Davis or any other man of color. That was typical of *Confidential's* style. The magazine sometimes hinted or suggested, without actually stating something to be true. In the Gardner-Davis case, *Confidential* omitted facts that would have suggested another reason for their liaison—that the two stars moved in the same Hollywood circles and were very good friends. Gardner's first husband was Mickey Rooney, with whom Davis toured early in his career. Her third and final husband was Frank Sinatra, to whom she was married when the *Confidential* story was published. Sinatra and Davis were longtime friends, eventually becoming known as members of the "Rat Pack," a group of actors who starred in films such as *Ocean's 11*, *Sergeants 3*, and *Robin and the 7 Hoods*.

9

"Have You Heard the Latest About Sammy Davis, Jr.?"

From Sunset and Vine to Broadway, the whispers go round and round about that engaging little bronze guy who used to wear a black patch over his left eye, Sammy Davis, Jr.

"Heard what he's up to now?" one curvy starlet will ask another. If the second shakes her head, she's in for an ear-tickling half hour of spicy chitchat, all adding up to the fact that Sammy's a sensation these days—in more places than on the stage.

Not so long ago the gossip columns snapped and crackled with items about his friendship with that globetrotting glamour girl, Ava Gardner. There were even published photos showing Sammy and Ava as a cozy twosome.

It was hard for some of Hollywood's top Don Juans to understand it all.

Sammy's no collar ad. His nose wanders down his face uncertainly and he has a lantern jaw that makes him look like he's always on the verge of picking a fight.

Instead he's picking off movieland's snappiest sirens. By no means all of these cozy conquests reach the public print. For instance, with the recent release of the Allied Artists picture, *Phenix City Story*, wolves from the Atlantic to the Pacific sat up to take notice of its curvy star, Meg Myles. Watching her wriggle in and out of scenes and hearing her sing the film's sexy theme, "Phenix City Blues," they one and all wanted to know where this bosomy babe had been hiding.

They'll get the answer—which was carefully deleted from Meg's booming press build-up—right here. It's too good a secret to bury.

The lowdown is that, when she wasn't on camera, the fully-packed Miss Myles was steaming it up with Sammy at the Sunset Colonial Hotel on Hollywood's famed Sunset Strip. What's more, their undercover blaze flared up within hours of first laying eyes on each other.

Excerpt from "Have Your Heard the Latest
About Sammy Davis, Jr.?"
(March 1956)

"I'm colored, Jewish, and Puerto Rican," Davis once joked, naming three reasons why bigots might hate him. "When I move into a neighborhood, I wipe it out!"

Given her stature, Davis's dalliance with Gardner ultimately had little impact on her. But the studios knew such stories could be devastating to minor players. *Confidential*'s story about Meg Myles and Davis, for example, effectively ended her career.

Myles, a pinup model, was better known for her 42–24–36 measurements than her modest film oeuvre when she landed the uncredited part in *The Phenix City Story*. Her previous two roles also had been uncredited: in 1954's *Dragnet* and in 1955's *New York Confidential*. She was already filming *Calypso Heat Wave*, which gave Myles her first screen credit, when the *Confidential* story hit the newsstands. The impact was immediate: Myles wasn't able to land another role until 1962, when she starred in the obscure *Satan in High Heels*, filmed in New York's old La Martinique cabaret and today a minor cult classic.

The stories didn't have an impact on Davis's career, and he never seemed bothered by them. Less than a month after the Ava Gardner story was published, Harrison was celebrating his fiftieth birthday at the Copacabana, where Davis was performing. Before the night was over the two were sharing a birthday cake that Davis delivered to Harrison's table. Al DeStefano recalls that on another occasion Davis gave Harrison a set of gold cuff links.

Confidential's stories about mixed-race romances weren't confined to Hollywood. In May 1955, the magazine reported that Doris Duke was having an affair with her chauffeur, describing him as "Prince David Madupe Mudge Paris, a 54-year-old, five-foot, brown-skinned royalist who claims his right to his title because his father was King of a tribe on Africa's Gold Coast.

"Madupe arrived at Falcon's Lair [Duke's Hollywood home] with his unique prescription for her insomnia," *Confidential* said. "He immediately started the tobacco tootsie on a course of involved breathing exercise, broken by sessions in African voodoo dancing . . .

"Madupe's training courses were strictly night-time events and the Prince seldom left Duke's Lair before four or five in the morning. On top of that, Doris apparently valued his soothing touch so much she left standing orders to the help that she was to be awakened by no one but him."

But Madupe, *Confidential* reported, attempted to extort money from Duke. "Unlike a gentleman—much less a Prince—he had tape-recorded their fancier ballets and suggested that they might make pretty fancy diversion, if distributed wholesale. Furthermore, he added, he'd kept diaries of his patient's progress and his sprightly treatment, which might be turned into a volume of interest to thousands—including non-medical researchers."

Duke promptly called private eyes who retrieved the recordings and diary and managed to lure Madupe to Mexico, where he was denied re-entry into the United States. "Miss Duke, meantime, has gone on to new adventures. She steers clear of royalists, to be sure, but has lost none of her interest in ebony boy friends," *Confidential* said.

"Not too long ago, she was startling her old friends in Manhattan by showing up at parties with Claude Marchand, a Negro ballet dancer who was her house guest in Hawaii for months on end."

In 1956, *Confidential* shocked proper New York with a story about New York society figure and real estate heir Robert Goelet, whose family was among the founders of Chemical Bank and once owned a sizable chunk of Manhattan from Union Square to Forty-seventh Street, and his affair with Gloria Carney, a black beautician. Goelet, the grandnephew of Mrs. Cornelius Vanderbilt, was seeking a divorce from actress Lynn

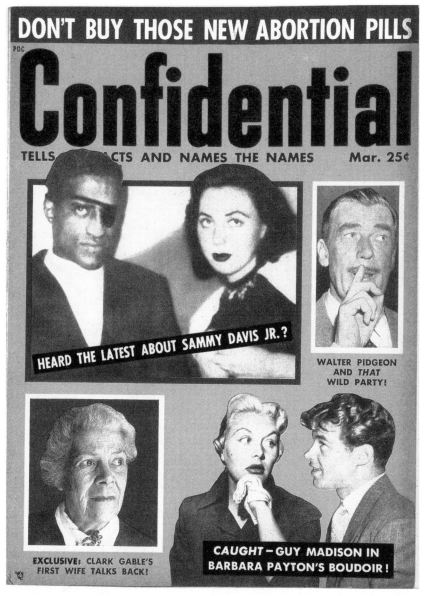

DON'T BUY THOSE NEW ABORTION PILLS

PDC

Confidential

TELLS ⬚⬚⬚CTS AND NAMES THE NAMES   Mar. 25¢

HEARD THE LATEST ABOUT SAMMY DAVIS JR.?

WALTER PIDGEON
AND *THAT*
WILD PARTY!

EXCLUSIVE: CLARK GABLE'S
FIRST WIFE TALKS BACK!

CAUGHT – GUY MADISON IN
BARBARA PAYTON'S BOUDOIR!

While *Confidential*'s stories about Sammy Davis Jr. and white actresses didn't hurt his career, the same can't be said for one of them, Meg Myles, with whom he appeared in a photo on the magazine's March 1956 cover. Myles didn't land another role until 1962, when she appeared in the camp classic *Satan in High Heels*.

Confidential occasionally shifted its focus away from Hollywood to celebrities such as tobacco heiress Doris Duke. Duke attracted attention for her marriage to Porfirio Rubirosa, a notorious playboy from the Dominican Republic. Duke reportedly secured Rubirosa's freedom to marry her with a gift of $1 million to his second wife, Danielle Darrieux.

Merrick when the story broke. *Confidential,* using the alliteration that Harrison loved, described Carney as Goelet's "tawny temptress" and "Harlem honey" and accused her of passing for white. "The burning question among bluebloods is . . . Will the grandnephew of the ultrasocial Mrs. Cornelius Vanderbilt marry his sepia sweetheart?" the magazine asked. "Bobby's Harlem honey may dream of sharing some day in the wealth represented by the Goelets' acres of skyscrapers, and of

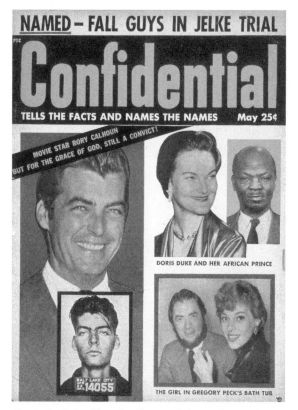

Doris Duke's alleged affair with her African chauffeur was the subject of a May 1955 *Confidential* story.

queening it in the 50-room family villa, Champ Soleil, in Newport, but it all depends whether she can keep Junior rockin' and rollin' until Lynn Merrick makes up her mind to a divorce.

"In the meantime, Gloria's life is necessarily transient. She moves from hotel to hotel, each more modest than the last—the Park Sheraton, the Woodward . . . *Sic transit* Gloria."

In none of its stories did *Confidential* actually question the propriety of black-and-white sex or romance; Harrison could count on his readers to do that on their own. In fact, Harrison himself seems to have been less a bigot than an opportunist, ready to print whatever it took to build cir-

77

culation. Interestingly, in the same issue in which the Gardner story ran, *Confidential* exposed the Bermuda Tourist Bureau's secret code for signaling its anti-black and anti-Jewish policies to travel agents (Gentiles were identified as Oleander, Jews as Hibiscus, blacks as Geranium, and Asians as Poinciana). In writing about Josephine Baker's attraction to white men, *Confidential*'s criticism was grounded in what it saw as her hypocrisy in opposing racism while not dating men of her own race. And Harrison once dated Dorothy Dandridge, the actress and lounge singer who later sued *Confidential* for alleging she had sex in the woods while on tour in Lake Tahoe. That story neglected to mention that Dandridge's unnamed lover (bandleader Dan Terry) was white, and was *Confidential*'s source.

10

"The Untold Story of Van Johnson"

Van Johnson came to Hollywood in 1941 and his slow, boyish smile sent millions of bobby-soxers screaming in juvenile ecstasy.

But there was a mask of tragedy behind that smile and the wide, innocent face of the Newport, Rhode Island lad who hoofed his way into the big time . . . Tragedy and heartbreak, because Van realized that there was another inner self that completely refuted the he-man husky he portrayed on the screen.

For the idol of the nation's gals of all ages during World War II was an admitted homosexual . . .

Often during those years when the Johnson star was blazing a trail of gold across Beverly Hills, Van sat in his room and sobbed. The virile hero of the big muscle and the fierce embrace was a scared, lonesome boy locked in his secret, whimpering and afraid.

Only a psychiatrist could explain the reasons that caused Van Johnson's abnormality, and certainly the men who study the mind would take into account his early boyhood. Van's father and mother separated when he was a youngster and he was raised by relatives.

The loneliness must have started then.

He found an outlet in singing and dancing and starred in high school plays and musical shows. Then came several years of a hand-to-mouth existence as a struggling young hoofer in the small towns and one-night stands.

Van has never revealed, except to the FBI, how his trouble started.

Among the other chorus boys with whom he worked, he might have found a friend to compensate for the father he had missed during his boyhood.

Excerpt from "The Untold Story of Van Johnson"
(September 1954)

Recurring themes in *Confidential* such as homosexuality and miscegenation were good for sales because they pandered to popular fears and preconceptions. Harrison's focus on gays was extreme in the eyes of at least one of his editors, who remarked that his boss was "queer for queers." "When it came to proving so-and-so actor or politician was a homosexual—a curious preoccupation of his—Harrison would spend thousands of dollars, if necessary, to check facts and line up witnesses," said Al Govoni, who was one of Harrison's top editors. Ronnie Quillan reported that when she met Harrison for the first time, in September 1954, he told her he was most interested in the sex lives of celebrities, particularly whether they were homosexual.

There were stories about homosexuality in most of the magazine's issues. After the fictitious gay wedding story in its first issue, issue number 2 featured "Is It True What They Say About Johnnie Ray?" alleging that the crooner had frequently performed in drag during the early days of his career. "There were scores of persons in Detroit who could swear they had seen this youngster cavorting on the stage of a nightclub made up and outfitted down to the last scarlet fingernail in a girl's attire," *Confidential* said. "A suave, sophisticated audience at New York's internationally known Copacabana Club also had seen him 'in drag,' a cynical Broadway term for a man who dresses as a woman." When Ray finally married, *Confidential* said, "a Broadway wit wired the bride's father: 'Don't feel that you've lost a daughter. You've really gained a daughter.'"

Issue number 3 featured three explicitly gay stories. One was about Sweden's King Gustav V and his male companion, Kurt Haijby, a petty thief who claimed to have been seduced by Gustav when he was fifteen and became the king's lover twenty years later. Haijby, sentenced to prison for blackmailing the Swedish royal family over the affair, "testified that Gustav liked his intimate pals on the youthful side," *Confidential* reported. "Haijby was in his mid-thirties when he became 'Mr. G's' constant companion—at a time when that ruler was pushing 70. But Kurt testified that Gustav was unbelievably gay and youthful at that age and inclined to sulk for days if there was the slightest suggestion made that he ought to slide into a wheelchair."

Another gay story in that issue, published as a travel piece, warned Americans about a Mexico City bar frequented by "sideshow types obscene in their sexlessness—the lesbians indistinguishable from the faggots." And there was a piece, likely written by Howard Rushmore under a pseudonym, that feigned outrage while putting into print what *Confidential* called "the foulest rumor ever circulated about a presidential candidate"—that unsuccessful Democratic presidential candidate Adlai Stevenson was gay. Stevenson was a liberal who had earned the enmity of FBI director J. Edgar Hoover, and thus of Rushmore, for his perceived softness on Communism. While the FBI was never able to develop evidence to prove Hoover's suspicions, *Confidential* found a way to get into print a rumor that wouldn't be reported again for another three decades, well after Stevenson's death, when the *Nation* revealed the FBI's suspicions about Stevenson, including an allegation that he "was well known as Adeline."

Confidential laid the accusation to a desire for vengeance on the part of Stevenson's former wife, Ellen, who reportedly confided in a reporter "the real reason" for their divorce, a reason that the magazine said, elliptically, "reflected on the manhood of the father of her three sons" and included a reference to a "lifelong friend of Adlai, whose character and happy relations with his wife are above reproach.

"It was the start of the nastiest, most widely circulated hearsay in the annals of rumor-mongering," the story said. "By phone, on planes and trains, from the racket of factory assembly-lines to the quiet of hospital rooms, from the big-town sharpies to unsophisticated villagers, it burned the ears of a nation."

A story in issue number 4 said Willie Sutton, America's most famous bank robber, had a penchant for drag, although the story's only evidence of that was a photo of him in an apron and an allegation that he kept house for fellow crook Tommy Kling. "Most people believe 'Willie the Actor' is a he-man who outbogeys Bogart," *Confidential* said. "But the truth is that this bank-robbing, jail-breaking stick-up artist is strictly a victim of *swish-ful* thinking!"

"There are plenty of reasons why seasoned criminals sometimes turn from the boy-girl department to the boy-boy variety," *Confidential* reported, acknowledging that Sutton had had his share of relationships with women.

"For one thing, criminals, perhaps more than any other classification of men, have learned that the wrath of a woman scorned or rejected is, indeed, terrible. Libraries could be filled with variations on this theme. Often just a sudden distaste for her lover can produce the same symptoms in a girl, as witness the cooperation that celebrated wench, the 'Woman in Red,' gave G-men who caught up with John Dillinger.

"On the basis of so many unhappy experiences with women, many law breakers decide it's far safer to confine their romantic interests to another man.

"Another equally practical reason is that a man facing many years in prison decides sordidly and cold-bloodedly that he may as well go for something more realistic than his rapidly fading dream of the good old days . . . Since Sutton has lived more than half his life in jail and will finish out the balance there, this is undoubtedly a factor in his case."

Other stories over the years took *Confidential* readers to sites expected (Liberace's bedroom) and unexpected (automobile heir Walter Chrysler Jr.'s quarters at a U.S. Navy base in Florida, where *Confidential* claimed he seduced young sailors). "Chrysler is known as 'Mary' by the other homosexuals," *Confidential* said, quoting a source in a Navy investigation of his activities as personnel officer at the Key West base.

One of the magazine's stranger stories, "When Harvard Was Home Sweet Homo," published in September 1956, alleged that Harvard University had a secret policy of segregating gay male students in Claverly Hall, built in 1893 as a private luxury dorm whose amenities included private baths, steam heat, and a swimming pool. It was the gay students, according to *Confidential*, who were responsible for a series of fires at Claverly in the spring of 1951. When firemen arrived at the first fire, the magazine said, they discovered "a special quintet of Harvard men. They

82

were dressed in a fashion best described as 'gay' and wore enough rouge, lipstick and eyebrow pencil to pass as short-haired coeds from neighboring Radcliffe College for Women." Subsequent fires turned up more suspiciously gay men.

Associate Dean Robert Watson explained that the university "had no sure-fire way of dividing the deviates from the red-blooded applicants for University entrance, especially since students' previous school records rarely showed anything as off-color as lavender. Once matriculated, suspect students merely got the corral treatment—at Claverly." The students, *Confidential* said, protested they were only trying to have fun. " 'We never wanted to hurt anyone,' the arguments ran. 'But we do love to see the flames . . . the people running . . . the sirens screaming . . . and the big red engines roaring. It's just—just thrilling!' "

Confidential's naming of prominent gay people, male and female, came three decades before controversy erupted over the practice known as "outing." For the most part, history has confirmed its revelations. Among the magazine's other closeted and alleged gay male subjects were Tab Hunter, Under Secretary of State Sumner Welles, and Peter Orton, a Vanderbilt heir. Orton, stepson of George Vanderbilt, fell in love with Christine Jorgensen, perhaps the era's most famous transsexual. "In all the months Peter dated her, he was heard to murmur only one minor complaint about his doctored doll," *Confidential* reported. "La Jorgensen, he confessed, was inclined to get a little bristly along the jawbone as the hour grew late in some fashionable restaurant they were attending, which made whispering in her ear a little like talking into a clothes brush."

But the most famous gay story, and today one of the best known, was the one that *Confidential* didn't print. It involved Rock Hudson, the most popular male movie star in the world, whose manly reputation *Confidential* spared in a deal with Hudson's agent, Henry Willson. Willson, gay himself, had learned that the magazine was offering as much as $10,000 to ex-boyfriends of Hudson for a tell-all story. Willson's solution, never revealed by Harrison but long rumored and amply documented by Robert Hofler in his book about the agent, was to offer a trade.

In May 1955, *Confidential* published "Rory Calhoun: But for the

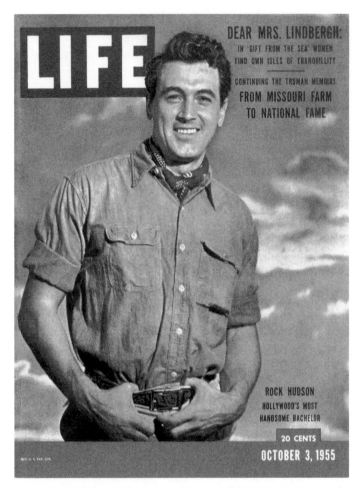

DEAR MRS. LINDBERGH:
IN 'GIFT FROM THE SEA' WOMEN
FIND OWN ISLES OF TRANQUILLITY

CONTINUING THE TRUMAN MEMOIRS
FROM MISSOURI FARM
TO NATIONAL FAME

ROCK HUDSON
HOLLYWOOD'S MOST
HANDSOME BACHELOR

20 CENTS

OCTOBER 3, 1955

Rock Hudson's sexual orientation was well-known in the Hollywood community. But Hudson's agent prevailed on Harrison not
to reveal in *Confidential* that Hudson was gay in exchange for a
story on Rory Calhoun.

Grace of God, Still a Convict." The story documented Calhoun's previous armed-robbery convictions, but ended on a note of redemption.
Calhoun came off looking like a he-man. "Once Rory's story was published," *Parade* magazine reported, "Hollywood made him a minor
hero. Parties were thrown in his honor. Television producers vied for his
services. He received more movie offers than he could accept."

Rory Calhoun was one of the few celebrities whose image was helped by a *Confidential* story. The magazine's May 1955 revelation that he once had been convicted for armed robbery oddly made him a minor hero.

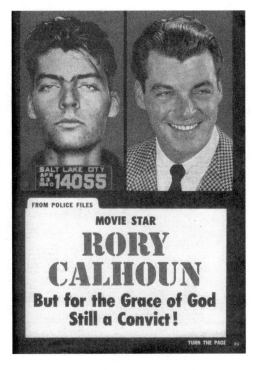

FROM POLICE FILES

MOVIE STAR
RORY CALHOUN
But for the Grace of God Still a Convict!

TURN THE PAGE

That *Confidential* could have had the Rock Hudson story is made clear by a chapter in Fred Otash's autobiography, *Investigation Hollywood!* Otash, one of the magazine's major informants, prints the transcript of a tape he surreptitiously made of a conversation between Hudson, whom he describes only as "one of Hollywood's most handsome of handsome leading men," and his wife, for whom Otash was gathering evidence for a divorce suit. Hudson admits his homosexuality, but denies some of his wife's allegations.

"WIFE: The whole town is talking about your activities. I've heard that one of the major studios doesn't consider you a good risk anymore. You have worked eight hard years on your career, and because of your abnormal sex drive you are destroying yourself. Can you deny that your pattern is that of a homosexual?

"STAR: (Crying) No, I can't deny it. But I never felt we were together on anything. I never felt you loved me.

Rock Hudson's marriage to Phyllis Gates, his agent's secretary, was typical of the ruses employed by gay actors who feared *Confidential* and its imitators would "out" them.

"WIFE: . . . How long after we were married did you have your first homosexual affair?

"STAR: Oh, I don't know. The next day."

The story behind the Rory Calhoun story made the rounds in gay Hollywood and terrified many a celebrity, and at least one journalist. "Two events during 1955, in particular, were too close for comfort in Connolly's life," wrote Val Holley of Mike Connolly, the prominent and gay gossip columnist for the *Hollywood Reporter*. "These were the publication of *Confidential*'s May 1955 issue, with its cover story of actor Rory

Calhoun's sordid early years as a car stealing juvenile delinquent (the issue actually would have been on the newsstands in early March 1955); and the November 9, 1955, marriage of Rock Hudson to Phyllis Gates, the secretary of Hudson's agent, Henry Willson . . .

"If Hudson could read the tea leaves, so could the seemingly untouchable Mike Connolly, who, owing to the 'journalistic sword over his head' revealed by [*Time* correspondent Ezra] Goodman, began to fear *Confidential* would turn the tables and hang out the dirty laundry of a trafficker in dirty laundry."

So Connolly too proposed marriage, to a surprised female friend. But at the last minute he backed out. "He'd heard that another columnist was going to print an item that said (in essence), 'Which columnist with the raised pinkie is going to shock all of Hollywood and get married?' " Holley wrote.

Tab Hunter, another Willson client, didn't escape *Confidential*'s notice. He had fired Willson in the summer of 1955 and found himself on *Confidential*'s cover in September of that year in a story entitled: "The Truth About Tab Hunter's Pajama Party." The story explained the heartthrob had been arrested on a morals charge in 1950 with two dozen other men. It was a difficult situation for Hunter and for Warner Bros., which earlier in the year had released *Battle Cry*, a film in which Hunter played a tough young Marine, and *Sea Chase*, in which he played a naval cadet.

"The real low down on Hunter . . . the build-up boys thought was safely locked in the records of the L.A. vice squad, confidential file Z-84254," *Confidential* wrote. "In it is the racy story of a night in October, 1950 when the husky Hunter kid landed in jail along with some 26 other good-looking young men, after the cops broke up a pajama party they staged — strictly for boys. Only a year later, Tab had zoomed to where he was being interviewed by front rank columnists like Earl Wilson, with whom he blushingly discussed how it feels to kiss Linda Darnell. But he was strictly an un-known on that night of October 14, 1950 — just one more of the scores of overly handsome youths who haunt the studios by day and get their kicks in an unusual style after sundown . . . Tab went by his real name, Art Gelien, and he was so far from fame and fortune that the cops found only 20 cents in his pockets when

Tab Hunter's publicity photos showed him on the town with beautiful women (here, starlet Venetia Stevenson), but *Confidential* revealed in 1955 that Hunter had been arrested on a morals charge at an "all male" pajama party. In a 2005 memoir, Hunter described the revelation as being "as serious as a heart attack."

they pinched him . . . Milling around him were two dozen of the gayest guys the vice squad had ever seen."

Hunter, who had carefully hidden his homosexuality, was stunned. "Ludicrous as it was, there was nothing laughable about the article," he recalled. "It was as serious as a heart attack.

"I'd all but forgotten about that ridiculous 1950 arrest. But it had taught me the importance of being circumspect. I'd seen how others in the business had toed the line, and I followed their example . . . The rule was, act discreetly, and people would respect your right to privacy. I'd mastered it.

Tab Hunter was working in a Hollywood drugstore when he first met Roddy McDowell in 1948. The men, both gay and closeted, hit it off. After Hunter was dragged out of the closet by *Confidential*, studio head Jack Warner offered his support. "Remember this," he told Hunter. "Today's headlines, tomorrow's toilet paper."

"Then *Confidential* blew all that out of the water.

"The irony wasn't lost on me. On one side of the newsstand there were dozens of innocent and naïve movie magazines, pitching me as the perfect specimen of young American manhood, every girl's dream. Those magazines created Tab Hunter, virtually out of whole cloth.

"Across from them, higher on the rack, up at Dad's eye level, nested the lurid new breed of tabloids, dedicated to gleefully making a buck by turning over every last rock in Eisenhower's buttoned-down America."

Hunter survived the outing, largely because of the support of studio head Jack Warner. "Warner's response was to simply let the whole nasty episode fade," Hunter wrote in his autobiography. "*Confidential*'s purported four million monthly readers may have sounded like a lot, but Jack Warner knew it was a drop in the bucket compared with the number of people who read *Photoplay*, bought tickets to *Battle Cry*, and watched *Climax!* [another Hunter film].

"He didn't panic, didn't issue retractions, didn't demand I start going on more 'arranged' dates. Best of all—he didn't tell me how to live my life."

But Jack Warner's support wasn't a sign that he was open-minded. "By the time *Battle Cry* was released, the studio already had invested an enormous amount of time and money in making a star of Tab Hunter," explained entertainment journalist David Ehrenstein. "It was in no mood to simply kiss it all goodbye."

"He wasn't a marginal performer on the cusp of a break, like Tucker Smith, whose turn as Ice in *West Side Story* was expected to jump-start a larger career had his 'private life' (exposed in a columnist's 'blind item') not supplied casting directors with a reason to give him the go-by."

It's unclear why, but *Confidential* treated Van Johnson more delicately, with what is best described as a story of redemption. Johnson, six feet two inches tall, was a blue-eyed, baby-faced redhead with the wholesome appearance of the boy next door. He was known as "the bobbysoxer's heartthrob," "the voiceless Sinatra." He had appeared in more than fifty films when the *Confidential* story broke, with *The Caine Mutiny* just then entering second-run theaters.

There was something about Johnson that had spurred questions about his sexuality from the very beginning of his career. "Do we have a situation here?" Benny Thau, MGM's personnel chief, had asked Martin Jurow, Johnson's agent, when he signed with the studio in 1942. Later there had been rumors that Johnson was carrying on an affair with actor Keenan Wynn, his best friend. Johnson, an awkward introvert, spent much of his time with Wynn and Wynn's wife, Eve. "Questions later circulated about the nature of this ménage à trois," wrote Johnson's biographer, Ronald Davis. "Many Hollywood insiders assumed or became convinced that Van's relationship with Keenan had a sexual component."

Wynn's father, comic Ed Wynn, reflected the confusion. "I can't keep them straight," he said in a 1946 interview. "Evie loves Keenan. Keenan loves Evie. Van loves Evie. Evie loves Van. Van loves Keenan. Keenan loves Van."

Still, it took *Confidential* to "tell the facts and name the names," albeit with a delicacy that must have left MGM's Louis B. Mayer uncharacteristically grateful.

The magazine reported that Johnson had revealed his homosexuality when he was called before the draft board in 1941 for induction into the Army. "The decision he made when he was called for induction took plenty of old-fashioned guts," *Confidential* reported. "Exactly what Van

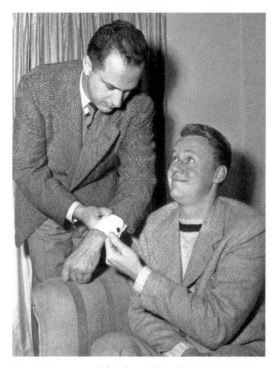

Van Johnson and his best friend, Keenan Wynn, were inseparable, leading to rumors that the two were having an affair. In its September 1954 story about Johnson's homosexuality, *Confidential* offered the happy news that a skull fracture suffered in a car accident had restored Johnson to heterosexuality.

In 1947, Van Johnson married Eve Wynn, his
best friend's wife, in an effort to deflect rumors
about Johnson's homosexuality.

told his draft board is still a secret, but a few days later, Selective Service
called the FBI [to investigate whether Johnson was faking his homosexuality to evade the draft]."

"Van told the FBI he didn't want to be a homosexual. And he added
that he was making a desperate effort to return to normal living," *Confidential* wrote. "Johnson reported to the Los Angeles field office of the
FBI that he was continuing his desperate effort to rid himself of his
abnormality . . . But it took another tragedy in Van Johnson's life before
he succeeded."

That tragedy was an automobile accident, which left Johnson with a
fractured skull. But, miracle of miracles, Johnson recovered his health,
and his heterosexuality, eloping to Juárez, Mexico, with Eve Wynn, his
best friend's wife, in January 1947. It wasn't until 1999 that Eve finally
explained the circumstances.

Eve Johnson blamed MGM's Louis B. Mayer for coercing her and Van Johnson into marriage. She claimed that Mayer said he wouldn't renew Keenan Wynn's contract unless Eve divorced him and married Johnson. The Johnsons had a daughter, Schuyler, in 1948 and separated in 1961.

"They needed their 'big star' to be married to quell rumors about his sexual preferences," she said in an interview years later, "and unfortunately, I was 'It'—the only woman he would marry."

Eve put most of the blame on Mayer. "For my money, Mayer was the worst of the lot, a dictator with the ethics and morals of a cockroach," she said. "Mayer decided that unless I married Van Johnson, he wouldn't renew Keenan's contract. I was young and stupid enough to let Mayer manipulate me. I divorced Keenan, married Johnson, and thus became another of L.B.'s little victims."

Eve Wynn separated from, reconciled with, and in 1962 finally divorced Johnson. That final act was precipitated, her son Ned Wynn later claimed, by Johnson's affair with a boy in the cast of *The Music Man*, in which Johnson was performing. Well into his eighties, Johnson

was still somewhat in denial about his sexual orientation. "In his opinion, he is still a conventional New Englander, and intimate friends say
that Van sometimes kids himself that he was never homosexual," wrote
Davis in his biography of Johnson. "Sexuality does not fit in the movie in
his mind, and like the films from Hollywood's golden era, Van would
rather ignore an aspect of his life that might cause controversy or damage his image."

11

"Lizabeth Scott in the Call Girls' Call Book"

It started out as merely one more vice raid for the two husky detectives who pounded through the back door of the swanky, four-story house at number 8142 on Los Angeles' Laurel View Drive.

The catch seemed run of the net, too. Chances are that few of the nation's newspaper readers gave more than a passing glance to the item reproduced elsewhere on these pages, detailing the arrest of Sandra Ann Betts, 22, with 20-year-old Joyce Hicks and a third scarlet sister whose tender age—17—prevented her name from being made public.

But what many an editor buried on page five or even tossed in his waste basket would have made banner headlines—coast to coast—had the whole story come out.

For when these frolicsome floozies were picked up, the arresting cops, W. R. Worthington and J. A. Randolone, also grabbed their traditional little black books, listing their near, dear and cash-on-the-line friends. And out of those pages tumbled a line-up of cinema greats which would have had even blasé Hollywood gasping.

In among the 'H's' was Lou Holtz, long-famed comedian of stage, screen and radio. Further down the alphabet, nestling among the 'J's' was Georgie Jessel, another international quipster. Lest you think it was just one big laugh after another at this swanky bordello though, the girls also had on their roster of roosters that dapper movie bad boy, George Raft.

But what stopped the men from the vice squad cold was an entry on the 'S' pages: Scott, Lizabeth (4) HO 2–0064 BR 2-6111.

The astounded cops at first refused to believe their eyes. Could that name be that of the honey-blonde star they'd seen in a dozen top movies? If so, what was it doing rubbing elbows with a zesty collection of customers for a trio of cuddle-for-cash cuties?

Excerpt from "Lizabeth Scott in the Call Girls' Call Book"
(September 1955)

Robert Harrison's fascination with homosexuality wasn't limited to men. Over the years the magazine occasionally published stories hinting to one degree or another that various actresses were lesbian. One story, about Katharine Hepburn, merely hinted. "Katharine Hepburn, Hollywood's Torrid Tomboy!" acknowledged an unnamed male lover (Spencer Tracy) but dwelled endlessly on her "tomboy" ways: "She once ripped off her panties and handed them to a stage hand. Another time she publicly bathed in the nude. Here's the story-behind-the-story of a gal whose lovelife has been a subject of vicious speculation for years," the story said.

The magazine was bolder in a story about Marlene Dietrich. "In the millions of words that have been written about Dietrich's dalliances you've never, until now, read that some of them *were not with men!*" it reported in "The Untold Story of Marlene Dietrich," published in July 1955.

"Dietrich going for dolls? Her adoring fans the world over will shriek, 'Impossible!' It's the truth, though. In the game of amour, she's not only played both sides of the street, but done it on more than one occasion."

Among Dietrich's lovers, according to *Confidential,* was Claire Waldoff, "a blonde Amazon who had become the toast of Germany's supper clubs for her skill with a risqué song and a naughty story."

Back in the United States, the magazine reported, Dietrich "picked up with Mercedes de Acosta, a writer who favored clothes that seemed

Marlene Dietrich "played both sides of the street," *Confidential* said in a July 1955 story about her bisexuality. Dietrich's only marriage, to Rudolf Sieber, produced a daugher, Maria Elisabeth, who had her own acting career under the name Maria Riva.

to be tailored by Brooks Brothers." De Acosta, a poet, playwright, and clothing designer, is known today for her affairs with Eva Le Gallienne and Greta Garbo. But the relationship with Dietrich was an amazing revelation in the 1950s.

"Mercedes had been the companion for other Hollywood double-standard dollies and fitted neatly into Marlene's pattern," *Confidential* said. "But this was the U.S.A., where publicity on such capers would have raised a storm, so the girls discreetly limited themselves to quiet get-togethers at each other's house. At parties, they were the acme of propriety."

But Dietrich was "really flamboyant in the girl-meets-girl department" when on a 1936 trip to Paris she met "a slim, brown-eyed girl, 20 years old and yearning to learn all about life. Frede was her name and she was destined to become the queen of Paris' Lesbians."

Frédérique Baule, nicknamed Frede, so entranced Dietrich that she helped bankroll her nightclubs, La Silhouette, which quickly became the gathering place for Paris's lesbians and other sophisticated members of the demimonde. Frede also featured in *Confidential's* story about Lizabeth Scott. "On one jaunt to Europe she headed straight for Paris' Left Bank, where she took up with Frede, that city's most notorious Lesbian queen and the operator of a night club devoted exclusively to entertaining deviates like herself."

Howard Rushmore had asked Ronnie Quillan to help verify the Scott story, supplying her with a wristwatch that concealed a microphone to capture an incriminating confession from the actress. It was a story that Harrison was hot for. Quillan said Harrison himself asked her to "get verification in any way possible, to go out to lunch with her, to use a Minifone to record the conversation." Quillan later testified that she didn't go through with the plan to verify the Scott story. But, she says, Rushmore agreed to publish it anyway, without the rigorous fact checking that had kept *Confidential* "suit proof."

Confidential claimed the cops never questioned Scott about why her name was in the call girls' little black book. If they had, the magazine said, "they would have learned that Liz was a strange girl, even for Hollywood, and from the moment she arrived in the cinema city. She never married, never even got close to the altar. With the exception of a longtime affair with a noted Hollywood producer, her life was startlingly free of the hectic, on-and-off romance rumors which are run-of-the-mill to movie beauties.

"This in itself was more than enough to cause much whispered speculation in the movie colony, but Liz herself raised Hollywood eyebrows with an interview she gave columnist Sidney Skolsky. She confided that she always wore male cologne, slept in men's pajamas and positively hated frilly, feminine dresses . . .

"As she neared 30 and her career moved deeper and deeper in its eclipse, she took to hard drinking, which didn't improve her fragile beauty.

Confidential in a September 1955 story claimed that the police had found Lizabeth Scott's name in a call girl's book of clients. The story alleged that she hung out "with Hollywood's weird society of baritone babes." Here Scott, left, is in Cannes with French actress Michèle Morgan.

"At about the same time, an even more startling change came over the gal they'd known back in Scranton as Emma Matzo. Liz, according to the grapevine buzz, was taking up almost exclusively with Hollywood's weird society of baritone babes." Scott denied *Confidential's* insinuation that she may be a lesbian and sued the magazine for libel.

A summer-stock actress and a fashion model in New York, Scott first came to the attention of fans in 1942 on Broadway, when she was understudy to Tallulah Bankhead in Thornton Wilder's *The Skin of Our Teeth*. Producer Hal Wallis brought her to Hollywood, where she starred in such noir films as *The Strange Love of Martha Ivers* (1946) and *Dead Reckoning* (1947). She became known for her blond hair, husky voice, and sultry sexuality, and eventually settled into a series of roles where she played a good girl turned bad.

And despite what *Confidential* said, her career didn't really move into eclipse until publication of its story. *Loving You*, a film she made in 1957 with Elvis Presley, was to be her last film for fifteen years.

12

"The Big Lie About Filter Cigarettes"

When filters hit the market with the biggest advertising barrage in years, did you believe what the ads told you—that now you could smoke your fool head off—and forget what the doctors said about cancer or heart disease? . . . Well, you're in for a rough awakening, buster. You've been had!

Tobacco companies will spend more than 52 million dollars this year on advertising. Countless publications, 30-odd radio shows, and 25 or more TV shows will shout the merits of various filter-tip brands. At least five million dollars will be spent by the industry for what is laughingly called "Public Relations."

A major part of these endless millions will try to convince you that if there really are harmful ingredients in cigarettes, then filters—and any and all filters—magically remove the impurities and make your favorite gasper as pure as the soap that floats.

The truth is that some filter cigarettes actually pass on more nicotine than ordinary unfiltered brands. Other filters act as a sieve, straining out more of the coarse tar particles than nicotine, thus enabling the unsuspecting smoker to get a "purer," more concentrated dose of nicotine than he would from a conventional smoke! . . .

During the past few years an overwhelming amount of medical evidence has been presented linking cigarette smoking to the increase in lung cancer. The tobacco industry, while screaming "not true," "not proven . . ." on the one hand, has tacitly admitted the facts by developing filter cigarettes and holders on the other hand—suggesting to a gullible public that "just in case there is something in all this fuss the doctors are making, we've already fixed the whole thing up by removing these supposedly harmful ingredients from your smokes. Now you can smoke filtered cigarettes with out fear!" . . .

This is a carefully fostered and deliberate fraud!

Excerpt from "The Big Lie About Filter Cigarettes"
(March 1955)

While *Confidential's* stories about miscegenation, homosexuality, and the sexual indiscretions of the powerful in Hollywood and Washington understandably upset their subjects, the magazine's consumer reporting kicked up a fuss in corporate boardrooms. Harrison took his magazine into American bathrooms, living rooms, and kitchens, turning up scandals involving deadly baby powders, carcinogenic cigarette filters, and flawed pharmaceuticals produced by some of the biggest companies in America.

Some of the consumer stories could only be called goofy. There was, for example, "Beware . . . the Davy Crockett Skin Game!" (September 1955), which warned mothers that the popular coonskin caps could carry parasites and cause skin and scalp infections. "Davy Crockett's scalp survived many a desperate adventure, but the greedy racketeers have got it at last," *Confidential* wrote. "In the process, they have also got the scalps of too many of our kids—as you may be shocked to discover when you lift that mangy blob of animal hair off Junior's itchy curls and take a good long look.

"Under a weird and nameless conglomeration of evil-smelling, scrofulous, dangerously dyed, even vermin-infested 'coon'-skin caps, alarmed and indignant doctors are discovering an appalling crop: aggravated and oozing eczema sores; deep-rooted skin and scalp infections; angry-looking and hard-to-check allergic rashes from cheap but powerful chemical dyes and from unsterile animal hairs. And parasites that are notorious disease carriers!"

Confidential also explored more serious issues. It revealed that carbon tetrachloride, a common spot remover, had been implicated in the deaths of a number of women and children ("Killer in Your Home!," May 1956). It revealed a pattern of unsanitary conditions at the plants of some of the nation's leading candy manufacturers ("Beware the 5¢ Candy Bar . . . Look Before You Bite!," January 1956). *Confidential* also warned parents that aspirin could be dangerous for kids ("Aspirin—No. 1 Poisoner of Children!," March 1955). And of course there was the story on filter cigarettes. As Cutter Laboratories was reeling from the impact of revelations that children vaccinated with its polio vaccine actually contracted the crippling disease, *Confidential* revealed that the company seven years earlier had been cited by the American Medical Association and the Food and Drug Administration for selling contaminated dextrose fed intravenously to ill hospital patients.

Some of that consumer reporting left the magazine vulnerable to legal action. Authorities in California, where publishing stories about male virility drugs was illegal, complained about "The Vine That Makes You Virile." "Don't Buy Those New Abortion Pills" brought unwelcome attention from authorities in several other states where any mention of abortion drugs was banned. That March 1956 story exposed the off-label use of aminopterin sodium to induce abortion and explained how it put both the mother and the unborn child at risk if the abortion wasn't successful.

Harrison thought those stories important. "We ran stories exposing how children were dying from eating candy-flavored aspirin, and how boric acid was poison, and a lot of things like that," he recalled years later. "But we had to have the other stuff, the gossip, to sell the magazine, or we could have never run these stories at all. Nobody remembers that part of it, but that magazine was a goddamned public service."

Harrison's own attempt to report on a cure for male sexual problems was responsible for one of the most bizarre episodes in his life and a spate of publicity that bumped off the nation's front pages a story about President Eisenhower, who was recovering from a heart attack, and reports on lawsuits against the magazine.

It all started with a September 1955 jaunt to the Dominican Republic, on which Harrison was accompanied by editor Al Govoni. While there, he stayed at the El Embajador hotel in Ciudad Trujillo, where Geene Courtney, 30, a nightclub singer who also was a former New York Miss Cheesecake and the reigning Miss Hot Dog of 1955, was performing. Harrison claimed to be conducting his own research on Pego-Palo, a drug made from "the vine that makes you virile," the subject of a January 1957 story in the magazine.

But his timing left much to be desired. *Confidential* had been researching a story about John Wayne and his wife, the Peruvian beauty Pilar Palette. The source for much of the story had been a naïve Richard Weldy, an airline pilot turned wild game hunter who had been married to Palette and had introduced her to his buddy Wayne. Wayne had fallen for Palette, and the two married, with Weldy's blessing. But there had been some messy details in between concerning Wayne's nights in a Lima brothel and attempts to seduce an underage girl. Weldy inadvertently had provided Harrison with information about his former wife and Wayne during a meeting that ostensibly was for planning a safari.

Weldy happened to be at the El Embajador when Harrison and Govoni arrived. The thirty-five-year-old hunter, standing six-two and weighing 205 pounds, towered over the slender fifty-two-year-old publisher and had to be restrained by hotel security guards and evicted from the premises when they got into a fearsome argument. That wasn't the last Harrison would see of Weldy. Improbably, Harrison and Govoni, this time with Geene Courtney in tow, bumped into Weldy two days later in the thick forests of the Jarabacoa Mountains, an area known as "the Dominican Alps," where Harrison was searching for the virility vine. "I heard an argument and saw Weldy was there," Govoni later recalled. "I was never so surprised in all my life. Weldy was shouting at Harrison in abusive language, gesticulating and insulting him for the magazine article." Then, suddenly, Weldy's gun went off. Harrison lay wounded on the forest floor while Weldy disappeared and Govoni went in search of help.

Finding his way through the Dominican forests wasn't easy for Govoni, and when he had found help, he and the rescuers couldn't find Harrison and Courtney. So the publisher and Miss Hot Dog spent a night and day in the mountainous forest, with Harrison clutching a flesh wound to the shoulder and Courtney clutching him. Luckily, Harrison had befriended Dominican dictator Rafael Trujillo, who assembled a force of five thousand civil guardsmen, police officers, and Boy Scouts to fan the forest and find Harrison and Courtney, who were briefly hospitalized for exposure to the elements and treatment of Harrison's gunshot wound.

The ensuing publicity more than made up for the pain of the gunshot. The Dominican newspapers published numerous photos of the wounded Harrison in his hospital bed, being greeted by government dignitaries. In the United States, the incident was an even bigger story, with front-page coverage ranging from the relatively serious "Wounded Publisher Found by Searchers" of the *Los Angeles Times* to the more jocular "Publisher Edited by Rifle?" of the *Los Angeles Mirror-News*.

Weldy, jailed for three days while the Dominican police investigated the shooting, maintained it had been an accident. He had run away, he explained, to summon help and because he feared being shot by Govoni. Harrison absolved Weldy, explaining, "The gun flew from his hand and hit a rock." John Wayne issued a statement saying he regretted Weldy hadn't done more damage: "Weldy is a nice fellow, but I deplore the fact that he is such a poor shot."

Days later, the Harrison party arrived at New York's Idlewild Airport to be greeted by throngs of reporters. "Wounded Publisher Home to Explain Blonde" was the headline that summed up the story's turn from that point. An angry June Frew, Harrison's longtime girlfriend, who frequently identified herself as his wife, showed up at the airport to let Harrison have it. "Take your wife next time," she yelled during the press conference. She described Courtney as an "old bag" and then went on to elaborate. "She's nothing but a fifth-rate performer . . . The papers say she is 30. She's 45 if she's a day." Courtney, who returned to the United States a week later, gave as good as she got. "I'm twenty-eight," she told reporters when asked about Frew's remarks. "God bless her. She started a little bit before I did."

Harrison's delight in the news coverage fed the suspicion of some journalists that the whole thing was a publicity stunt. It seems unlikely, however, that even Harrison could have convinced Trujillo to spare five thousand men and boys for a two-day search through mountain forests

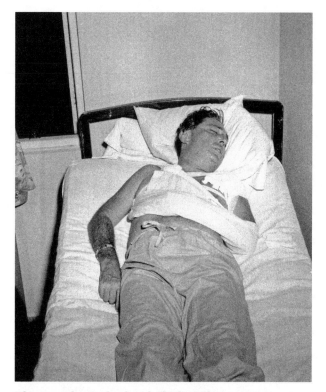

The angry former husband of Pilar Palette, a minor actress then married to John Wayne, shot and slightly wounded Robert Harrison during an encounter in the Dominican Republic that turned into a publicity bonanza for *Confidential*. Wayne said he regretted that Harrison's assailant was "such a poor shot."

to support a prank. The fact that Harrison was photographed with bandages in a hospital bed, not to mention that Weldy was held for three days in a very unpleasant Dominican jail, seems to argue that the event was real. Mike Wallace, who interviewed the publisher on television shortly after the Dominican Republic trip, accused him directly of faking the shooting, which prompted Harrison to rip off his shirt on air and invite the cameraman to film the wound to his shoulder.

The incident cast the first real public light on Harrison's love life. He was known for squiring chorus girls to various Broadway openings and to dinners at the Colony, the Stork, and the Harwyn. But, with the exception of Frew, the blond Canadian model, and later in life a long-term engagement with a blond beauty queen (from Eastern Europe by way of Canada) named Reggie Ruta, Harrison's girlfriends seemed mostly for show.

Sherry Britton, a stripper famed for her 38–18–33 measurements, recalled meeting Harrison because her agent's office was next door to his. Britton described herself as being his "hostess" for a while, and says Harrison photographed her for one of his girlie magazines and let her drive his car. Initially she found him attractive, if a little artificial. "He had the biggest, squarest whitest teeth you've ever seen—which just screamed 'caps,'" she recalled years later. But Britton, who liked the idea of settling down and having a family, soon realized that wasn't what Harrison was all about. They never had sex. And when he betrayed certain kinky desires ("He wanted to be my slave," she remembered), she ended the relationship.

Frew was the closest thing Harrison had to a wife. He met her in the late 1940s, when she was one of a group of models assembled in his office for a photo shoot. As lawyer Al DeStefano remembered, "She was his toy." She was an expensive and difficult toy. Harrison paid the $600-a-month rent on the hotel suite where they spent their time together. One writer described her as "somewhat possessive in temperament . . . a retiring sort [who] rarely left her quarters except to use some charge accounts Harrison had gallantly provided her and, of an evening, to attempt to catch Harrison night clubbing with some other member of the informal chorus line he has maintained ever since he first could afford it." The Idlewild Airport incident illustrated her possessiveness. Another example was a tirade that got both of them banned briefly from El Morocco. "She was a little nutty," remembered Al DeStefano. "She wanted to be Mrs. Harrison . . . She would call me at home at three in the morning and rave to me that I was preventing Bob from marrying her." While Harrison told the press he and Frew had married, DeStefano insists that never happened, and indeed there are no records of a marriage license in New York or nearby states.

Why did Harrison never marry? "To be frank," he explained, "when I was a kid things weren't too good, money-wise. My mother always had to work so hard, I decided this would never happen to my wife. I set out to make me some dough. In doing that I never did have time to get married. I still don't. I work twenty hours a day, most days."

Perhaps another obstacle to marriage was Harrison's family—six members of which were on his staff. In addition to sisters Helen and Edith, there were brother-in-law Dan Studin, the circulation manager; brother-in-law Michael Tobias, on the advertising staff; and niece Marjorie Meade and her husband, Fred, in the Hollywood bureau. Any woman who wanted to get close to him had to contend with the sisters, who shielded him from trouble and reality and governed every aspect of his life except his nightly outings to the clubs. To them, Harrison still was the baby brother. "Any time some real unpleasantness came up, they acted as buffers," one Harrison friend explained. "If he had to fire someone or if someone asked for a raise, he would ask them to handle it."

The *Confidential* office was an extension of the Harrison family. Even editors, with the notable exception of Howard Rushmore, were treated like family. Harrison summoned the staff for a meeting when Edythe Farrell, who quit her job at *Confidential* with some regularity, finally made her resignation permanent. "There's been a death in the family," he announced. "It's the kind of thing nobody talks about." Farrell, a staffer recalled, was never mentioned again.

Robert Harrison arrived in the office each day in the early afternoon, a schedule dictated by his love of clubs such as the Harwyn, the Colony, El Morocco, and the Stork. Helen, his secretary, and Edith, the office manager, would flutter around him. The sisters would barrage their younger brother with questions about his health and how he'd slept even as they dusted lint from his suit, whisked away his hat, and escorted him into his office. Helen, ten years older than Bob and a devotee of Gayelord Hauser, the health food faddist whose *Eat and Grow Beautiful* was a 1936 best-seller, would start in on Bob's diet. She had prescribed a routine of vegetables, sour cream, wheat germ, and fruit salads, something Harrison had trouble sticking to, given that he dined and partied until late every night at nightclubs. Still Harrison, a hypochondriac, tried to obey. Edith, five years older than Harrison, was no less attentive, worrying, for example, that a brief cough might be the start of something serious. "They treat him like a two-year-old," one friend observed. "But he goes along with it." Niece Marjorie, as flamboyantly outspoken and argumentative as her flaming red hair would suggest, occasionally turned up to offer her opinions on stories.

The sisters also comforted Harrison when he felt he had been wronged. "There were days when Bob felt everyone in the world was conspiring against him," one former *Confidential* editor recalled. "If it rained the day he was supposed to hit the newsstands, he would come in wringing his hands and everything was so tragic. He'd call in Helen and Edith and say, 'Oh, this is the end, I'm being ruined, I can't take it any more.'

"Then they would pacify him in a very curious way. They never tried to talk him out of it. Instead they would agree that the world was conspiring against him and they'd tell him how unfair it was that it rained that day. That always brought him out of it."

The office staff, initially composed solely of Harrison family members, grew to seventeen full-timers. The routine was enlivened by the presence of a "reader," who came in before publication of each issue to read every story aloud. "The Reader, whatever his name was, had a truly great voice, like Sir Ralph Richardson reading Lear soliloquies at a Bauhaus Modern lectern under a spotlight," wrote Tom Wolfe. "Great diction, great resonance, etc. Harrison hired him just to read out loud. Harrison had a theory that if you read the stories out loud, every weak spot in a story would stand out. So there would be the Reader with a voice like Sir Ralph Richardson enunciating such works as 'Errol Flynn and His Two-Way Mirror,' and 'White Women Broke Up My Marriage' (to a Negro entertainer), and 'How Mike Todd Made a Chump of a Movie Mogul.'" The reader also gave voice to Harrison's puns. "Harrison dotes on puns," one of his editors explained. "For him, puns are a mark of sophistication. If he's about to run a picture of a girl holding a knife, the caption comes to him immediately—'Knife Work If You Can Get It.' If there's a shot of a girl swathed in bandages, 'I got it,' Harrison shouts. 'My Mummy Done Told Me.'"

Charlie, the elevator operator in Harrison's building, was as important as the reader to the editorial process. He also attended the *Confidential* story conferences, filling the role of "man in the street." "We wouldn't do a final story conference without him," one Harrison employee confided. "If he likes the story, we know we got a winner."

13

"The Wife Clark Gable Forgot!"

You have to park your illusions with your car when you drive up to 12746 Landale Street in North Hollywood.

One glance tells you the building before you is a converted barn—and not much changed at that. Paint is peeling from its sides, its roof sags dejectedly. Inside are two large rooms, drafty and cold when the winter rains and fog roll in from the Pacific.

The furniture is worn and dilapidated. Wherever your eye turns, it picks up the giveaway signs of poverty. The penny-pinching, tomorrow's–rent-day, got-to-pay-the-gas-bill kind of poverty.

The tall, kindly gray-haired woman who comes to the door might be someone's grandmother. But she isn't.

She's Mrs. Clark Gable. The first—and the forgotten—Mrs. Gable. She's 71 now, a time of life when most women sit back with their memories and rock away their few remaining years. But that's not for Mrs. Gable. She works hard with, and desperately needs, the few drama students she coaches these days—to keep the wolf from the door. And it's just as well there's not much time for reminiscing; the memories would be more bitter than sweet.

Just three blocks away from the Landale Street barn is Ventura Boulevard, one of California's super-highways. When he's in Hollywood, commuting to and from his luxurious home at 4525 Pettit Street in Encino, Gable uses it daily.

Sometimes he zooms by in one of his half-dozen racing cars, on his way to the studio where he makes those he-man movies that have the world's women swooning at his feet. Nights, he's in the back of a sleek, chauffeur-driven limousine—bound for one of his new and youthful conquests.

Only a block. But it might as well be a continent, because forgetting comes easy to Gable. He's "King" Clark now, the unquestioned monarch of movieland. And a king can do no wrong.

. . . Or can he?

Is it wrong to ignore the woman who launched you on your way to the top, while showering gems, furs, gowns and money on a little French model? Is it wrong to hand one wife a million-dollar settlement—and let another grub to pay the grocer?

Excerpt from "The Wife Clark Gable Forgot!"
(July 1955)

It was the summer of 1923 and Josephine Dillon had been tapped to stage the pageant that was a focal point of Portland, Oregon's Rose Festival. Dillon, thirty-eight, was a logical choice: She had acted on Broadway before moving west, and she was in the process of setting up the Red Lantern Players, a theater group. Hard at work on the pageant one day, she discovered the telephone at the Red Lantern Theater had stopped working. The local telephone company promptly dispatched a repairman who, Dillon later recalled, had big ears, a captivating grin, and an interest in the theater.

Fixing telephones was the latest in a string of odd jobs young Clark Gable had held since leaving his Ohio home and a dreary job in a tire factory. Gable had made his way across the country to Portland, occasionally hopping freight trains, with a stop along the way in Butte, Montana, where he joined a touring theatrical company. In Portland he first worked selling ties at Meier & Frank, Portland's prestige department store.

Dillon, variously described as ten, seventeen, and twenty years his elder, became not so much Gable's acting teacher as his Pygmalion, teaching him to speak properly, to project, to carry himself like the King of Hollywood he later would become. In 1923, having done all she could for him in Portland, Dillon took her student to Hollywood. There Dillon married Gable, becoming the first of his five wives.

Gable spent six years in minor roles, eventually returning to the stage. He made his Broadway debut in September 1928 in *Machinal,* a play inspired by Ruth Snyder's sensational 1927 trial for the murder of her husband, which resulted in her becoming the first woman electrocuted at Sing Sing. Eventually he separated from Dillon and took up with Ria Langham, a wealthy Houston socialite who was instrumental in Gable's landing the role of a young villain in the 1931 Western *The Painted Desert*, where he was a sensation. Gable divorced Dillon in 1931 so he could marry Langham. "Clark told me frankly that he wished to marry Ria Langham because she could do more for him financially," Dillon recalled. "He is hard to live with because his career and ambition always came first."

Dillon was living in a dilapidated barn in North Hollywood when *Confidential* found her on a tip from Francesca de Scaffa, who claimed to have once been Gable's lover. *Confidential* reported that Gable had ignored Dillon after the divorce, even insisting she quit using his last name. Eventually she fell ill and asked Gable for help paying her hospital bill.

"Although King Gable was earning $300,000 a year at M-G-M, her plea went in one big ear and out the other," the magazine said. Gable was one of Hollywood's top ten box-office draws when this story appeared, and he was starring in two Twentieth Century–Fox films (*The Tall Men* and *Soldier of Fortune*) and one from MGM (*Betrayed*). This was another slap at a major star, two major studios, and at the powerful Joe Schenck, chairman of Twentieth Century–Fox. The studios now were taking *Confidential* seriously. MGM's publicity department mobilized, and stories appeared in the *Los Angeles Mirror-News* and in *Look* magazine disputing Dillon's account. *Confidential* responded with a second story. This one was written by Dillon herself and recounted the publicity campaign against her and the humiliating negotiations she underwent with Gable's private secretary, who finally agreed that the star would buy the dilapidated house from Dillon at a discount, fix it up, and let her continue to live there.

"It must have rattled skeletons in a few closets when *Confidential* came out last May with an article titled 'The Wife Clark Gable Forgot,' " Dillon wrote. "They described me as virtually penniless and Clark as a multimillionaire who had chosen to wipe his memory clean of the woman who gave him his first boost on the road to fame, and often paid for the food he ate.

Josephine Dillon, the first of Clark Gable's five wives, was variously said by reporters to be ten, seventeen, and twenty years his senior. His first acting teacher, she took him to Hollywood and served as his Pygmalion, teaching the telephone repairman to speak and carry himself like an actor.

"Then the storm broke. From coast to coast, newspapers and magazines joined up with Hollywood's 'trained-seal' gossip columnists to label the article a pack of lies. I remember reading where the *Los Angeles Mirror-News* called it 'unfair and untrue.' There was also a biography of Clark in *Look* magazine where the writer even charged Clark's age had been misstated, making him 61 when he was really only 54. And that same publication rhapsodized that 'Gable recently purchased Miss Dillon's house, arranged to have it painted and repaired, and leased it back to her, rent-free, for the rest of her life.'

"I've read enough of that sort of stuff. It's time the truth was told, and I don't think there's anyone better qualified than I am to tell it.

"To begin with, let's get one thing straight. I've been reading for years that I'm supposed to be 20 years older than Gable. It isn't so and *Confidential* had it right. I'm 71; he's 61.

"As for that house deal, there are two sides to the story, the one you read in the papers and my side. And to me, the entire negotiations added up to one of the most sordid and depressing experiences in my life. The 'generous gesture' Clark supposedly made was, in reality, nothing more than a good business deal for him.

"At no time during the proceedings was I ever able to reach and speak directly to Clark himself. His part of the trading was handled by Howard Strickling, the publicity boss of Metro-Goldwyn-Mayer, and a long-time pal of Clark's, together with Mrs. Jean Garceau who has been Gable's private secretary for years.

"They lost no time in putting me in my place. On one of the first get-togethers we had, to discuss selling the house, Jean coldly told me, 'After all, Miss Dillon, Mr. Gable has every right to forget you; it was 30 years ago.' "

The July 1955 issue of *Confidential*, which went on sale in early May, set another record. The *Wall Street Journal* reported that 3.7 million copies had been sold on newsstands—"history's biggest sale through newsstands of any single magazine issue." That's not to say that *Confidential's* overall circulation was greater than that of titans such as *Look*, which claimed an average of 970,000 newsstand copies, or *Ladies' Home Journal*, which averaged 1.6 million copies in 1955. Those magazines mailed most of their circulation directly to subscribers. However, in an America where most people knew their postman, *Confidential's* readers were not likely to subscribe.

The *Journal* also reported that *Confidential* had made Harrison rich. The newspaper estimated that Harrison Publishing, of which Harrison was the sole owner, netted four or five cents a copy before taxes. That $148,000 to $185,000 was supplemented with $55,000 in advertising revenue for correspondence schools, negligees, hernia supports, and other down-market goods and services. Thus Harrison Publishing netted $1.2 million to $1.4 million a year, equivalent today to $8.5 million to $10 million a year—a big step up from the $100,000 a year (equivalent

Clark Gable left Josephine Dillon to marry Ria Langham, a wealthy Houston socialite who helped him
land a role in *The Painted Desert*. Dillon said Gable
told her he wanted to marry Langham because she
could help him financially.

to $800,000 in 2009) from Harrison's girlie magazines. On top of that there was income from *Beauty Parade*, the only one of Harrison's stable of girlie magazines that he continued to publish, and *Whisper*, a second-tier *Confidential* look-alike. "Lots of magazines imitate *Confidential* and are doing well on the newsstands," Harrison explained to the *Journal*. "So we also imitate ourselves with *Whisper*, which is doing fine, with per issue sales of 700,000."

While Harrison and *Confidential* were thriving, in 1955 Hollywood clearly was in decline. By nearly every measure, the film industry was losing ground to television and other forms of entertainment, such as bowling and miniature golf, that thrived with the development of the suburbs. For example, the number of feature films released by the eight major distribution companies had declined to 215 in 1955 from 263 in 1950. Americans spent only 9.4 percent of their recreation dollars on movies in 1955, down from 12.3 percent in 1950. Clearly people had found other ways to entertain themselves. Many of the big studios had special problems of their own. Howard Hughes sold troubled RKO in 1955, and it stopped all production in January 1957. Paramount, the first of the major studios to comply with the court decision to split off their distribution arms, saw profits fall from $20 million in 1949 to $6 million in 1950. MGM was beset by turmoil in the executive ranks and the separation of the studio from its Loew's theater chain. Battles between the Warner brothers disrupted their eponymous studio. Fox was successful, in large part because of income from leasing films produced in the 1940s to television.

Then there were those nasty stories in *Confidential*. With *Confidential*'s massive circulation, the studios and their publicists found themselves outgunned in publicity battles over stories like the Gable exposé. Making matters worse, *Confidential*'s success had inspired a host of imitators. "For 25 cents each, you can buy *Uncensored, Top Secret, Inside Story, Suppressed, On the QT, Behind the Scene, Inside, Hush-Hush, Exposed, Private Lives, Rave, The Lowdown, Dynamite* and *Dare*," wrote Jack Olson in a *Chicago Sun-Times* series on *Confidential* titled "Titans of Trash." One of the magazines, *Suppressed*, was edited by Edythe Farrell, who had studied under Harrison in his girlie magazine days.

"All of them appear to be selling well," Olson reported. "*Uncensored*, second of its type in the field, boasts a circulation of 800,000. *Whisper*, converted from a 'girlie' magazine to an 'exposé' type by Harrison Publications . . . is up to 700,000. Three others—*Top Secret, Inside Story* and *Suppressed*—are in the 300,000–500,000 bracket, and climbing."

Confidential and its competitors also had given rise to blackmail. Even Harrison conceded that problem and offered to help. "Cops are after a new kind of racketeer," wrote one journalist. "And *Confidential* mag is offering a reward for info leading to the arrest and conviction of

Clark Gable promptly forgot Josephine Dillon after divorcing her in 1931. But *Confidential* reminded him, and his fans, of his elderly and impoverished former wife with a story that alleged Gable had refused to help pay her medical bills.

blackmailers who contact players and tell them: '*Confidential* is working on a story about you but I can get it killed for $500.'"

The fan magazines, long supported and encouraged by the studios, also felt pressured by *Confidential*. "You can see the fix they were in," wrote Olson in his *Sun-Times* series. "They would come out with an article entitled 'The Happy Homelife of Peter Screenstar,' and on the same newsstand would appear an 'exposé' magazine whose cover screamed: 'Peter Screenstar's Other Woman.'"

In his *Sun-Times* series, Olson spelled out the dangers to Hollywood, and made clear that Harrison knew what he was doing. "Overnight, some of Hollywood's biggest stars have been tagged as deviates, rakes, nymphomaniacs, lunatics, drunks and hopheads," Olson wrote. "Theater bookings have been canceled because of certain 'exposés' . . . [An] actress, heretofore cast as a sweet-young-thing type, will never again play such a role because of 'exposé' publicity about her nighttime escapades. Other actors, similarly tarbrushed, have silently slipped away.

"Robert Harrison, career publisher of nudity and the man who began the 'exposé' trend with his *Confidential* magazine, takes cognizance of all that in a proud statement: 'Sure, they're scared in Hollywood. I feel for those guys. You take a producer. He makes a star out of some guy and then he finds out the guy is a (queer). The producer stands to make a million bucks offa this (queer). So why shouldn't he be afraid?' "

Harrison argued that his magazine was a force for good, helping to clean up Hollywood. As *Confidential* investigator Fred Otash put it: "Kick all the Communists out of Hollywood, kick out the homosexuals, enforce marital fidelity on both husbands and wives, and you won't have any scandal—and no scandal magazines."

Robert Harrison and *Confidential* certainly weren't a problem on a par with the movie industry's wrenching economic and structural changes. But, faced with the spread of television, the Supreme Court decision that forced the studios to divest their theater holdings, and court rulings that weakened their hold on talent, the *Confidential* problem at least was a comprehensible one. And magazines mattered. In an era before nightly TV shows such as *Access Hollywood*, magazines were the primary way young moviegoers learned about movies.

It wasn't as if Hollywood hadn't dealt with this problem before. In the 1930s, the fan magazines had alarmed the studios with a spate of stories with headlines such as "Unmarried Hollywood Husbands and Wives." In response, studio publicity chiefs met on August 9, 1934, and developed a "white list" of writers "known for their honest and clean writing." Only writers on the so-called white list could get access to stars. For their part, fan magazine editors signed a pledge "to cleave to a policy of clean, constructive and honest material." "As a result," wrote Ezra Goodman, the Hollywood correspondent for *Time*, "the fan magazines, instead of taking raps, have been operating under wraps." Even the newspaper coverage of Hollywood was beholden to the studios, Goodman said. "It is strictly a second-rate fourth estate subsisting—with negligible exceptions—on press-agent handouts of mostly trumped-up fact, freeloading (another name for payola) and general incompetence. The professional standard of journalism, as it is known in Washington, D.C., New York or London, is almost nonexistent."

Thus Goodman found value in *Confidential* for its accuracy, if not its prose style. "I have always been of the opinion that *Confidential* was decidedly underrated," he said. "It was easy to indict the magazine for its sensationalism and for its sloppy writing. But what *Confidential* proved was that there was too much pallid, punches-pulled reporting elsewhere and that the average, untutored reader was probably wise to it and instinctively knew that he was being hornswoggled. He undoubtedly realized that *Confidential,* in its own way, was giving him a glimmer of the truth."

The studios soon discovered the solution to the PR problem of the thirties wouldn't work in the fifties. *Confidential* didn't need access to stars to write its stories. The magazine wasn't dependent on studio advertising for revenue. It kept its list of confidential sources very confidential. And *Confidential* really stood out in a business characterized by inaccurate reporting, puffery, and collusion with sources. *Confidential's* promise that it "Tells the Facts and Names the Names," printed on every cover, was its biggest business asset.

14

"Robert Mitchum . . . the Nude Who Came to Dinner!"

They say you can tell a man's character by whom he pretends to be at a masquerade ball.

The late, unlamented Serge Rubinstein loved to dress up like Napoleon, for instance, and in real life desperately wanted to be a conqueror like the Little Corporal. Winston Churchill used to go to such make-believe functions in a purple toga, wearing a wreath of laurel leaves, obviously his way of saying he wished he were Julius Caesar.

But what about that handsome he-man Rob Mitchum who takes off all his clothes and . . .

Maybe we'd better prepare you for all this, because it's a pretty crazy story, even for a guy who did time in a Hollywood clink on charges of flying too high with marijuana Airlines.

This Mitchum lad, as everyone knows, is easily the world's No. 1 fun lover these days. Only a few months ago he got bounced from a movie he was making because he tossed a fellow worker in San Francisco Bay—just to get a chuckle from two bystanders, Lauren Bacall and Anita Ekberg. But that's not Bob at his best. For the tops in entertainment, one has to turn to a night in February, shortly after completion of his latest opus, *Night of the Hunter*.

. . . Two other workers in the same film decided to throw an elegant binge for members of the cast. Their only trouble was that they'd worked with rambunctious Robert, but never played with him. They

120

had a lot to learn. Charles Laughton, the evil-hearted "Captain Bligh" of *Mutiny on the Bounty,* was one of the hosts. Sharing the honors was celebrated producer Paul Gregory.

. . . Mitchum was late for cocktails but proceeded to make up for that by grabbing up a bottle of Scotch . . . which he nursed as he wandered around Gregory's living room greeting fellow guests.

Mitchum's girl friend did a fine job of piloting him to the dining room when the bell rang, and was intent on her appetizer when a deathly hush fell over the dinner table. Looking up, she choked on her last bite as she identified Bob, several steps removed from the festive board, slowly but solemnly removing every bit of his clothing — down to his socks.

She and the other celebrants watched in hypnotized silence as Mitchum then returned to the table to seize a bottle of catsup.

Backing off, he liberally sprinkled himself with the stuff as he retreated. After thoroughly spattering his six-foot-two-inch frame with the thick red goo, he stared haughtily at the assemblage and inquired:

"This is a masquerade party, isn't it?" The rest of the customers, who had come as themselves, just giggled. "Well, I'm a hamburger," Mitchem observed, forgetting to add, "well done."

> *Excerpt from "Robert Mitchum . . . the Nude*
> *Who Came to Dinner!"*
> *(July 1955)*

The Mitchum story, whose likely source was Fred Otash, *Confidential's* favorite private eye, came across to the average reader as a tale of a dope-smoking drunk gone wild. That was bad enough. But Hollywood insiders, who knew that Charles Laughton and Paul Gregory were gay, and a couple, could read more into it.

The novelist James Ellroy was later to tell David Ehrenstein, a chronicler of gay Hollywood, that the episode took place on the set of *Night of the Hunter,* which Laughton directed, and was a lot more explosive. Ellroy said Otash had told him: "It's a lunch break, and

Mitchum pours ketchup on his dick and says, 'Which one of you fags wants to eat this?' "

Mitchum, unlike other actors, who feared stirring up more dirt with a court battle, filed suit as soon as the July issue of the magazine hit the newsstands in late May. Perhaps, having already endured and survived negative publicity over his 1948 arrest and conviction for marijuana use, he was more willing than most to take the risk. Or maybe he was emboldened because, as his counsel, he had engaged Harold Lee "Jerry" Geisler.

Geisler, a balding lawyer, then sixty-eight, had represented many of the biggest stars in the Hollywood firmament. He guided Marilyn Monroe through her 1954 divorce from Joe DiMaggio. He had gotten Errol Flynn and Charlie Chaplin declared innocent of rape charges in the 1940s. He had defended Robert Mitchum on the marijuana charges, managing to secure a sixty-day sentence in a case that could have put the actor away for two years. Geisler was known as a fierce advocate who could get so emotional in his address to a jury that he would pound the jury rail until he broke bones in both his hands.

Geisler declared himself disgusted at the movie industry's timidity. He argued that the *Confidential* "problem" was only going to grow. "Heretofore the circulation of these magazines has been rather small," he explained in a television interview in July 1955. "But recently one of them in particular has grown to quite some dimension and because of that it cannot be ignored longer. Therefore, people have to, to protect their good name, come out and bring the action."

Geisler convinced two more celebrities to join his campaign. From May to July of 1955, he filed three lawsuits against *Confidential*, on behalf of Mitchum, Lizabeth Scott, and Doris Duke, claiming damages of $1 million, $2.5 million, and $3 million, respectively. He filed another suit, on behalf of Sammy Davis Jr. for $3.5 million, against *Hush-Hush*, a *Confidential* imitator. The Lizabeth Scott suit was based on the allegations that she was a lesbian. The Doris Duke suit stemmed from the May 1955 story about her affair with her African chauffeur. Geisler also announced he would take his battle to Congress, where he would ask that "scandal sheets" be banned.

"These magazines are a major threat to the movie industry," he said.

Robert Mitchum, whose career had survived an arrest for marijuana possession, was one of the first actors bold enough to sue *Confidential* for libel. The suit was over a bizarre story that claimed Mitchum had stripped, covered himself with ketchup, and said he was a hamburger at a Hollywood party. Insiders knew that the story was a coded reference to an antigay tirade by Mitchum against the party's hosts, Charles Laughton and Paul Gregory.

"They must be treated as such. My clients have decided to fight, which is more than I can say for the industry as a whole. We'll hound them through every court in the country. We'll file civil suits and criminal libel complaints. We'll sue the publishers, the writers, the printers, the distributors. We'll even sue the vendors. This smut is going to stop."

The studios, whose campaigns against the exposé magazines had been few and ineffectual, were delighted that Geisler was riding to their

Prominent Hollywood attorney Jerry Geisler represented Robert Mitchum in his libel suit against *Confidential* and challenged the timid studios to go on the offensive against the magazine. Soon he was representing actress Lizabeth Scott and heiress Doris Duke in libel actions against *Confidential.*

rescue. "Short of being involved in a conspiracy ourselves, I believe we should take every step toward ending these smears," said Dore Schary, head of MGM. But, he acknowledged, the industry "didn't know what the hell to do. We felt a little lost. Thank God a few courageous individuals have shown us what can be done."

In a speech to the Audit Bureau of Circulations, which confirmed magazine sales figures for advertisers, Schary said Hollywood deplores "the shoddy contents of *Confidential* and its bevy of imitators that live off the sad, tragic mistakes of some or the indulgences of the maladjusted few."

"I have not as yet been the victim of an article in *Confidential* magazine," he said, "though at this very moment I guess I'm on my way. And so I speak not as a personally aggrieved spokesman, but rather for the host of my co-workers who live decent and purposeful and religious lives."

Schary called on his audience to find ways to "inhibit this kind of journalism . . . To accomplish the downfall of such publications would bring honor to your profession. Edmund Burke said the only thing necessary for the triumph of evil is that good men do nothing. Mr. Burke was, in modern jive talk, hep."

Confidential wasn't without defenders. Victor Lasky, the conservative columnist for newspapers such as the *Chicago Sun* and the *New York World-Telegram*, thought the attacks on *Confidential*'s right to publish were so outrageous that he wrote the American Civil Liberties Union and asked it to help. "I am no devotee of *Confidential* but . . . I am troubled by some of the methods being employed by well-meaning citizens in their efforts to put *Confidential* out of business," he said in an August 1955 letter to the ACLU's director. The ACLU responded with a press release supporting *Confidential*, which drew thanks from Edward Bennett Williams, who had represented the magazine in its successful suit to reverse an obscenity charge that had briefly barred it from the U.S. mails.

Rather than ease up, Harrison geared for a fight. In July, his niece Marjorie and her husband, Fred Meade, opened Hollywood Research Inc., *Confidential*'s first permanent base in the film capital. Marjorie, whose loan of $400 years earlier had helped her uncle get his girlie magazine business off the ground, in February had gone to California with her husband to explore the possibility of opening a fiberglass business like the one they had operated in New York. Now Uncle Bob proposed a permanent move and provided $5,000 for expenses. In the Harrison family, when duty called, kin responded. The Meades promptly bought a glamorous house in Beverly Hills that was suitable for entertaining. Not surprisingly, they quickly discovered they were persona non grata at many Hollywood gatherings.

Nevertheless, word spread among hotel bellhops, studio extras, prostitutes and hustlers, and even minor stars hungry for publicity that the

Meades would pay well for "the story behind the story." By incorporating Hollywood Research separately from the magazine, Harrison hoped to insulate *Confidential* from lawsuits in the movie colony. But by staffing the operation with members of his family he eventually exposed himself to more trouble than he ever could have imagined.

15

"How Long Can Dick Powell Take It?"

It was the night of the Photoplay Awards and the big banquet room in the Beverly Hills Hotel was jammed to capacity with the great and near great of Hollywood, on hand to pick up new laurels or cheer those who did. But as it turned out, there was more on the program than handing out medallions. There was a choice bit of gossip that set tongues wagging all around the room.

Dapper Dick Powell started it, when he was asked to take a bow at the shindig. The one-time musical comedy singer made the usual thank-you comments and then snapped the big room to attention with a remark no one had anticipated. "For those of you who were worried," he said, "everything's okay again at the Dick Powells."

It was a double-action bomb because there were many at the party who had no idea they should have been worried about the Powells. There were others, though, who knew just what his problem was. Whispered conversations started buzzing around the banquet hall like a rocket. The subject was June Allyson, that five-foot-one-inch, petite little blonde who looks nice enough for an angel award.

But she is one little book that can't be judged by its cover. Insiders know that Powell has been plucking his pretty bride out of tangles with other men for most of their 10 years of married life . . . The one-time Broadway chorus dolly is 31 years old now, a veteran of nearly 10 years marriage with Powell, and has an uncontrollable itch to push the sugar bowl aside and reach for the spice shelf . . . Every time they assigned her a new leading man in a movie, her flirtatious ways gave patient Powell something new to sit up nights biting his nails about.

Excerpt from "How Long Can Dick Powell Take It?"
(July 1955)

Ginger Rogers described June Allyson as "the girl every man wants to marry and the girl every woman wants as a friend." In 1955, Allyson was so popular that she and Grace Kelly were the only women among a list of the top ten box-office draws compiled by motion picture exhibitors. It was an image MGM had carefully crafted. In addition to giving Ella Geisman a more melodious name, the studio turned her hair a light brown, softened her makeup, and dressed her in simple clothes with Peter Pan collars.

"June Allyson is to the 1950s what Myrna Loy was to the 1930s," wrote Jeanine Basinger in *The Star Machine*, her look at how the studios created their talent. "Loy provided glamour and escape. She was the sophisticated, well-dressed companion, ready to go out on the town, hit the spots, and slug down her own round of martinis . . . Allyson's wife was the loyal, steadfast homebody, always loving, always supportive, always keeping the home fires burning while wearing a reasonable little outfit."

Confidential was only too happy to put the lie to Allyson's carefully manufactured reputation for sunny innocence.

"Think June Allyson is too nice to be naughty?" the magazine asked in July 1955. "Dick's been hitched to her for ten years but that doesn't keep June from busting out all over." *Confidential* alleged that Allyson had many lovers, naming Dean Martin and Alan Ladd in particular. "June's fans—and they number in the millions—will howl their heads off at the charge that the cutie with the page-boy bob and the Peter Pan collar could ever be a hubby-snatcher," *Confidential* wrote. "Nor can they be blamed, after swallowing years of a publicity build-up typing her 'as the girl next door,' 'cute as a button' and just too nice to be naughty."

Dick Powell, thirteen years Allyson's senior, was outraged. But the fear of more publicity, which long had kept Hollywood in check, stopped him from taking action. "What can you do when a pack of lies appears about your wife?" he asked. "I was told legally that to sue for libel is just blowing up a lot of wind. This is a job for the government."

The Allyson story didn't even rate a cover line in an issue filled with juicy items such as the story about Clark Gable's forgotten wife and a piece that insinuated that Walter P. Chrysler Jr., heir to the automobile empire, was forced to resign his Navy commission after an investigation into his habit of entertaining young sailors at his navy quarters. But it added to the growing tension between Harrison and Rushmore, who complained about the salaciousness of the story. In a piece published in the *Christian Herald* in January 1958, Rushmore said he had become ashamed to bring *Confidential* home, for fear his two teenage stepdaughters would find it. The magazine was, he wrote, "the Peeping Tom of American Journalism."

Harrison also had problems with Rushmore. A major one was Rushmore's disinclination to check facts, evident in the Lizabeth Scott case, when he published a story even though Ronnie Quillan had failed to vet it. Rigorous fact checking had been key, along with attorney DeStefano's practice of securing sworn affidavits from sources, to keeping *Confidential* "suit-proof." Harrison bragged that he would pay an individual as much as $500 to verify a fact, and once spent $2,500 (equivalent to about $17,000 today) to send a lawyer to Europe "to nail down just one important fact."

Harrison also was uneasy with Rushmore's success in garnering the sort of media attention that formerly had been focused solely on him. Rushmore, for example, had been front page news across the country for several days in July 1955 when he mysteriously disappeared from a Chicago hotel room while on a trip to interview an underground Communist Party operative. The FBI was called in to help search for Rushmore, and newspapers reported that members of the Communist Party had threatened his life. Rushmore turned up in a hotel in Butte, Montana, telling police and FBI agents that he had to go "underground" in pursuit of a story that attempted to tie the death of Navy Secretary James

MGM had carefully manufactured June Allyson's image. She was, said Ginger Rogers, "the girl every man wants to marry and the girl every woman wants as a friend." *Confidential* begged to differ in a July 1955 story.

Forrestal to "Communist violence." Forrestal had jumped to his death in 1949 from the sixteenth floor of a hospital, but Rushmore remained convinced he had been killed by Communists.

At the *Confidential* offices, staffers saw the Rushmore "disappearance" as a publicity stunt. Clyde Tolson, associate director of the FBI, was scathing in a comment he scrawled in the margin of a Bureau report on the disappearance. "Rushmore must be a 'nut.' We should have nothing to do with him," he wrote. Bureau director J. Edgar Hoover, with whom Rushmore had tried to curry favor in a series of obsequious letters, added his own scrawl: "I certainly agree."

But the biggest clashes between Rushmore, the passionate ideo-

"How Long Can Dick Powell Take It?" *Confidential* asked in July 1955, in a story that alleged his all-American wife, June Allyson, had been involved with other men for most of their ten-year marriage. Among those it cited as her lovers were Dean Martin and Alan Ladd.

logue, and Harrison, who knew nothing about politics or world affairs and cared less, were ideological. One battle was over Harrison's attempt to woo Murray Kempton, the famously liberal columnist for the *New York Post*, as a contributor. The *Post*, in Rushmore's mind, was a nest of Communists and fellow travelers. Its editor, Jimmy Wechsler, had had the temerity to attack in print U.S. Senator Joe McCarthy, Walter Winchell, and J. Edgar Hoover—the Anti-Communist Trinity so far as Rushmore was concerned.

Another fight was over Rushmore's plan to publish stories about former first lady Eleanor Roosevelt's sexual "indiscretions," a plan that par-

NY Z8 INP SOUNDPHOTO....1-3-58...NEW YORK...HOWARD RUSHMORE, 44, (ABOVE) NOTED EX-COMMUNIST WHO ONCE EDITED CONFIDENTIAL MAGAZINE, KILLED HIS WIFE, FRANCES, 40, AND HIMSELF WITH A .32 CAL. REVOLVER IN A NEW YORK TAXI CAB TONIGHT. (FILE PHOTO).

Howard Rushmore, six feet five inches in height, was different from his much shorter boss, Robert Harrison, in every respect except for their shared lust for fame, which exacerbated their many other conflicts.

ticularly incensed DeStefano, who not only was Harrison's lawyer but one of his closest confidants. DeStefano said Rushmore was working on a story that, improbably, claimed Mrs. Roosevelt was both a lesbian and having an affair with her black male chauffeur. "I killed it on the ground that you don't besmirch the First Lady of a great president," DeStefano remembered. Meanwhile, Al Govoni, who had been with *Confidential* since its founding, was warning Harrison about Rushmore's growing drinking problem.

That the two men would clash shouldn't have come as a surprise, for in most ways Rushmore was Harrison's absolute opposite. While Harrison's parents were Jewish refugees who settled in crowded and polyglot

Robert Harrison thought of himself as debonair. But he was described by a writer for *Esquire* as having "the face of a lordly asthmatic falcon. . . . His voice is low and underscored by ill-concealed snorts and hacks. His clothes are those of an immensely prosperous manufacturer of nail enamel, wrought of expensive fabrics and a trifle sharp."

New York City, Rushmore's mother and father were early homesteaders in the sparsely populated West who traced their ancestors back to the Pilgrims. The decidedly apolitical Harrison's ethnic background made him a New Deal Democrat almost by default; Rushmore had a youthful flirtation with Communism that was an anomalous departure from the conservative American nativist tradition that he returned to with a vengeance. Harrison, whose lifelong companions were elder sisters who served as his secretaries, consorted with a succession of pretty blondes, none of whom he married or took seriously; Rushmore married two women whom he loved intensely—one with a deadly passion. Harrison was relentlessly social; Rushmore had few friends and displayed an awkwardness in social settings signified by a twitching nose. Harrison was a dandy, a fashion plate; Rushmore's height and scarecrow physique made him the object of jokes. Harrison's childhood was poor but comfortable; Rushmore's family was so poverty-stricken that his few Depression-era friends would remark on it years later. Harrison took a childlike delight in publicity about his playboy life; Rushmore had pretensions to rectitude.

About the only thing they had in common was that both generally were considered homely. Rushmore, six feet five inches tall and skinny, was described as having the face of Mephistopheles. And Harrison, as one writer put it, didn't look like the most successful publisher of all time. "He has the face of a lordly asthmatic falcon," wrote Richard Gehman in an *Esquire* profile published at the height of Harrison's success. "Heavy hoods of skin hang down over the corners of his eyes, his nose is a sharp beak, and his expression is one of indignant disdain. His voice is low and underscored by ill-concealed snorts and hacks. His clothes are those of an immensely prosperous manufacturer of nail enamel, wrought of expensive fabrics and a trifle sharp."

In September 1955, Rushmore agreed to leave *Confidential* with severance pay and the magazine's promise to assume any liability Rushmore faced for libel suits over stories published under his watch. He had struck a good deal, as eventually suits seeking a total of $1 million in damages were named with him as defendant. For his part, Rushmore pledged that he bore neither *Confidential* nor Harrison any ill will.

But Rushmore, who had turned against his conservative Midwestern family to join the Communist Party, then turned against leftist friends Jack Conroy and Nelson Algren to join Senator Joe McCarthy's anti-Communist crusade, then turned against Roy Cohn and was forced off the McCarthy committee, once again switched sides. "Mr. Harrison gave Rushmore $2,000 when he left *Confidential*," DeStefano remembered. "Rushmore used this money to fly to California where he met with attorney Jerry Geisler, who then was representing Robert Mitchum, Doris Duke, and Lizabeth Scott in suits against *Confidential* amounting to $6 million."

Once again Rushmore was out of a job. Things were difficult on the home front. His beloved mother, Rose, had died in January, leaving him only a few hundred dollars. And in September his wife, Frances, battling depression and a drinking problem, hurled herself into Manhattan's East River, where the police rescued her.

16

"The Real Reason for Marilyn Monroe's Divorce"

The Los Angeles private detective eased his car into the curb a few feet past 754 Kilkea Drive and took a drag on his cigarette as he watched the world's most famous set of curves wiggle up to an apartment house door and vanish inside. As he stepped from his car, a dark-colored convertible slid up and came to a stop behind him.

Out stepped Joe DiMaggio, the famed Yankee Clipper and—as of that moment—the newly divorced ex-husband of the "Shape," luscious Marilyn Monroe. By the light of a corner street lamp, the detective could see Joe's face was set in hard, angry lines.

"Well, where is she?" DiMaggio growled at the private eye. There was no need to identify "she."

For weeks the dick had been tailing the nation's sexiest blond. Time and time again the trail had led to this address and the apartment of Sheila Stewart, a little-known Hollywood bit player. Cocking a thumb at this now familiar door, the detective, said, "She's in there again."

"Who else is in there with them?" DiMaggio demanded.

"I don't know," was the detective's reply. "I just got here when you drove up."

"Well, I'm not fooling around here any longer," Joe said. "Let's kick the door in and find out."

Excerpt from "The Real Reason for Marilyn Monroe's Divorce"
(September 1955)

On a moonless night on November 5, 1954, Frank Sinatra found himself standing under the Chinese elms on a quiet West Hollywood street trying to reason with Joltin' Joe DiMaggio, the Yankee Clipper himself, whose judgment had been clouded by too many stiff ones at a club on nearby Sunset Boulevard. Standing with them was Barney Ruditsky, a private investigator whose bespectacled and friendly face seemed ill matched to his terrier disposition, and Phil Irwin, Ruditsky's cocky young sidekick. It was an impressive gathering for Kilkea Drive, a street that would never appear on anyone's map of Hollywood stars. Their focus was the house at number 754.

It was and is an unremarkable house, built in the postwar construction frenzy for a single family. Its two stories of stucco with red tile trim are an homage to California's Spanish heritage contradicted by a fake mansard roof and a vaguely Dutch entry. By the early 1950s it had been carved into three apartments to better suit the changing character of the neighborhood, where single young men and women whose careers were waxing mixed with oldsters whose lives were on the wane. One of those young women was Sheila Stewart, who lived upstairs.

This quiet block was familiar to Ruditsky and Irwin, who had kept a close watch on Stewart's apartment for weeks. But it wasn't Sheila they were interested in. On DiMaggio's behalf, the two private investigators had been tracking "the Shape," the swivel-hipped glamour girl whose marriage to the ballplayer ten months earlier had been Hollywood's most celebrated wedding since Mary Pickford swapped rings with Douglas Fairbanks. Marilyn Monroe had become a frequent guest at 754 Kilkea Drive, and, as Ruditsky put it, "these weren't just girlish bunking parties."

In a sense, DiMaggio had no claims on Monroe. Only months after their marriage, it became clear that he wasn't going to realize his ambition to turn America's favorite sex kitten into a retiring homemaker and mother. Instead of settling into DiMaggio's home in San Francisco, Monroe had headed to New York after the marriage to film *The Seven Year Itch*. The film's publicity photo of Marilyn standing over a subway

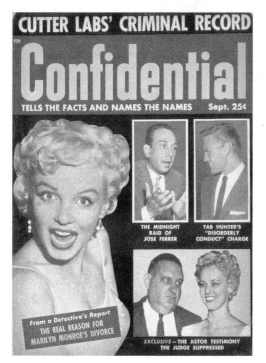

With an August 1955 story that promised the real reason for Marilyn Monroe's divorce from Joe DiMaggio, *Confidential*'s circulation soared above that of magazines such as *TV Guide* and *Life*. It was the best-selling newsstand publication in America, and the Hollywood studios realized they no longer could ignore it.

grating, her skirt billowing to the top of her thighs, infuriated the possessive DiMaggio. In late September, they had separated. And on October 28, Monroe stood before a judge in Santa Monica to testify that the famed baseball player had treated her with "coldness and indifference" when she had expected "love, warmth, and affection." She walked out of the courthouse with an uncontested divorce.

But DiMaggio couldn't let her go. He still loved Marilyn, and the possibility of another man nagged at him as he drank on the Strip that Friday night in November. The other man he had in mind was Hal Schaefer, a vocal coach who had coached Marilyn for hits such as *There's No Business Like Show Business* and who, according to Ruditsky, was a regular visitor at Sheila Stewart's apartment. When Irwin bumped into DiMaggio at the Sunset club, the ballplayer was brimming with liquid courage, and he demanded that Irwin come with him for a showdown.

A panicked Irwin called Ruditsky, who called Sinatra, who dragged along his manager, Henry Sanicola, and Pasquale "Patsy" D'Amore, the owner of the Villa Capri, the restaurant where he and Sanicola had been dining. By the time their cars crept onto Kilkea, DiMaggio had formulated a plan, and none of his friends could dissuade him. One of them would stand on the sidewalk to see who ran out the front door while the rest of the men crashed through the back.

Ruditsky was afraid of what DiMaggio would do if he caught Schaefer with Monroe. So he convinced DiMaggio to stand outside and let him lead the attack. Ruditsky put his shoulder down and charged the rear door, four or five times in all. Finally it crashed to the floor, and Barney and his buddies tumbled over one another into the apartment. Shrill screams led the posse to a bedroom, where Ruditsky flung open the door while Irwin hoisted his camera and set off a blinding flash. Then Ruditsky flicked on the bedroom light to reveal the terrified countenance of one Florence Kotz Ross, clutching her bedclothes around her and howling like a banshee. It took only seconds for the men to realize they'd busted into the wrong apartment. And it took only minutes for them to hit the street, leaving behind the frightened Miss Ross and a badly damaged door. As they piled into their cars and sped away, they could hear the siren of an approaching police car.

The incident at 754 Kilkea was rated an ordinary breaking and entering. Miss Ross didn't know what had hit her. If L.A.'s notoriously corruptible cops knew the identity of her late-night guests, they weren't talking. The sordid details went into a locked file cabinet in Barney Ruditsky's office to which only Barney and his trusted associate, Phil Irwin, had the key. Ruditsky could relax knowing the file cabinet, a tainted police department, and a lazy and compromised Hollywood press corps would protect the reputations of America's most famous crooner and most beloved athlete, not to mention his own private investigator's license.

But while Ruditsky was breathing a sigh of relief, the perpetually broke Irwin spent the next few months thinking about the cheaply printed magazine with the lurid red and yellow covers that was turning the town on its ear. Every private eye in Los Angeles knew that *Confidential* would pay well for information about scandals that no one else could or would touch. Irwin, known for letting his affairs with the bottle and an occasional skirt get in the way of his good sense, used his key to slip the Monroe/DiMaggio file out of Ruditsky's file cabinet.

In early August 1955, ten months later, hundreds of trucks fanned out across America carrying more than four million copies of *Confidential* with a cover that promised to give its readers "The Real Reason for Marilyn Monroe's Divorce: From a Detective's Report." The story was written by Al Govoni, using the pseudonym J. E. LeClair, the name of his brother-in-law. Fred Otash called it "the most explosive story in that publication's history." Baseball fans who thought the Pride of the Yankees could do no wrong saw a cuckold crazed by jealousy. Bobby-soxers who swooned when Ol' Blue Eyes opened his mouth saw a candidate for the Three Stooges. Barney Ruditsky lost his private investigator's license. Phil Irwin was beaten and dumped in a telephone booth by Sinatra's friends. *Confidential*'s newsstand sales soared above those of *TV Guide* and *Life*, cementing its reputation as the best-selling magazine on America's newsstands. The magazine that a Marilyn story had helped launch had used her to achieve its biggest triumph.

17

"What They 'Forgot' to Say About . . . Kim Novak"

The Big Build-Up

When the Hollywood hucksters set out to give a new starlet the build-up treatment, they hand out a lot of hokum to the press. Take the case of curvy blonde, Kim Novak.

Life said: She got into pictures when her agent, Louis Shurr, discovered her riding her bicycle in Beverly Hills.

Look said: A dreamy, 22-year-old, green-eyed blonde, Kim Novak . . . earns $250 weekly and rents a $19.50-a-week room at the YWCA's Hollywood Studio Club. So far, her life has been so uncomplicated that she can say she finds an outlet for all her emotions in acting.

Kim Novak said: "I wasn't really mad for a Hollywood career, but since it fell in my lap, I'd like to try my hand at it for a while."

The Lowdown

There must have been half a dozen Hollywood wolves who choked on their highballs while reading such undiluted malarkey about the chesty, little Czechoslovakian cutie they knew back in the good old days when her name was Marilyn Novak. They'd have hardly known the kid from her press clippings, though.

She may, for instance, know what the inside of the Hollywood YWCA looks like by now, but she was flying considerably higher—and faster—when she arrived in movieland early in the summer of 1953 and checked into the Beverly Hills Hotel with a girl friend.

A neatly–moulded nymph of 20, Marilyn had abruptly resigned as the principal attraction in a touring demonstration of refrigerators, where she was erroneously titled "Miss Deep Freeze." Kim wasn't even chilly, as she soon demonstrated to a slick-haired fellow she met in the hotel lobby, and to whom she confessed that she was down to her last two dollars.

He was Michael (alias Laslo) Benedict, a Sunset and Vine hanger-on with a long record for bad check manipulations, and a talent scout himself, although the kind who talked in whispers. It just so happened, he told Marilyn, that he could introduce her to a romp-loving Rumanian munitions baron, Edgar Ausnit, who dearly loved to help curvaceous girlies.

Excerpt from "What They 'Forgot' to Say About . . . Kim Novak"
(January 1956)

While Columbia's publicists, and the major magazines that lapped up the studio publicity, portrayed Novak as an innocent, hardworking career girl, *Confidential* claimed she was a manipulative kept woman. And kept by a Romanian munitions merchant to boot.

Edgar Ausnit, who fled to the United States before World War II and lost much of his property to the Yugoslavian government after the war, became a naturalized, and still quite wealthy, U.S. citizen in 1948. Bespectacled, with a pencil-thin mustache and partial to homburg hats, he wasn't a handsome man. But, as *Confidential* pointed out, his money gave him a certain allure to young starlets. The magazine claimed that Novak not only profited from Ausnit's "generosity," but also simultaneously carried on an affair with a younger and more attractive man, Ted Cooper, like Novak an aspiring actor.

The stories in *Life* and *Look* were typical of the way major magazines lapped up studio publicity. Novak, who came to Hollywood with

Confidential gave the lie to Kim Novak's image as an innocent, hardworking career girl with a January 1956 story that alleged she was a manipulative woman kept by a mysterious Romanian munitions merchant. The story contrasted sharply with more adoring accounts published, with Columbia Pictures' help, by *Life* and *Look*.

plans to model and then pursued her film career with a vengeance, was very much a creation of Harry Cohn.

"Girls like Kim Novak, Marilyn Monroe, and Jayne Mansfield—the most popular actresses in movies—all reflect the times we are living in," a Beverly Hills psychiatrist explained to Ezra Goodman, the *Time* magazine correspondent. "They are blobs, faceless wonders, poor lost souls that go well with an era that suffers from a loss of identity. They reflect their times . . . They feel they have no tie to anything."

"Kim Novak was created not so much by her own talent, which is debatable, but by her diligent application and what Harry Cohn rightly called 'the studio,' " explained Goodman. "A great many people put in their own highly specialized talents, from Cohn's propensity for making use of the right people, to the lowliest technician who pitched in, as part of his or her job, to build up the glamorously monstrous creation that was Kim Novak."

For example, the story that Novak was discovered riding her bicycle was crafted by George Lait, who was head of publicity at Columbia when Novak arrived. "The bicycle thing caught on great," Lait said. "I got her a lavender bicycle and she'd wear lavender shoes, slacks and sweater and she'd drive the bicycle to the studio and park it in my office."

By the time *Confidential* published its story, Novak had left the YWCA, and Edgar Ausnit, far behind. She had drawn attention from fans and critics for her role in *Pushover* (1954), where she played opposite Fred MacMurray. She became even more popular after appearing in *Phffft!* (1954) opposite Jack Carson, Judy Holliday, and Jack Lemmon. But 1955 was her biggest year, when she starred in *Picnic* opposite William Holden, winning a Golden Globe award, and in *The Man with the Golden Arm* opposite Frank Sinatra.

Novak, like many Hollywood hopefuls, had left skeletons in the closets of the many small apartments she'd inhabited on her way to the top. In addition to the affaire Ausnit, Columbia had to help her take some nude pictures off the market (for which the studio paid a reported $15,000). And there was a bit of a flap when she posed nude for columnist Earl Wilson during her first publicity tour of New York. She also dated Ramfis Trujillo, son of the Dominican dictator, who was so noted for his generosity to beautiful actresses that, for a while, some women took to using a bumper sticker that read: "THIS CAR WAS NOT A GIFT FROM RAMFIS TRUJILLO." Novak's was a case where the negative publicity seemed to do no real harm, although doubtless it vexed

Kim Novak of Hollywood was fashioned from Marilyn Pauline Novak of Chicago by Columbia Pictures boss Harry Cohn. A Beverly Hills psychiatrist claimed Novak was typical of the "blobs, faceless wonders, poor lost souls" that Hollywood fashioned into stars in the 1950s.

the studio publicists like Lait who were paid to make sure *Life* and *Look* and the tame fan magazines presented the authorized version of Novak's life. She made the cover of *Time* in 1957, and in 1958 scored her best-known role, a dual engagement as shopgirl Judy Barton and wealthy brunet Madeleine Elster in Alfred Hitchcock's *Vertigo*.

The absence of an uproar over the Novak revelations led some observers to suggest the filmgoing public was taking all this negative publicity in stride. They averred that it was too late to return to a more innocent past—that the exposé magazines marked a major and irreversible change in American public discourse. Clearly, with some sixteen magazines now in the category, there was an audience.

18

"The Left Hook That Unhooked Lana Turner from Bob Topping"

It is currently husband No. 3 in the life of Lana Turner, but now the story can be told of the fuse which led to the explosion of matrimonial project No. 2.

If you're listening, Lex Barker, don't ever belt your pretty wife. Your predecessor, Bob Topping, tried it and in a matter of months he wound up losing one of Hollywood's all-time glamour girls. It all started over that perennial straight man, Mr. Black Magic himself, Billy Daniels, who seems to have the unhappy faculty of being around when knives are flashed, shots are fired or husbands break in unexpectedly.

It was one fatal evening back in the days when all was idyllic in the Topping-Turner household. Lana and Bob were entertaining a couple from the East. A close friend and his date dropped in and they all decided to do a little pub-crawling. After making a few rounds they wound up at Mocambo, one of the Sunset Strip's glitter joints. The star attraction was Billy Daniels.

Lana Couldn't Get Enough of Billy's Singing

Mr. B. was his usual smash, directing most of his show to the Topping table. After the show Topping motioned to Billy to sit down and have a drink with them . . . It wasn't long before the joint was empty, except for the one party. No one in the group was feeling any pain at

147

the moment, least of all Mr. Topping. He took one bleary look at the desolate room and recommended that they all move on to the cheery fireplace at his plush Holmby Hills manse.

[There] the logs in the fireplace crackled, the ice cubes in the glasses tinkled, and Billy's velvety voice crooned of amour, making the whole thing a real romantic little symphony. Lana just couldn't get enough of Billy's singing and if anybody in the party was concentrating, it would have been obvious that William was singing directly at Lana.

Of a certainty, Mr. Topping wasn't concentrating. He got to his feet shakily and asked to be excused. It had been a long, wet night and his friend had to help him up to bed. The singing went on for a while, but suddenly it stopped—for a very good reason. The singer had disappeared—and so had Mrs. Lana Turner Topping.

*Excerpt from "The Left Hook That Unhooked
Lana Turner from Bob Topping"
(September 1956)*

There was a sudden scream from the den, *Confidential* reported, and when the other guests raced into the room they discovered a furious Topping. "He hit Lana with a left hook that caught her on the chin and knocked her across the room and onto a couch," the magazine reported. "The names he called her never would have gotten by the movie censor."

Topping also lashed out at Daniels. "Get out of my house, you no good— —" *Confidential* wrote, in a rare bit of self-censorship.

"There wasn't much peace in the Turner-Topping household after this debacle. One row led to another and ultimately to the divorce."

Turner had separated from Topping in 1951 and divorced him in 1952. By the time this *Confidential* story appeared, Julia Jean Mildred Frances Turner, whom her fans knew as "Lana," was on husband number four, not three. She was, of course, to have even more tempestuous marriages and affairs, not least with Barker, whom she divorced after allegations he molested Turner's daughter. The mistake in counting Turner's husbands was uncharacteristic of *Confidential*. What was typi-

Lana Turner, who had been dropped by MGM in February 1956 because of her poor box-office showing, was dealt another blow in September of that year by *Confidential.* The magazine recounted an incident in which ex-husband Bob Topping, whom she divorced in 1952, had slugged her in front of guests. Turner had married Topping after her divorce from Stephen Crane, father of her only child, Cheryl. By the time the story appeared, Turner was on to husband number 4, Lex Barker.

cal was that it had dredged up dirt from the past and published it at an inopportune time for its subject. When the story appeared Turner's career was in real trouble.

Turner had prospered for years at MGM, where mentor Mervyn

149

LeRoy took her in 1938. But by 1954 things began to slow. She was cast in two poorly written films at MGM (*Betrayed* in 1954 and *The Prodigal* in 1955) and loaned out to Twentieth Century–Fox for two inauspicious films (*The Sea Chase* and *The Rains of Ranchipur*) in 1955. She returned to MGM to make *Diane*, also in 1955, which was poorly received. The studio dropped her in February 1956, when Turner was thirty-five.

"I didn't know how to make a hotel or airline reservation," Turner said of that difficult time. "For a long time I waited for my limousine that never came to pick me up. I was an orphan. MGM had prepared me for stardom, but not for life."

19

"Joan Crawford's Back Street Romance with a Bartender"

You wouldn't have believed it, either. Here the guy was, tending bar at a plush restaurant in Beverly Hills, when a waiter walked up and said a dame wanted to talk to him on the telephone.

Answering it, the barman heard a low, throaty woman's voice announce, "This is Joan Crawford."

Well, what would you have done? Just before slamming down the receiver, he said, "Yeah? Well, I'm Robert Taylor."

"No, really this is true," the husky voice continued.

And would you like to know something? It was true. What's more, only a few days later the amazed bartender ended up with Joan at seven in the yawning—in Joan's very own house at 426 Bristol Avenue in Brentwood.

What did the acknowledged Queen of Hollywood want with a bartender? She was a gal bachelor in those days—before her marriage to Pepsi-Cola king Alfred Steele—and could have had half the leading men in the movies at the snap of a finger.

But it happened—a dizzy, daffy romance which began with that telephone call to a man Joan Crawford had never even met.

What Her Cinema Highness had in mind didn't come out at first. Smoothly, she explained she was having a party for some friends and the cast of her movie, *Sudden Fear*. Would he come around and tend bar? The bartender agreed and, later, was ushered to the side of La Crawford's swimming pool, where they discussed what was to be poured in the punch for the party the following Saturday.

Favorite Drink Was Vodka on the Rocks

Joan was careful about the recipe but she didn't touch the stuff when the wingding got rolling . . . Half a dozen times during the course of the evening Joan would stop by the bar, pat the bartender's head and coo, "Baby, you're doing a swell job!" . . . By twos, threes and fours, the guests left, then the extra help. . . . Taking him by the hand, Joan led him into the living room and over to the couch. They'd barely met. Could this be—the Empress of Hollywood and a bartender?

It not only could be, but the bartender soon discovered one other thing: Joan is even younger than she looks. The sun was shining brightly before Queen Crawford bade her boy friend good night. What's more, she was on the phone the very next night to arrange another party—this one a simple little thing for two—herself and the Martini mixer.

Excerpt from "Joan Crawford's Back Street
Romance with a Bartender"
(January 1957)

Joan Crawford may have gotten a pass from Howard Rushmore when he was assigned to investigate rumors she was abusing her children, but she wasn't so lucky when it came to her sexual antics.

By the time the *Confidential* story appeared, Crawford had left behind a life of sexual profligacy and alcohol abuse. She was alleged to have had affairs with men ranging from Yul Brynner (likely) to Rock Hudson (highly unlikely) and longer relationships with Greg Bautzer, a lawyer, and Vincent Sherman, a married director. Her fights with daughter Christina were so fierce that once the police were called to intervene. Son Christopher had run away from home multiple times. But in 1955 she married Pepsi-Cola chairman Alfred Steele, who provided her with a level of financial and emotional security that transformed her.

Again, as it had done with Kim Novak, Lana Turner, and so many others, *Confidential* had dug up an embarrassing story from the past.

As with so many of its stories, the source for *Confidential*'s article about Joan Crawford's liaison with a bartender was the bartender himself. When the story appeared, in January 1957, Crawford had stopped her heavy drinking and sleeping around and had settled into domesticity with husband Alfred Steele, chairman of Pepsi-Cola.

Not that the magazine's readers, ever eager for a titillating peak at the shenanigans of the rich and famous, seemed to mind. Circulation continued to grow.

Conventional thinking was that *Confidential*'s audience was mostly female, and largely middle- to lower-middle-class. There was anecdotal evidence that it actually was an economically and culturally diverse audience. Howard Rushmore described a dinner party where an old friend, "a lady of distinct charm, refinement and culture," confessed that she enjoyed *Confidential*. Rushmore, trying to conceal his surprise, offered that he tried to have an article about the Communist threat in every issue. "Oh, pshaw!" his elderly friend replied. "Those articles are all right, Howard, but what I really get a kick out of are the saucy stories on Hollywood. I can't wait until the next issue."

On another occasion, Rushmore said, he was on a plane to the West Coast, sitting next to "a distinguished gentleman, well dressed, impeccable in his speech and his deportment. He had refused cocktails offered by the stewardess and I noticed that in his lapel he wore an emblem indicating his membership in a great religious organization. Yet, snuggled between the covers of a financial magazine, my seatmate had a copy of *Confidential.*"

Rushmore, who at the time of his writing was trying to dissociate himself from *Confidential,* said many subscription orders were from "people of dignity and reputation, asking that *Confidential* be sent 'in plain wrapper.' Apparently ashamed to buy it on the newsstands, they hoped the 'plain wrapper' would take care of things." Finally, as if to expiate his own guilt by laying it on others, Rushmore described a sidewalk encounter with "a nicely dressed, pleasant-looking woman" who bought a copy of *Confidential,* carefully slipping it out of view under a copy of a "popular family magazine."

"I watched her leave, headed no doubt for a pleasant home full of children and morality," he recalled. " 'Without her,' I thought, 'Harrison can't publish.' That quarter she paid for *Confidential* doesn't add much to the money in Harrison's pocket. But it keeps his circulation up, keeps the 'respectable' magazines copying his money-getting techniques, inspires TV shows to become Peeping Toms, and has the newspapers frantically trying to cash in on *Confidential's* secret of refining gold from dirt."

Harrison obviously had a more positive view of his audience and his magazine. He told *Writer's Yearbook* that subscribers to the magazine included sex researcher Dr. Alfred Kinsey; Henry Ford II; Rafael Trujillo, president of the Dominican Republic; Sophie Tucker; and Bob Feller, the famed Cleveland Indians pitcher.

In addition to his arguments that *Confidential* was helping clean up Hollywood, Harrison claimed that the magazine had a liberating effect on its mostly female audience. "Now, most women for the most part are much inhibited," he said. "Men have a certain freedom . . . Men can go to a night club alone. Women can't. Women's lives are on the more inhibited side. So they live in their minds to a great extent. When they read about other women who are doing the things that they think about, perhaps what they might want to do . . . this is great excitement to them . . . I talk to educated women who read *Confidential* all the time, and they tell me that they get a tremendous amount of enjoyment out of it because here is freedom that they don't have."

Other, less biased, writers also tried to explain the appeal of *Confidential* and its imitators. John Sisk, writing in the June 1956 issue of *Commonweal*, said *Confidential* and its competitors appealed to baser instincts. "The easiest explanation for the success of the exposé magazines is that the public is generally envious of successful and prominent people . . . " he wrote. "Yet the exposé magazines also represent symbolic participation masked as morally indignant discovery, with the exposed one conveniently bearing off the guilt."

Whatever the reason, Harrison was confident that what he had created was here to stay. "*Confidential* . . . is permanent," he told *Writer's Yearbook*. "The format may change with the times. In other words, people generally will always be interested in the story behind the story . . . The desire to know that which is not told, and that's *Confidential*—will continue. That I place my life on."

20

"Here's Why Frank Sinatra Is the Tarzan of the Boudoir"

He's had the nation's front-rank playboys dizzy for years trying to discover his secret. Ava Gardner, Lana Turner, Gloria Vanderbilt, Anita Ekberg—how does that skinny little guy do it? Vitamin pills? No. Goat Gland Extract? Nope.

Wheaties! That's the magic, gentlemen. Where other Casanovas wilt under the pressure of a torrid romance, Frankie Boy just pours himself a big bowl of crispy, crackly Wheaties and comes back rarin' to go.

How he does it might have remained a mystery forever, if it weren't for a curvy, dreamy-eyed little pigeon who met "The Voice" on the Coast just a few months ago . . .

They dined at the fashionable Dunes restaurant in Palm Springs after arriving from Hollywood, and the gal noted that Frank just picked and pecked at his food. Back at the house, though, he tore into the kitchen, wolfed down a big bowl of those nourishing flakes and then led her to the boudoir. The frolic that followed was as nice a little ad for Wheaties as you could ever want, General Mills, but that was only the beginning.

While the tootsie was catching her breath, Frankie excused himself and padded back into the kitchen for a refill of that "Breakfast of Champs." The girl was still wondering what was going on when he came charging back into the play room humming "I'm In the Mood for Love," and proceeded to prove it.

It had been a very nice evening but the doll never got a chance to say so after the second inning because her commuting Casanova bounced out to the kitchen once more for another pick-me-up and came striding back with that old love light in his eye.

Believe It Or Not—Frankie Was Shuffling into His Slippers Again!

When Frankie made his fourth visit to the Wheaties bin the gal began to cross her fingers. Something, she was sure, was going to explode. Her worries were groundless, though. They cut another caper and she finally nuzzled her weary head into the pillow for some shut-eye—until—she heard a noise.

Believe us, General Mills, it was Frankie shuffling into his slippers again. Out to the kitchen he went. Back in her little nook, the unbelieving babe could plainly hear the crunch, crunch of a man—eating Wheaties.

Excerpt from "Here's Why Frank Sinatra Is
the Tarzan of the Boudoir"
(May 1956)

The Wheaties story, a paean to sexual prowess, would have pleased many a *Confidential* subject. But Sinatra, already furious over the "Wrong Door Raid" story, was incensed and threatened to sue the magazine. Eight months after the Wheaties story appeared, he became embroiled in a California Senate committee hearing that generated more negative headlines for weeks.

The Senate Interim Committee on Collection Agencies, known as the Kraft Committee after its chairman, State Senator Fred Kraft of San Diego, was formed to look into allegations of misconduct by private detectives. Kraft made a successful bid for publicity by announcing that his investigation would focus on the "Wrong Door Raid" and the scandal magazine business, ostensibly out of concern that the money being paid to tipsters by Harrison's operatives was compromising the integrity of the state's private detectives. Kraft told reporters that he intended to subpoena the records of Hollywood Research Inc., *Confidential*'s source of Hollywood information. His witness list included Marjorie Meade, Frank Sinatra, and Joe DiMaggio, the latter two of America's biggest celebrities.

DiMaggio, who was on the East Coast and out of range of state subpoenas, filed a deposition with the committee instead of appearing personally. Sinatra was required to testify in person. He told the committee that he had sat in a car and not participated in the raid, an account contradicted by private detective Phil Irwin and Virginia Blasgen, owner of the apartment house at the corner of Kilkea and Waring drives. "It was definitely Sinatra," she said. "He was laughing and standing next to another exquisitely dressed man across the street just before it happened."

"About 11:15, I heard a crash, like thunder. I grabbed the phone to call the police and looked out my kitchen window. I saw four of them rush out the back of Waring Drive."

Los Angeles District Attorney William B. McKesson asked Kraft to drop the scandal magazine portion of his Senate committee inquiry for fear that those on Kraft's witness list, including Marjorie Meade, might try to bargain for immunity from later criminal prosecution. After several weeks of study, the committee recommended federal legislation to curb magazines like *Confidential*. "They're a national disgrace. The field is beyond the scope of a single State Legislature," Kraft said.

But the inquiry wasn't over. McKesson then convened a grand jury to consider whether Sinatra, DiMaggio, and others mentioned in the "Wrong Door Raid" should be indicted for conspiracy to commit criminal mischief or, in the case of Sinatra and Irwin, for perjury in their comments to investigators. Los Angeles police raided Sinatra's Palm Springs home at 4 a.m. on a Saturday in search of more evidence. McKesson announced that it was obvious to him that either Sinatra or Phil Irwin had lied to the committee. The government was responding to Hollywood's request to turn up the heat on *Confidential*. Now, as the temperature rose, it was the stars and the studios that began to feel uncomfortable.

21

"It Was the Hottest Show in Town When Maureen O'Hara Cuddled in Row 35"

Almost anyone who's ever been to the movies knows about Hollywood's famous Grauman's Chinese Theatre. That's where the stars go to get their footprints recorded in cement. That's where they stage some of movieland's gaudiest premiers.

But you'd have to be an usher to get the real lowdown on what goes on in this celebrated movie house. Garbed in your flashy uniform and equipped with your tiny flashlight, you'd discover something to make your eyes pop. Because Grauman's is also the theater where the stars go—not to watch the movie but to bundle in the balcony. And the show that goes on in the back seats often beats anything that's flickering on the screen.

. . . A gentlemanly assistant manager at Grauman's didn't give it a second thought one November evening not so long ago when he greeted lovely, green-eyed Maureen O'Hara at the head of the main aisle . . . He got the shock of his life an hour later, though, when the usher in charge of aisle "C" came rushing out to report that there was a couple heating up the back of the theater as though it were mid-January. Easing down the aisle, he saw the entwined twosome. It was Maureen and her south-of-the-border sweetie . . . He saw even more than that. Maureen had entered Grauman's wearing a white silk blouse neatly buttoned. Now it wasn't.

The guy had come in wearing a spruce blue suit. Now he wasn't . . . Moreover, Maureen had taken the darndest position to watch a movie in the whole history of the theater. She was spread across three seats—with the happy Latin American in the middle seat.

Excerpt from "It Was the Hottest Show in Town
When Maureen O'Hara Cuddled in Row 35"
(March 1957)

The Maureen O'Hara story was so relatively unimportant in Harrison's eyes that it didn't rate a cover line in the March 1957 issue. It was a big deal, however, to O'Hara. Outraged by the magazine's insinuation that she had practically had sex in row 35 of Grauman's Chinese with a Latin lover, she brought a $5 million libel suit against *Confidential*. Two Grauman's employees, assistant managers James Craig and Michael Patrick Casey, testified to seeing O'Hara doing something with a man in the last row of Grauman's, although each gave a different date for the incident. Craig, an Irishman, had given the story to *Confidential's* London-based Michael Mordaunt-Smith and was paid seventy pounds, then worth about two hundred dollars. "I understood that practically an act of sexual intercourse had taken place in the back seat of Grauman's Chinese Theatre," Mordaunt-Smith later said.

Hollywood insiders knew O'Hara was seeing Mexico City hotel man Enrique Parra, who fit the description of O'Hara's movie date. It was a relationship that displeased *Hollywood Reporter* columnist Mike Connolly, who some believe may have been another source for the *Confidential* story. "Word wafts up from Mexico City that Maureen O'Hara is having a whirrrrl," he wrote in his column. "If Maureen O'Hara has her heart set on that Mexican, she should know (1) he's married and has a seventeen-year-old daughter, (2) Mexicans don't divorce easily in Mexico and (3) he doesn't own that hotel or that bank but merely works for the people who own them."

But O'Hara sued with confidence, knowing there was a stamp in her passport proving that she had been in London on the day the magazine said the incident took place. This was another sign that *Confidential*, now feeling the heat from a bevy of imitators and scrambling for its own Hollywood exclusives, had let its rigorous fact-checking system slip.

Harrison had gotten through 1955 and 1956 relatively unscathed, except of course for the flesh wound to the shoulder in the Jarabacoa Mountains and lawsuits claiming more than $8 million in libel damages. Nineteen fifty-seven, however, was to be one of the worst years of his life. It opened with the February debut of *Slander,* an MGM film about a scandal magazine that starred Steve Cochran, Van Johnson, and Ann Blyth. The film ended with the magazine editor's own mother shooting him, declaring him "unfit to live." A superstitious person might have seen the film as an ominous sign of Hollywood's willingness to fight back.

"On the face of it, the picture is just Hollywood's way of swatting one of its more irritating fleas: most of the people who have been smeared by the scandal magazines are movie stars," *Time* magazine said. "But in a deeper sense the moviemakers have served the public too. For in the pursuit of the principal villain they also take a swipe or two at his accomplices—at the readership which settles in cloudlike millions on the garbage which the scandal sheets provide."

On March 27, the Los Angeles grand jury handed the "Wrong Door Raid" matter back to the Los Angeles Police Department for further investigation. Harrison, the Meades, and the rest of the *Confidential* family didn't have long to savor the passing of this particular public relations nightmare. The next morning Assistant Attorney General Clarence Linn met with District Attorney McKesson to discuss further grand jury action. McKesson announced that he had been quietly studying the scandal magazine business for the previous eight months and was considering whether to take action. Alarmed, Harrison decided to close Hollywood Research after only a year and a half of operation. Marjorie Meade and her husband, Fred, went into real estate.

Shortly thereafter, California governor Goodwin Knight publicly condemned exposé magazines and called for them to be banned. Holly-

Maureen O'Hara was outraged by a *Confidential* story that alleged she had misbehaved in the back row of Grauman's Chinese Theatre with her Mexican lover. O'Hara's passport showed she was out of the country on the date of the alleged incident. For once, *Confidential*'s vaunted fact-checking system had failed it. O'Hara sued for libel and won.

wood power brokers, aware that Attorney General Edmund G. "Pat" Brown was considering a gubernatorial bid and would need their financial support, now pushed him to take a stand. Brown soon made his own speech in which he denounced exposé magazines in general, and *Confidential* in particular, as a threat to the state's important movie industry. Working with McKesson, he impaneled a grand jury to hear testimony about *Confidential*'s operations. O'Hara announced that she'd be delighted to testify. The rest of the grand jury witness list was a veritable Who's Who of Hollywood, with names such as Liberace, Walter Pidgeon, Corinne Calvet, Buddy Baer, and Mae West volunteering their testimony. What was worse, a bitter Howard Rushmore approached Assistant Attorney General Linn and volunteered to tell all about the inner workings of the magazine.

Rushmore really had nothing to lose. At the age of forty-four, he had had difficulty finding work after leaving *Confidential*. His reputation as a "turncoat" didn't stand him in good stead with potential employers. The best job he'd been able to land was as editor of *Uncensored*, a *Confidential* imitator, which he resigned from after five months. He then freelanced for *Tipoff*, another scandal magazine, and did occasional stories for outdoors magazines and the *Police Gazette*. No longer was he commanding the attention of millions with his stories of Communists hiding in high places. Now he was making his living writing the sort of stories he claimed to despise. His personal life also was on the shoals. His wife, Frances, continued to suffer from depression, although her attendance at Alcoholics Anonymous meetings helped her curb her drinking. Rushmore, who coworkers had noticed was drinking heavily at *Confidential*, stepped up his consumption of alcohol. From time to time his arguments with Frances erupted into physical violence that left her afraid for her life. An earlier offer to Jerry Geisler to testify about his work with Harrison in return for a job in the film industry had been unproductive. Linn, however, was more than happy to give Rushmore the public platform he'd been missing since he left *Confidential*.

22

"Why Liberace's Theme Song Should Be, 'Mad About the Boy!' "

There are few show business personalities today with a gaudier sense of theater than the Kandelabra Kid himself, Liberace. You know the routine—grand piano, glittering suit, glimmering candles, Brother George on the violin, and so on.

But the pudgy pianist's many faithful fans would have popped their girdles if they had witnessed their idol in action last year in an offstage production that saw old Kittenish on the Keys play one sour note after another in his clumsy efforts to make beautiful music with a handsome but highly reluctant young publicity man.

In one of the zaniest plots in theatrical history, this comedy of errors rang up the curtain in Akron, Ohio, played a crazy Act Two in Los Angeles, and closed in Dallas, Texas with the wildest finale since *Hellzapoppin'*. The show had everything: unrequited love . . . conflict . . . mob scenes . . . low comedy. And through it all throbbed the theme song, "Mad About the Boy."

Excerpt from "Why Liberace's Theme Song
Should Be, 'Mad About the Boy!' "
(July 1957)

"Why Liberace's Theme Song Should Be, 'Mad About the Boy!' " In the summer of 1957 *Confidential* accused Liberace of making moves on a handsome young press agent in Akron, Ohio, and later in Dallas. "Arriving at the Sheraton-Mayflower Hotel, he wasted no time persuading the press agent to join him in his suite for a drink," *Confidential* said of Liberace's Akron shenanigans. "The latter went along with the invite, figuring it was his job to keep Dimples happy. He had no idea that in a few short minutes he would be fighting for his honor."

The magazine described a tussle that followed Liberace's attempt to sit in the press agent's lap. "Dimples clamped on a headlock. His victim fought to keep from being pinned, but he was at a disadvantage. For one thing, he was outweighed. For another, he needed a referee. A referee certainly would have penalized the panting pianist for illegal holds."

Walter V. Liberace, known to one and all by his last name, had steadfastly maintained that he wasn't homosexual. In fact, he had successfully prosecuted a suit against the *Daily Mirror* of London for even insinuating as much in a September 27, 1956, story that described Liberace as "this deadly, winking, sniggering, snuggling, chromium-plated, scent-impregnated, luminous, quivering, giggling, fruit-flavored, mincing, ice-covered heap of mother love."

A preposterous claim on his part? Perhaps. But the *New York Times* played it straight, as it were, headlining its coverage of the *Daily Mirror* suit "Liberace Denies He Is Homosexual."

Fresh from victory in London, Liberace was ready to do battle with *Confidential.* This time he was armed with an important fact—he could prove he was elsewhere on the dates when he was alleged to have been wrestling for the affection of his young press agent. Shades of Maureen O'Hara. Once again the vaunted *Confidential* fact-checking system, its practice of soliciting sworn affidavits from tipsters, had failed the magazine. Now *Confidential* faced libel suits claiming just under $10 million in damages.

Confidential certainly was used to lawsuits. But never before had it faced so many of them. Harrison always had held fast to DeStefano's pol-

Liberace fought rumors that he was gay, successfully winning a lawsuit against London's *Daily Mirror* for insinuating as much. A *Confidential* story in July 1957 accused him of making passes at a young male press agent. Liberace sued *Confidential*—he was elsewhere when the alleged incidents occurred—and won.

icy of never settling a suit. But the sheer volume of damages sought, and the number of actions pending against *Confidential*, seemed overwhelming. There also were lawsuits pressed in Elizabeth, New Jersey, and Chicago, Illinois, both aimed at determining whether the magazine violated community mores and should be banned as obscene. And Attorney General Pat Brown had, to all intents and purposes, stopped distribution of *Confidential* in California by threatening distributors with prosecution. *Confidential* eventually won the Chicago suit, and the Elizabeth suit fizzled before the California trial was over, replaced by an appeal to newsstands by the local district attorney to forswear distribution of *Confidential*. But for the first time, Harrison decided to settle a suit, paying Dorothy Dandridge $10,000 in May to settle her $1 million claim without a trial. DeStefano argued that fighting the suit would be a waste of the magazine's time and money.

Confidential's business structure had provided it some protection from legal action. The magazine's corporate offices were in New York City, its printer was in another state, and its entire press run typically was purchased by a wholesale distributor based elsewhere for circulation. Most of its Hollywood gossip had been gathered by Hollywood Research

The successful lawsuits by Liberace, the ultimate mama's boy, and others—Robert Mitchum, Lizabeth Scott, Doris Duke, Maureen O'Hara, and Dorothy Dandridge—spurred Hollywood's studio chieftains to press California's attorney general to act against *Confidential*.

Inc., a separate company. That meant a Hollywood plaintiff didn't have the standing to sue *Confidential* under California law in New York. But it looked as if even that barrier might be breached.

In May, Pat Brown announced that he would attempt to indict *Confidential* and Robert Harrison for conspiracy to commit criminal libel and to publish indecent material. Brown said he would prove that Hollywood Research Inc., the business run by Harrison's niece Marjorie and her husband, Fred, actually was a *Confidential* subsidiary. On May 15, a grand jury handed down indictments against eleven people and five companies. In addition to Harrison and Fred and Marjorie Meade, the individuals accused were Harrison's sisters Edith and Helen; Edith's son, Michael Tobias Jr., listed as vice president of Hollywood Research; Helen's husband, Dan Studin, the magazine's circulation manager; editor Al Govoni; tipster Francesca de Scaffa; and two executives of Kable Publishing Co., which printed the magazine. The companies indicted were Hollywood Research, Kable, Confidential Magazine Inc., Publishers Distributing Corporation, which distributed the magazine, and *Whisper, Confidential's* sister publication.

Confidential was in the fight of its life.

23

"Hollywood Vs. Confidential"

That this magazine is under assault in the California courts is, we assume, a fact known to most of our nine million readers. We have been indicted by a Los Angeles County grand jury on charges of:

1. Conspiracy to commit criminal libel;

2. Conspiracy to publish obscene and indecent material;

3. Conspiracy to disseminate information about abortion;

4. Conspiracy to disseminate information about male rejuvenation.

A California Assistant Attorney General has stated to the press: "In my opinion, *Confidential* is finished."

This is a determined effort, initiated by a segment of the motion picture industry, to "get" this magazine. We hold no secrets from our readers. In our first issue, nearly five years ago, we promised to "publish the facts" and "name the names." We have kept that promise; and our readers have made us successful. We have the world's largest newsstand sale. We sell more than three million copies per issue; and each copy, conservatively is read by three adult, free Americans.

Nine million Americans are worthy of respect. We respect them. Our success is due to their appreciation of our efforts to establish the truth and to maintain the right for them to have the truth.

Excerpt from "Hollywood Vs. Confidential"
(September 1957)

Harrison used an unusual editorial in the September 1957 issue of his magazine to speak to his nine million readers, nearly all of whom had spent the summer following the legal machinations of what came to be known as "Hollywood vs. *Confidential*." "California has accused us of a crime," he wrote, "the crime of telling the truth." "Hollywood is in the business of lying. Falsehood is a stock in trade. They use vast press-agent organizations and advertising expenditures to 'build-up' their 'stars.' They 'glamorize' and distribute detailed — and often deliberately false — information about them . . . They have the cooperation of practically every medium except *Confidential* . . . They can't influence us. So they want to 'get' us."

Most of the summer had been consumed with various pretrial motions, including unsuccessful efforts by the State of California to have Harrison and his sisters extradited to Los Angeles to stand trial. Even though Harrison and his sisters won that battle, they were keenly aware that the State of California held Marjorie and her husband hostage. The two faced a penalty of up to three years in jail and a $5,000 fine. No doubt the possible jail term was in Harrison's mind when he agreed to talks about a settlement in which *Confidential* would agree to drop its exposé format, or at least cease distribution in California. Superior Court Judge Herbert V. Walker rejected those efforts and set a trial date of August 2, 1957.

The two sides quickly put together powerful legal teams. While Brown officially led the state's case, in the courtroom it was to be handled by Assistant Attorney General Clarence Linn and Deputy District Attorney William (Bill) Ritzi. Harrison's defender was Arthur Crowley, Hollywood's pre-eminent criminal defense lawyer, with DeStefano and one of his law partners, Jacob Rosenbaum, assisting as "observers." It was a cast of characters made for the movies. Judge Walker had, in fact, been an actor earlier in his life, as an extra in a silent film called *Bill the Office Boy*. He was known among the press as "the Phumpfer," for his habit of mumbling. Reporters speculated that Walker had rejected efforts to settle the case outside the courtroom because he relished the attention the

170

trial would bring to him. Crowley, prematurely bald at thirty-two, and a judo practitioner, represented Hollywood Research Inc., the prosecution's proxy for *Confidential* and Harrison. Linn and Ritzi were models of Christian rectitude. A Sunday-school teacher, Ritzi spent his off hours "delving into the effects of salacious literature on kids." Linn used stories from the Bible to illustrate some of his courtroom points.

While reporters from around the world made plans to gather for the opening of *People of the State of California vs. Robert Harrison et al.*, people in Hollywood quickly made plans to leave town. Crowley had announced he would issue subpoenas to as many as two hundred members of the film community with the intent of forcing them to acknowledge the truth of what *Confidential* had written.

"Filmland Bigs Hiding Out to Duck Subpoena," wrote Florabel Muir in the *New York Daily News*. Frank Sinatra headed for Las Vegas, where he huddled with the likes of Gregory Peck, outside the reach of Fred Otash's subpoenas. Dan Dailey, who *Confidential* revealed had a penchant for wearing women's clothes, slipped out a back exit of the Hollywood Bowl after a performance to avoid a subpoena from one of Otash's operatives. Others weren't so lucky. An unwary Tab Hunter, for example, answered his own front door to find he was wanted to testify as to the truth of his involvement in the "all-male pajama party" he thought he had put behind him. Others subpoenaed included Dean Martin, Rory Calhoun, Corinne Calvet, Buddy Baer, Lana Turner, Gary Cooper, and Josephine Dillon, Clark Gable's long-neglected first wife.

The actors being subpoenaed weren't the only worried ones. Also nervous were the journalists and waiters and prostitutes and police officers and jilted lovers who had tattled to *Confidential* and now feared their perfidy would be revealed. More than a few friendships ended as gossip spread about who *Confidential*'s real informers were. Harold Conrad, the boxing promoter and screenwriter, lamented how Jackie Gleason avoided him after Mike Todd suggested, in grand jury testimony made public in a pretrial filing, that Conrad was the source of a *Confidential* story.

The rash of subpoenas alarmed the studios as well. George Murphy, MGM's public relations chief, met with Assistant Attorney General

Linn to demand that he find a way to avert possibly embarrassing testimony. Otherwise, the studio bosses said, Pat Brown could expect no campaigning or cash from Hollywood in his bid for governor. Of course, plenty of titillating details already had emerged from the 143-page grand jury transcript that the prosecution planned to enter into evidence. Ronnie Quillan, for example, had told the grand jury that Harrison "primarily was just interested in the sexual activities of the stars and celebrities and whether they were homosexuals or they weren't. In other words, the most lurid phases of their lives that he could expose."

While the studios were worried about testimony that would embarrass stars, Harrison worried about testimony that would expose the identities of *Confidential*'s anonymous tipsters, the key to its success. Rushmore, of course, knew them all.

As a counter to *Confidential*'s subpoena strategy, Attorney General Brown and Linn put pressure on distributors to stop carrying the magazine. In the process, they made "Hollywood vs. *Confidential*" a classic First Amendment battle. Harrison protested loudly, but a voice that once would have made Hollywood quiver now was the butt of jokes on radio and television. *Confidential* had made too many enemies; now, sensing its vulnerability, they simultaneously pressed for advantage. The usual defenders of freedom of the press, who might have been expected to defend this publishing renegade on First Amendment grounds, declined to step forward.

On July 29, on the eighth floor of L.A.'s downtown Hall of Justice, perspiring sheriff's deputies tried to keep order as spectators vied for seats at what was, to put a contemporary label on it, the O. J. Simpson trial of its time. Reporters from dozens of newspapers, including four from London, and a correspondent from *Paris Match* filled front-row seats for the opening of *People of the State of California vs. Robert Harrison et al.* After a jury of seven men and five women was impaneled, the first witness was called on August 7. It was Howard Rushmore.

Rushmore, looking the model of rectitude in a blue suit and rep tie, told the jury that Harrison wanted "stories that would make its readers whistle and say 'We never knew that before.'" More damaging, he offered that Harrison pushed for " 'hotter and hotter' stories . . . the kind family newspapers do not print." And most damaging of all, he listed the names of many of *Confidential's* confidential sources and correspondents. Among other sources on *Confidential's* payroll, Rushmore said, were two or three New York City police officers; Aline Mosby of United Press International; Agnes Underwood of the *Los Angeles Herald Express*; Florabel Muir of the *New York Daily News*; and Mike Connolly. Mosby was in the courtroom, covering the trial, when Rushmore outed her. A defense attorney, elaborating, revealed that she had written twenty-four stories for *Confidential.* United Press quickly assigned another reporter to cover the trial while the humiliated Mosby left town.

Rushmore made clear that any libel was the fault of Harrison, who, he testified, was "the sole, I would say, editorially responsible person for *Confidential.*" He named Francesca de Scaffa as the magazine's main source in Hollywood. De Scaffa was responsible for "90 percent" of the Hollywood material used in the magazine, he said, including material about Clark Gable's former wife, Josephine Dillon, gleaned after she had slept with him. Like Quillan, she had been provided with a wristwatch tape recorder. Rushmore testified that the story about Desi Arnaz's infidelity came from one of Ronnie Quillan's prostitutes.

Rushmore was forced to take credit, under cross-examination, for his own work for *Confidential,* published under various pen names. In addition to the Robert Oppenheimer story, he had penned gems such as "Batista's Eight Million Dollar Divorce," "A Cop Tried to Blackmail Marilyn Monroe," and the story exposing Rory Calhoun's criminal past. For all of his expressed distaste for the exposure-magazine genre, Rushmore confessed under questioning from Arthur Crowley that he had edited or written for two *Confidential* competitors: *Uncensored* and *Tipoff.* Now, he testified, he was a freelancer writing for men's adventure magazines.

Rushmore's testimony was followed by that of Ronnie Quillan, the "soiled dove," who had been in protective custody since the state announced she would be called as a witness. Quillan, now forty-one, with a mane of red hair that fell over the shoulders of her white, V-necked shift, caused a stir in the courtroom as she calmly identified herself as a prostitute. She verified Rushmore's story about Desi Arnaz, but noted that her affair with him had occurred while he was estranged from Lucille Ball. She added that she had been the source for stories on former boyfriend Billy Daniels, the singer she had knifed, and Herb Jeffries, the actor she had cut with a razor.

Next to come were a minor Hollywood writer who testified that he had been the source of a tip on his neighbor, the actor Sonny Tufts; a Hollywood detective, H. L. Wittenberg, who had worked for *Confidential*; and a reporter for the *Los Angeles Herald Express*, who had succumbed to an offer of $300 to check out a *Confidential* story when he was down on his luck.

But the real excitement was to come the following week, when Deputy District Attorney Bill Ritzi began his lengthy reading of some of *Confidential*'s more salacious stories into the court record—a treat for Californians who had missed the magazines since the state had started leaning on its distributors. On Monday, August 15, the largest crowd of spectators lined up in hopes of scoring seats to hear the dramatic reading of stories like "Only the Birds and the Bees Saw What Dorothy Dandridge Did in the Woods" and "Can a Guy Have Too Much of a Good Thing? Ask Alan Dale—He Played House with Two Girls."

"Judge Walker propped his head up with his hand. One elderly juror stared earnestly at the ceiling. Two other jurors who had been taking copious notes put away their pencils," reported the *New York Daily News*. "Spectators drank in the testimony avidly—it was the first time many of them had heard *Confidential*'s scandals, for the publication is banned in California."

It was the sort of spectacle that *Confidential* would have loved to have covered, if only it weren't the focus of it. Theo Wilson, writing for the *New York Daily News*, perhaps said it best: "In this make believe town, where phonies sell baloney by the yard and adjectives grow like palm trees, they have finally produced the show they can't find words for—the show that's too big for even those king-size Hollywood rumors and that at last gives some life to all the worn-out clichés of moviedom."

While the trial was the main event, there were plenty of sideshows. Shortly after the grand jury returned its indictments, a pregnant Francesca de Scaffa escaped to Mexico, where she hoped her marriage to celebrated bullfighter Jaime Bravo would protect her against extradition. She left behind her four-year-old daughter, Alphonsine, the product of her brief marriage to Bruce Cabot. Having children and leaving them was not an unusual habit for de Scaffa, who claimed to have borne a son named Antonio after a liaison with the Shah of Iran. Antonio was stashed in Italy, a *Confidential* story claimed, "because Francesca feared the Shah would spare no effort in a kidnapping attempt." Headlines about the exotic de Scaffa interrupted the routine of the trial coverage: "Scandal Mag's Girl Twice Tries Suicide," reported the *New York Daily News,* which said she took an overdose of pills and then slit her wrists in a fit of depression over the "cruel" attacks against her in court. "Comb Filmland on Tip Francesca Slipped In," the *Daily News* reported three months later, claiming de Scaffa had secretly entered the United States in the trunk of a white Jaguar to visit her ailing daughter. "Mexican Puzzle: So Where Is Francesca?" the *Daily News* asked two days later, reporting that Mexican authorities wanted to deport her as an undesirable alien. "Rumors put her possible destination as Cuba, Venezuela or New York," the newspaper reported.

Then there was the mysterious death of Chalky White, the former world featherweight champion and chauffeur of Mae West. In a story entitled "Mae West's Open Door Policy," *Confidential* had insinuated the black boxer had had more than a professional relationship with West. White was scheduled to testify, but his body was discovered in his bathtub on August 12 in what the coroner ruled was an accidental death. An already suspicious Hollywood grew more so when White's ex-wife, Gertrude Arnold, also subpoenaed for the trial, claimed she received a threatening phone call from a "gruff-voiced unidentified man," who told her: "Gert, if you know what's good for you, you'll clam up about this whole thing." Arnold said she was frightened, but not of *Confidential.* "I want to die a natural death. That crowd has too much power and money for me to fool with," she said, without explaining exactly who she feared.

Another untimely death was that of prosecution witness Polly Gould, a private investigator who had consulted with Harrison. Before she could testify she was found dead in her apartment, apparently of an overdose of sleeping pills. More headlines were generated when actress Corinne Calvet, another prosecution witness, accused Fred Otash of threatening her outside the courtroom.

Meanwhile, much of Hollywood tried to bravely soldier on. Dick

Powell and June Allyson hosted a party for 150 people at their Mandeville Canyon home. "The Powells' party ostensibly was to honor German actor Curt Jurgens and Bob Mitchum," reported Florabel Muir of the *Daily News*. "Actually, the party was Hollywood's way of showing a stiff upper lip."

"If I got myself into an uproar every time stories are told or rumored about me, I wouldn't have time left to attend to the important things in my life," Powell told Muir, belying his outraged protests in 1955 when *Confidential* wrote about his worry that Allyson was unfaithful. "June and I have never been happier. I think we will stay that way, in spite of that disgusting thing that was written about her."

The trial's dominant personality, however, remained Robert Harrison. Three thousand miles away in New York, he was conspicuous by his absence from Hollywood and safe from California process servers. Harrison kept up with the proceedings by reading the newspapers and with daily updates from Al DeStefano. The news wasn't good. It was clear that Howard Rushmore had destroyed *Confidential*'s valuable network of informants by revealing many of their names to the prosecution. Several tipsters already had lost their jobs after their work for *Confidential* was revealed in grand jury testimony. While Rushmore himself had named de Scaffa and Quillan, prosecutor Bill Ritzi delighted in forcing Harrison's nephew-in-law, Fred Meade, to confirm a longer list. The biggest of the names was producer Michael Todd, husband of Elizabeth Taylor. Todd provided information, and photos of himself, for a March 1957 story about a practical joke he'd played on an unnamed studio boss. The other tipsters were less prominent than Todd, if no less interesting. Donald Bledsoe, a Hollywood bartender, had blabbed for cash about a night he spent with both Lana Turner and Ava Gardner in Palm Springs. Robert Tuton, a maitre d' and former bartender, was paid for confirming details of his liaison with Joan Crawford. Vera Francis, a black actress, was paid for a story on her affair with socially prominent John Jacob Astor. Allan Nixon, ex-husband of actress Marie Wilson, famed for her portrayals of the classic "dumb blonde," made money by providing information on several unnamed people. Stella Shouel, a former prostitute, was paid for her stories on Dan Dailey, Walter Pidgeon, Fredric March, and Dane Clark. Among others said to have tipped off

Robert Harrison's niece, Marjorie, and her husband, Fred Meade, managed a Hollywood office that provided scoops for the magazine. It was the Meades who stood trial in Los Angeles in 1957 for conspiracy to commit criminal libel. Harrison, based in New York City, was out of the prosecutor's reach.

Confidential were press agents George Shaw and Bruce Jones and Mitchell Lewis, a minor actor from the silent film days.

Bandleader Dan Terry, the white man with whom black singer and actress Dorothy Dandridge supposedly had canoodled in the woods, had been the source for that story. Chalky White, Mae West's driver, had signed an affidavit supporting the magazine's story that implied she was having an affair with him. Meade also fingered Aline Mosby, the United Press correspondent, as the source of *Confidential*'s story about June

Allyson and Dick Powell. He named Harold Conrad, proving that Jackie Gleason's decision to shun the writer and fight promoter had been justified. Conrad, Meade said, wrote stories for *Confidential* and had been paid $3,950 in one seven-month period.

But Harrison's biggest concern, as always, was family. He and his sisters worried about Marjorie, who faced up to three years in jail. The family back in New York struggled to get out a November issue whose contents betrayed the impact of the trial.

24

"Believe It or Not, There Are Ten Near-Crashes in the Air Every Day"

Aviation progress has extended so far and so fast that a new kind of suicidal game has evolved. One might feel prompted to call it an aerial form of Russian roulette. Or you might liken it to the deadly "chicken" game that teen-age drivers play, aiming their cars head-on at each other at high speeds.

Only difference is that airline pilots are playing this in the air, but not by choice. What it amounts to is that they're having a harrowing time of it keeping out of each other's way in a traffic-laden sky that's fast resembling the New Jersey Turnpike on a Labor Day weekend.

In short, this country is fast running out of airspace—to the point where pilots are riding in constant fear of flying their passengers into a mid-air collision similar to the horrible occurrence over Grand Canyon last summer between United Air Lines and TWA.

Excerpt from "Believe It or Not, There Are Ten Near-Crashes in the Air Every Day" (November 1957)

From outing blacks passing for white and gays passing for straight and hookers passing for happy homemakers, *Confidential* had come to this.

The November issue, written and edited while the Los Angeles trial was in full swing, was dominated by consumer stories. While there was a smattering of Hollywood gossip ("When Joan Collins Was the Perfect Hostess," "Jayne Mansfield's Wacky Weekend in the Catskills"), the magazine was mostly filled with stories about curing hernias, cigarettes and lung cancer, finding a job overseas, and bungled medical lab tests.

Lacking its usual editorial sizzle, this issue of *Confidential* was tangible evidence that Robert Harrison felt beleaguered. Uncharacteristically, he even indulged in a bout of public self-pity. "Why do they pick on me?" he asked in an interview with the *New York Post*. "I'm not the only one that's doing this kind of stuff. What about *Look*? What about the jobs they did on Sinatra and Gleason? What about the *Saturday Evening Post*? What about your paper? That's cruelty! You take a man's whole life apart! . . .

"No one speaks of the good we've done. It's the most unjust thing in the world. It's all slander! Is this the price of success?"

For all Harrison's woes, the man who had emerged as his archenemy was in more desperate straits. Howard Rushmore's history of betrayal had caught up with him. Rushmore blamed his testimony against *Confidential* for the fact that he'd been unable to land a permanent job. He had fingered newspaper reporters as secret *Confidential* sources and so couldn't expect to find jobs there. And while few magazine editors had much sympathy for Robert Harrison's problems, they also weren't interested in hiring a man who would voluntarily testify in court against his employer. Even his old anti-Communist cronies had turned against him after Rushmore's public assaults on Roy Cohn.

Rushmore's freelance writing for *True War* magazine wasn't sufficient to pay the rent on his apartment, which was seriously overdue. He was having trouble keeping up alimony payments to Ruth, his first wife, which cost him forty dollars a week. He had been quarreling with his current wife, Frances, who now worked in public relations. Their relationship long had been troubled, in part because of Frances's drinking and an attempt at suicide, and later because of Rushmore's drinking. Both of them were under psychiatric care.

Rushmore also may have felt the weight of trying to reconcile a public image of moral rectitude with a private life marked by violence.

He had assaulted Frances, whose psychiatrist had warned her and Rushmore's two stepdaughters that it wasn't safe to continue living with him, noting that Rushmore kept six rifles as well as a handgun at home. His bitter cruelty stunned fellow reporters who heard Rushmore happily take credit for the death of a Greenwich Village schoolteacher who had killed herself after Rushmore exposed her Communist Party leanings in a newspaper story. Howard Rushmore, once on top of the world, as he saw it, had fallen far. He was a *Confidential* story waiting to happen.

Back in Los Angeles, courtroom spectators finally were reminded that Marjorie and Fred Meade, who were occupying seats at the defense table, were the ones on trial. Producer Paul Gregory testified that Marjorie had approached him in 1955 and asked for a $1,000 bribe in exchange for keeping a story out of the magazine. The flame-haired Meade staged a dramatic collapse during the testimony, and a doctor was summoned. "It's not true. He's a liar," she cried.

Gregory had been the subject of a May 1956 story in the magazine titled "The Lowdown on Paul Gregory," which alleged he had romanced a widow and then cheated her out of her savings. After taking title to her home, *Confidential* said, Gregory had entertained himself with "a steady parade of soldiers and sailors who talked uncouthly and cavorted around the place in a manner that had her eyes bulging."

Meade declared herself ready to take a lie detector test to prove that she had never offered a bribe. The defense soon found a press agent for the Beverly Hills Hotel to testify that Meade had been sipping a drink in the hotel lounge when the bribe attempt was alleged to have occurred at a distant restaurant. Otash's former girlfriend Jackie O'Hara confirmed that story, saying she had been with Meade at the time.

When Fred Meade was put on the stand, he seized an opportunity under cross-examination to point out the hypocrisy of *Confidential*'s Hollywood persecutors. "If they took care of their business and exercised morality clauses there would be no need for all of this," he said from the witness stand.

"Take Robert Mitchum. He's a convicted narcotics user, has served time on a Georgia chain gang, posed publicly and for publicity with a woman stripped nude to the waist and was tossed out of his last picture for being obnoxious.

"His income continues to increase since the *Confidential* story. He wasn't hurt by that story.

"Corinne Calvet publicly stated that everything in the story about her was true and not unflattering. She has not been hurt.

"Maureen O'Hara was accused by her husband of openly consorting with a married man while she herself was married and her own child with her. She has not been hurt.

"Mae West's name has been synonymous with sex from the time I was a little boy. Her theme song was 'Come Up and See Me Sometime.' She has done nothing but surround herself with prize fighters. She's not been hurt."

The prosecution worked hard to tie the Meades to Robert Harrison. With a handmade genealogical chart, prosecutor Ritzi outlined the Harrison family tree, arguing that *Confidential* and Hollywood Research were parts of a multimillion-dollar enterprise controlled by one New York family—a sort of media mob enterprise. He reminded the jury that Hollywood Research had received $150,000, its only source of income in its eighteen-month life, from *Confidential*. Finally, the prosecution rested its case without ever calling a celebrity witness.

The studios initially had been grateful for the focus on the Meades and Robert Harrison, however brief. Now they were nervous that testimony would shift back to which star had done what as Crowley pursued his strategy of proving the truth of *Confidential*'s stories.

Outside the courtroom, some industry figures argued for a compromise that would end the trial and its embarrassing testimony. Some, explained the *New York Times*, "would like to see the trial expedited, with the chips—other people's chips—falling where they might, in hopes of putting *Confidential* out of business. Others are afraid that if *Confidential* is muzzled, other publications will spring up in its wake—as long as there's scandal in Hollywood."

Actor and singer John Carroll, who *Confidential* claimed had made love with a woman upstairs during a party, voiced some of Hollywood's concerns. "I don't think it will hurt me much," he said of the story. "But

I feel sorry for the fellows who are mentioned [at the trial] who are already having domestic beefs. Such yarns aggravate the trouble.

"Now that the whole world is reading what first appeared only in *Confidential,* it looks to me as if it were a mistake to bring this action into court.

"There is one thing more for sure: the folks aren't going to be thinking from now on that we show people are like the boys and girls next door."

In a step that many saw as too little and too late, a group of Hollywood organizations met in the third week of the trial to form an association to fight exposé magazines. The group, headed by MGM's George Murphy, included the Association of Motion Picture Producers, the Screen Actors Guild, the Writers Guild, and the Society of Cinema Photographers, among others. Billy Graham also offered Hollywood his support, telling a crowd of sixteen thousand at Madison Square Garden that *Confidential'*s readers were to blame for its sinful existence.

Inside the Hall of Justice, Crowley managed to produce more headlines by introducing James Craig, former assistant manager at Grauman's Chinese Theatre, to testify in sensuous detail to Maureen O'Hara's activities there. Craig said O'Hara had arrived with a "short, dark man" and appeared to have had a lot to drink. "The man was sitting facing the screen and she was across his lap," said Craig. He described O'Hara as being disheveled. When jurors appeared not to grasp Craig's word picture of that night at Grauman's, Judge Walker authorized a field trip and later invited Craig to demonstrate the couple's position in the courtroom with an attractive newswoman. Craig's awkward demonstration drew peals of laughter from the spectators. Walker was not amused. "This is a serious matter," he told the courtroom as he gaveled the onlookers into silence.

Soon the studios got a break, albeit a minor one. Walker decided only to permit testimony concerning the fifteen *Confidential* articles already read into the record, seven alleged to be criminally libelous, six to be obscene, and two—stories on abortion and male virility—to be in violation of the state professional and business code. Still, that left room for testimony by an array of Hollywood figures. The list included Maureen O'Hara, Dorothy Dandridge, Dick Powell, Mae West, Robert

Mitchum, John Carroll, Corinne Calvet, Alan Dale, Eddie Fisher, Frank Sinatra, Jayne Mansfield, Billy Daniels, and Anita Ekberg. Crowley eventually decided against calling any of them, reasoning that the testimony of such hostile witnesses wouldn't help his case.

Happy as the studios were about that, there was concern that even those who hadn't testified were keeping the case on the front pages by giving interviews to eager newspaper reporters outside of court. In one such interview, Corinne Calvet labeled *Confidential* a "malignant growth." Actor John Carroll, accused in *Confidential* of hosting a particularly wild party, declared he was "a romantic, not an exhibitionist." Josephine Dillon speculated that Francesca de Scaffa was seeking revenge when she offered up the story about Clark Gable abandoning her. And Mae West scoffed at the notion that she had been romantic with Chalky White.

In addition to asserting the truth of the stories *Confidential* had printed, and proving they had been published without malice, Crowley had to contest the prosecution's assertion that six of the articles were obscene. He introduced into evidence, for the sake of comparison, Frank O'Hara's *Appointment in Samarra*, John Steinbeck's *East of Eden*, James Jones's *From Here to Eternity*, Norman Mailer's *Naked and the Dead*, and a host of newspaper clippings. To the evident disbelief of the courtroom audience, Daniel Ross, one of DeStefano's law partners, asserted that he and Harrison had had many conversations about these works of literature in an effort to ascertain what was obscene and what was not. Many of the books and newspaper articles, Ross testified, would make "*Confidential* stories sound like *Grimm's Fairy Tales.*"

After four weeks of testimony, Bill Ritzi opened his Bible to begin two days of closing arguments. He turned to the Old Testament Book of Daniel to tell the story of Susanna. The Hebrew maiden, as the story goes, refused to be blackmailed by lecherous voyeurs who threatened to falsely accuse her of a dalliance with a young man unless she had sex with them. *Confidential* and its owners, he suggested, were the lecherous voyeurs. And the virtuous maiden? That would be Hollywood.

Crowley's summation, equally lengthy, trod more secular ground.

He argued that the state couldn't possibly prove *Confidential* guilty of conspiracy to commit libel, given the magazine's expenditure of at least $100,000 a year on lawyers to vet stories and its vaunted fact-checking system. What's more, he contended that *Confidential*'s stories were no more obscene than those found in any of a dozen other magazines (many of which were launched in *Confidential*'s wake).

25

"Confidential's New Policy"

Pardon us while we take a bow.

It's a proud bow.

We're proud because we like our new look which begins with this issue.

If *Confidential* seems changed . . . if you've noticed a new complexion, it's because we've broadened our outlook.

We're quitting the area of private affairs for the arena of public affairs. Some found fault with the private affairs. Some criticized.

But many eulogized and admired.

Where we pried and peeked, now we'll probe, and occasionally we'll take a poke.

If wiseacres say that we've retreated from the bedroom, we'll say yes, that's true . . . From now on we'll search and survey the thoroughfares of the globe for stories of public interest that are uncensored and off the record . . . It's a big world, a foolish world, a crazy world . . . and we'll be taking you on an inside tour, telling the facts and naming the names.

Robert Harrison, Publisher
(April 1958)

After two weeks of deliberation, the *Confidential* jury returned to the courtroom on October 1 to declare itself unable to reach a verdict. The jurors had split seven to five for conviction, and their debate had included some "big fights," according to a report from one juror.

LaGuerre Drouet, one of the jurors who had pressed for acquittal, said he based his vote on a concern for freedom of the press. Other jurors refused to comment. Prosecutor Ritzi announced his intention to take the case to court again, and Judge Walker set October 10 for a hearing to choose a new trial date. Crowley boarded a plane for New York, where Harrison hosted a celebration at Mamma Leone's, the raucous and kitschy Italian restaurant in Times Square. Harrison, ever the showman, turned up at Crowley's hotel the next morning at the uncharacteristic hour of eight o'clock with a violinist who played "Mr. Wonderful." He kept up the serenade all the way to Crowley's gate at Idlewild.

Then Harrison went back to his office to take stock of what the trial had done to him, his family, and his magazine. It had cost him an estimated $500,000, a sum equivalent to $3.5 million today. His sisters, worriers by nature, had endured incredible stress. The magazine's distribution system was a shambles. *Confidential* was all but unavailable in California, where news dealers feared prosecution under obscenity statutes. District attorneys and attorneys general in states such as New Jersey and South Carolina also were pressuring distributors to keep the magazine off the newsstands. Hollywood Research's doors were closed, with Fred and Marjorie Meade embarked on a new career in real estate. Perhaps most important, *Confidential's* deep pool of tipsters had evaporated as soon as it was exposed to the light of day by Howard Rushmore in Herbert Walker's courtroom.

The studios had no stomach for the retrial that Ritzi had promised, with its threat of another round of screaming newspaper headlines about Hollywood scandal. Negotiations ensued. On November 12, eight days before the new trial was to begin, Harrison agreed that *Confidential* and *Whisper*, its younger sister, no longer would publish exposés of the private lives of movie stars. The state, for its part, agreed to drop all charges against the defendants except for the claim against *Confidential* and *Whisper* of conspiring to publish obscenity. The maximum fine would be $5,000.

Hollywood celebrated Harrison's defeat, with toasts to the end of scandal mongering raised at Ciro's, Mocambo, and Chasen's. But the celebrations were premature. With *Confidential* and its wide shadow gone, imitators such as *Hush-Hush, The Lowdown, Exposed, Uncensored*, and *On the QT* were able to thrive. For the fan magazines, "*Confidential* gave the lie to this story that you could not get out a book dealing with the studios and personalities unless you played ball," one fan-magazine editor observed. "Not only did they get out a book, but it had the biggest circulation in the country. They didn't have to go to the studios for art, for stories, for anything." And with the dawning of the contentious sixties, America was developing a bitter cynicism about celebrity and power that no amount of Hollywood sugar could coat.

Within three months of his April 1958 announcement of a new "hands off Hollywood" policy, Harrison sold the magazine, whose circulation plunged to roughly 200,000 before it closed in the early 1960s. Harrison had lost much—the publication that guaranteed him a table at the Stork Club, the Harwyn, and El Morocco, the fearful respect of Hollywood, the attention of Walter Winchell. But he still had money, his sisters, and the companionship of other attractive young women. Howard Rushmore wasn't so fortunate.

"My mother and stepfather were both under psychiatric care," recalled Jeannie Dobbins, one of Rushmore's two stepdaughters, in an interview in 1958. "Two days before Christmas he chased my mother and Lynn [Rushmore's other stepdaughter] out of the house with a shotgun.

"They moved temporarily to my apartment in Greenwich Village. Mother was very upset.

"She told me that our psychiatrist had told her that my stepfather had reached a breaking point and it was not safe to stay with him.

"Mother said that, on several occasions, he had threatened to kill her. He said that if he couldn't have her, nobody else would."

Frances Rushmore eventually agreed to meet her estranged husband for dinner on January 3, 1958. It had been a difficult holiday for Rushmore, broke and alone. Edward Pearlman recalls the couple arguing outside the taxi he was driving when he pulled over to pick up Frances on the corner of Ninety-seventh Street and Madison Avenue. Both Howard and Frances entered the cab. Moments into the ride, at 102nd Street and Lexington Avenue, a gunshot rang out, and then two more. When Pearlman pulled up at the police precinct headquarters on 104th Street, it was evident that Frances Rushmore was the last person Howard Rushmore would betray. When police opened the taxi door they discovered a .32-caliber Colt revolver, a commando knife with a seven-inch blade, and the six-foot-five-inch corpse of Howard Rushmore draped over his dead wife's body.

With the murder of the woman he loved and his own suicide, Rushmore, that bundle of contradictions, again had made the front pages. The headlines this time were full of scorn and pathos: "Jobless, He Wouldn't Borrow; On Top, He Was Cold and Cruel," "Failed in His Biggest Role: Turncoat of Many Colors."

Many of the remembrances were equally grim. "Rushmore was a really mixed-up guy," recalled Roy Cohn, a man not known for compassion and kindness himself. "He had a mental quirk which resulted in his trying to hurt everyone he had ever worked for. He had a personality defect. It made him turn particularly on anybody who had ever been nice to him."

Old friend Jim Sterner lamented Rushmore's tragic passing. "I did and do regard it as a tragedy that one capable of so much became entrapped in that Communist-to-AntiCommunist to McCarthy to *Confidential* slide, which kept on going all the way down to that taxi. It was a terrible waste."

Harrison, who had resented the way Rushmore competed with him for headlines, got the news in the back of a taxi on his way from Idlewild Airport. "Hey, did you hear that?" the cabbie asked. "The publisher of *Confidential* just shot himself."

"The publisher of *Confidential*?" Harrison asked, thinking of himself. "Where did the publisher of *Confidential* shoot himself?"

"In the head, in a cab," said the cabdriver. "He shot himself through the head, right in the back of a cab!"

Flush with cash from the sale of *Confidential* and some good investments, Harrison turned to entertaining a succession of beautiful women at New York nightspots, dabbled in the stock market, and plotted a comeback, testing the waters with one-shot magazines such as *Menace of the Sex Deviates* and *Naked New York*. He tested a tabloid called *Inside News* and considered becoming a book publisher.

Howard Rushmore shot his wife, Frances, twice before shooting himself in the head in a taxi on New York City's Upper East Side on January 3, 1958. The murder-suicide was front-page news in all of New York City's newspapers. Frances Rushmore's psychiatrist had warned her to leave her husband because of his propensity for violence.

Harrison was to live another twenty years, sliding slowly into obscurity until his death in 1978 at the age of seventy-three. Only the occasional waiter now recognized him. Girlfriend Reggie Ruta made cruel jokes about his age. Walter Winchell gave him only a passing wave, where once he would have joined his table for the night. A story by Tom Wolfe in *Esquire* in April 1964 gave him his last big headline: "*Confidential* Magazine: Reflections in Tranquility by the Former Owner, Robert Harrison, Who Managed to Get Away with It."

Harrison died quietly at the age of seventy-three with Reggie Ruta by his side. His sisters and Marjorie survived him. There was a modest funeral at the Frank E. Campbell Funeral Home in Manhattan, and he was buried at Riverside Cemetery in Saddle Brook, New Jersey. The obituaries also were modest. By the time Harrison passed on, the original *Confidential* was a distant memory, its gaudy newsprint covers an object of amusement when they turned up at used book and magazine shops. What had seemed shocking when *Confidential* first published it now seemed commonplace on America's newsstands and on its television screens. Of course, it was *Confidential*, for better or worse, that had helped make it so.

Edith and Helen lived another few years. Marjorie, who once had been a fearsome figure in Hollywood, never left Los Angeles, where she lives today. A series of marriages (Marjorie Tobias Meade Bernheim Roth) helped obscure her identity to new friends and acquaintances. Today her name appears in neighborhood newspapers noting her attendance at charity luncheons. But she never forgot the value of a good story. Today she won't discuss her past with *Confidential*—unless she's paid for it.

Acknowledgments

The inspiration for this book was another that I began reading on a flight from New York City to Istanbul in 1997. I landed in that exotic city and spent the next two days in my hotel room, unable to pull myself away from James Ellroy's bizarrely fascinating *L.A. Confidential*. Back in New York I started looking for a book on *Confidential* magazine, which figured in Ellroy's story. Not finding one, I decided to write my own.

This book, for better or worse, is very much a group effort, although any errors of fact or stylistic faults are solely my own. The group that made this possible includes Luke Janklow, my agent, to whom I'm indebted for his enthusiasm and patience. It also includes Vicky Wilson, my editor, a source of encouragement and much more patience than any first-time author deserves. And it includes David Groff, a friend and poet who made me wise to the ways of book publishing and pushed me to keep at it when I wished the whole project would go away.

There were a host of people who generously shared information they had about *Confidential* and its dramatis personae. Among them are Susie Schrenck, who passed along articles she had discovered while writing a thesis on *Confidential*; Ted Gottfried, who handed over tape recordings and correspondence from his aborted effort to profile Howard Rushmore; Al DeStefano, who spent many hours telling me about his friendship with Robert Harrison and the magazine's legal troubles; the late Sherry Britton, who gleefully shared photos of her life as a burlesque star and tales of her dates with Harrison; Bill Taft, who talked about his boyhood friendship with Howard Rushmore; and countless librarians and archivists in New York, Los Angeles, Chicago, Washington, D.C., and Mexico, Missouri, who found this project fascinating.

Acknowledgments

Finally, I benefited from the support of my two families. They include my mother, Flora, and my sister Barbara and her husband, Gary, who have taken an inordinate delight in the fact that I have written this book; and my dearest Linda and Rich and Robin, whose love and support have meant more to me than they will ever know.

Notes

1. "Why Joe DiMaggio Is Striking Out with Marilyn Monroe!"

7 "No picture shall be produced"   Doherty, Hollywood's Censor, 353.

8 theater attendance by 1950 had declined   Peter Lev, History of the American Cinema, Volume 7, 1950–1959 (Berkeley, University of California Press, 2003), 5.

10 "Half-fictionalized as they are"   Camille Paglia, "Ask Camille," Salon, September 1997.

10 "I sincerely believe the basic vehicle"   Unbylined interview with Robert Harrison, "Fair Game," Writer's Yearbook, 1956, 2.

2. "They Started in Their Birthday Suits!"

12 To Harrison's amusement and amazement,   Alvin Davis, "The Confidential Story: Politics and Peek-a-Boo," New York Post, September 17, 1953.

13 It was about a dancer Harrison fancied   Richard and Paulette Ziegfeld, The Ziegfeld Touch: The Life and Times of Florenz Ziegfeld, Jr. (New York: Harry Abrams, 1993).

13 The afternoon paper was launched in 1924   Mallen, 4.

13 Although based in New York City, Martin J. Quigley   Quigley Publishing Co. Web site, http://www.quigleypublishing.com/AboutUs.html.

13 He also, oddly enough, helped write   Ibid.

14 "Silent smut had been bad"   Daniel A. Lord, Played by Ear (Chicago; Loyola University Press, 1956), 295.

14 It was a "deeply Catholic text"   Thomas Doherty, "The Code Before Da Vinci," Washington Post, May 20, 2006.

14 The result, says   Doherty Doherty, Hollywood's Censor, 172.

14 "I hated it," Harrison remembered   David Gelman and Edward Katcher, "The Man Behind Confidential," article 1, New York Post, September 3, 1957.

15 It was a family enterprise   Davis, op. cit.

15 Harrison also began to indulge   Gelman and Katcher, "The Man Behind Confidential," article 4, New York Post, September 6, 1957.

16 "a high-tension number"   Gelman and Katcher, "The Man Behind Confidential," article 2, New York Post, September 4, 1957.

16 "Edythe was a Hunter graduate"   Ibid.

16 "The place was just nuts"   Ibid.

16 For his covers, Harrison hired   Reimschneider, preface [n.p.].

17 Especially gripping were eight days of testimony   "The U.S. Gets a Good Look at Crime with Kefauver Committee Hearings," Life, March 26, 1951.

195

17 *"It was then that I believe"* Unbylined interview with Robert Harrison, "Fair Game," *Writer's Yearbook*, 1956, 19.

18 *Thus was born the magazine that Tom Wolfe* Thomas K. Wolfe, "Public Lives: *Confidential* Magazine: Reflections in Tranquility by the Former Owner, Robert Harrison, Who Managed to Get Away with It," *Esquire*, April 1964.

3. "Winchell Was Right About Josephine Baker"

22 *But also caught up in the controversy was Winchell* Gabler, *Winchell*, 419–420.

22 *"Though Winchell had had premonitions of his demise"* Ibid, 405.

22 *Winchell was furious . . . the night Baker was at the Stork Club* Ibid, 405–419.

23 *Asked once about his political position* Alvin Davis, "The *Confidential* Story: Politics and Peek-a-Boo," *New York Post*, September 17, 1953.

23 *"Bob Harrison's mind has been broadened"* David Gelman and Edward Katcher, "The Man Behind *Confidential*," article 3, *New York Post*, September 5, 1957.

23 *"Harrison gave us orders to write"* Jack Olson, "Titans of Trash: Who Is Bankroll for *Confidential*," *Chicago Sun Times*, October 18, 1955.

23 *"In America this very minute 1,000 Benedict Arnolds"* Howard Rushmore, "Red Murder Inc.," *Confidential*, November 1953, 38.

23 *"Harrison saw the story and a light lit up"* Olson, op. cit.

24 Confidential *"started running a Winchell piece"* Thomas K. Wolfe, "Public Lives: *Confidential* Magazine: Reflections in Tranquility by the Former Owner, Robert Harrison, Who Managed to Get Away with It," *Esquire*, April 1964, 152–153.

25 *Winchell delivered no fewer than sixteen plugs* Olson, op. cit.

25 *"With* Confidential, *I have finally gone respectable"* Gelman and Katcher, "The Man Behind *Confidential*," article 4, *New York Post*, September 6, 1957.

26 *"His father always pooh-poohed his aspirations"* Gelman and Katcher, "The Man Behind *Confidential*," article 1, *New York Post*, September 3, 1957.

26 *"Na-a-ah! I'm not trying"* Ibid.

26 *Harrison said his attraction to publishing* Unbylined interview with Robert Harrison, "Fair Game," *Writer's Yearbook*, 1956, 17.

26 *a life of poverty and brutal oppression that had grown worse* Howe, 61.

28 *By then penniless (the passage in steerage . . .)* Ibid., 39.

28 *After passing through Castle Garden, the Harrisons* U.S. Census, 1900.

28 *522 inhabitants per acre in 1890* Howe, 69.

28 *joining nearly 100,000 other Russian Jews* Jeffrey S. Gurock, *When Harlem Was Jewish, 1870–1930* (New York: Columbia University Press, 1979), 1.

28 *Paula gave birth to a second daughter* U.S. Census, 1897.

28 *Thus little Max Harrison* Birth certificate, New York.

4. "Exclusive Photos! How Rita Hayworth's Children Were Neglected"

32 *"The facts are that not just one night"* Alfred Garvey, "Why Rita Hayworth Walked Out on Dick," *Confidential*, January 1956, 14.

32 *"Harry Cohn, as absolute a monarch"* L. J. Lasky, *Whatever Happened to Hollywood?* (New York: Funk and Wagnalls, 1973), 289.

35 *Before the lower court could rule* Ibid, 326–328.

36 *Where box-office grosses totaled $1.7 billion*   Christopher H. Sterling and Timothy R. Haight, *The Mass Media: The Aspen Institute Guide to Communications Industry Trends* (New York: Praeger, 1978), 187.

36 *Profits of $121 million in 1946*   Irving Bernstein, *Hollywood at the Crossroads: An Economic Study of the Motion Picture Industry* (Hollywood: Hollywood AFL Film Council, 1957), 17–18.

36 *The advent of television, the suburbanization*   Schatz, *Boom and Bust*, 295.

36 *"Confidential . . . would get tips from starlets"*   Goodman, 51.

36 *In December 1950, she was in the headlines again*   Florabel Muir and Theo Wilson, "How V-Girl Dug Up Desi Smear," *New York Daily News*, August 14, 1957.

37 *In Hollywood, rumor had it*   Telephone interview with Anne Robinson, June 18, 2000.

37 *She offered to have an affair*   Unbylined, "Putting the Papers to Bed," *Time*, August 26, 1957.

37 *While still a cop, Otash managed*   Otash, 8.

37 *By 1955, Otash was making*   Theo Wilson, "Sleuth Declares Mag Told Only Half of It," *New York Daily News*, August 25, 1957.

37 *Their work was facilitated, according to* Time   Goodman, 51–52.

39 *One of the most colorful, Michael Mordaunt-Smith*   www.slick.org/deathwatch/mailarchive/msg00839.html.

39 *Mordaunt-Smith claims to have vetted*   Victor Davis, "The Father of Scandal," *British Journalism Review* 13, November 4, 2002, 74–80.

39 *and was kept on a retainer of $350 a week*   Art White, "Film Stars May Escape Testimony in Scandal Trial," *Los Angeles Mirror-News*, August 18, 1957.

39 *He was assigned to interview Uruguayan Esteban Larraura*   Davis, op. cit., 74–80.

40 *He taught* Confidential *that another way to ward off*   Interview with Albert DeStefano, February 24, 2000.

40 *Otash concurred*   Wilson, op. cit.

40 *"We controlled the fan magazines"*   Scott Eyman, *Lion of Hollywood* (New York: Simon & Schuster, 2005), quoted in Jeanine Basinger, *The Star Machine* (New York: Knopf, 2007), 55.

40 *"Right at the beginning, one of the things"*   Interview with Albert DeStefano, February 24, 2000.

40 *It was a rule Harrison broke only once*   Alvin Davis, "The Story of *Confidential* Magazine: *Confidential* Backs Down," *New York Post*, September 16, 1953.

41 *"The . . . problem was that Muscarella"*   Jack Olson, "Titans of Trash: How *Confidential* Curves Angles to Create Stories," *Chicago Sun-Times*, October 19, 1955.

41 *Bennett later described Muscarella*   Andrew Billen, "Whaddaperformer!" *Glasgow Sunday Herald*, May 28, 2000.

5. "The Strange Death of J. Robert Oppenheimer's Red Sweetheart"

44 *"My friends, both in Pasadena and in Berkeley"*   "The Storm Breaks," *Time*, April 19, 1954.

45 *All that changed by the fall of 1936*   Priscilla J. McMillan, *The Ruin of Robert Oppenheimer, and the Birth of the Modern Arms Race* (New York: Viking, 2005), 4.

45 *"Beginning in late 1936, my interests"* In the Matter of J. Robert Oppenheimer: *Transcript of Hearings Before Personnel Security Board and Texts of Principal Documents and Letters* (Cambridge: The MIT Press, 1971), 8.

45 *Perhaps one reason Tatlock turned him down* McMillan, 6.

46 *"Oppenheimer, when asked about his girlfriend"* Howard Rushmore, "The Strange Death of J. Robert Oppenheimer's Red Sweetheart!" *Confidential,* November 1954.

48 *There was that time, for example, at Mexico High School* Interview with William Taft, Columbia, Missouri, May 2000.

48 *Rushmore maintained it was his search* Howard Rushmore, "Rebirth of an American," *American Mercury,* April 1940.

49 *Jim Sterner recalled a visit* James Sterner, interview with author, Columbia, MO, May 2000.

51 *"It is in the Village and surrounded by fairies"* Howard Rushmore, letter to James Sterner, April 24, 1935.

51 *"Have a little girl trouble now"* Howard Rushmore, letter to "Woody," December 6, 1935.

51 *He got into an argument with David Ingram* "Howard Rushmore of Mexico and His Fight on Communism Dramatized by NBC Broadcast," *Mexico Daily Ledger,* March 8, 1954.

52 *"Our decision to drop Rushmore as a contributor"* Unbylined, "Notice to Our Readers," *Daily Worker,* December 22, 1939.

52 *"Thanks to David Selznick and Margaret Mitchell"* Howard Rushmore, "Red Paper's Lies Bared by Ex-Critic," *New York Journal American,* December 23, 1939.

53 *"For once in my life I didn't care"* Howard Rushmore, letter to Jim Sterner, December 23, 1939.

53 *"Got all the god-damned publicity in the world"* Howard Rushmore, letter to Jim Sterner, January 4, 1940.

6. "Does Desi Really Love Lucy?"

55 *Quillan was later to say she received* Florabel Muir and Theo Wilson, "How V-Girl Dug Up Desi Smear," *New York Daily News,* August 14, 1957.

55 *"Desi met our dark-eyed temptress"* Brad Shortell, "Does Desi Really Love Lucy?" *Confidential,* January 1955, 46.

56 *"I remember Lucy wanted to get a copy"* Sanders and Gilbert, 118.

56 *At forty-four, Ball, six years older* Ibid, 117.

57 *"What he does in his private life"* Howard Rushmore, "I Worked for *Confidential,*" *Christian Herald,* January 1958.

58 *"Our information is that she's mean to the kids"* Ibid.

58 *"She was a woman whose occupation had been halted"* Ibid.

58 *"Bob is rude, crude, unlettered"* Edward Gelman, "Confidential File on *Confidential,*" *Esquire,* November 1956.

59 *That same year, he testified before* Associated Press, "Ex-Red Says Mrs. Roosevelt, Hull Helped Mrs. Browder Re-enter U.S.," *New York Times,* September 15, 1949.

59 *Rushmore's testimony, and his writing for the* Journal-American   Federal Bureau of Investigation file on Howard Rushmore, no. 100-13058.

59 *After all, Wechsler and Dorothy Schiff*   Curt Gentry, *J. Edgar Hoover: The Man and the Secrets* (New York: W. W. Norton & Co., 1991), 462.

60 *Rushmore said his firing was retaliation for*   "Rushmore v. Cohn," *Time*, November 1, 1954.

7. "A Tale of Two Chippies . . . the Day Hollywood Trembled!"

63 *"They [the studios] say it's up to the individual"*   Jack Olsen, "Titans of Trash: Smeared Stars Fight Back," *Chicago Sun-Times*, October 22, 1955.

63 *Joan Bennett, profiled in a* Confidential *competitor*   Ibid.

64 *But Connolly's biographer, Val Holley, suggests*   Val Holley, *Mike Connolly and the Manly Art of Hollywood Gossip* (Jefferson: McFarland & Company, 2003), 28–29.

64 *Eventually the studios concocted a scheme*   Unbylined, "Private Eye Aims Blast at Collection Agencies," *Los Angeles Mirror-News*, March 1, 1957.

64 *They also enlisted an unnamed star*   Art White, "H'wood Pulls Cloak-Dagger Trick on Scandal Magazine," *Los Angeles Mirror-News*, February 21, 1957.

65 *The studios then approached Fred Otash*   Unbylined, "Private Eye Aims Blast."

65 *Finally, the trade journal* Hollywood Reporter *announced*   Olson, op. cit.

8. "What Makes Ava Gardner Run for Sammy Davis, Jr.?"

68 *"Some girls go for gold"*   Horton Streete, "What Makes Ava Gardner Run for Sammy Davis Jr.?" *Confidential*, March 1955.

68 *Many Catholic moviegoers were upset*   Roland Flamini, *Ava* (New York: Coward, McCann & Geoghegan, 1983), 154.

68 *The Motion Picture Code had dropped its ban*   Doherty, *Hollywood's Censor*, 319.

68 *In 1947, for example, Binford rejected*   Ibid., 242.

69 *MGM, where Gardner was under contract*   Mike Connolly, *Hollywood Reporter*, March 17, 1955.

70 *"Even my own family criticized me"*   Server, 305–306.

9. "Have You Heard the Latest About Sammy Davis, Jr.?"

73 *"I'm colored, Jewish, and Puerto Rican"*   Max Rudin, "The Rat Pack Is Back," http://www.ratpackvegas.com/cast_the_original_rat_pack.

73 *Less than a month after the Ava Gardner story*   Interview with Albert DeStefano, February 24, 2000.

74 *In May 1955, the magazine reported that Doris Duke*   Grant Peters, "The Untold Story of Doris Duke and Her African Prince," *Confidential*, May 1955.

74 *Robert Goelet, whose family was among*   Gustavus Myers, *History of the Great American Fortunes*, volume 1 (Chicago: Charles H. Kerr, 1911), 245.

76 Confidential, *using the alliteration*   "Bobby Goelet's Rock n Roll Romance," *Confidential*, January 1956.

10. "The Untold Story of Van Johnson"

80 *"When it came to proving so-and-so actor"*   Steve Govoni, "Now It Can Be Told," *American Film*, February 1990.

80 *issue number 2 featured*   Jay Williams, "Is it True What They Say About Johnnie Ray?," *Confidential*, April 1953.

80 *Issue number 3 featured three*   Svern Vroomler, "King Gustav . . . Sweden's Royal Scandal," *Confidential*, August 1953.

81 *the* Nation *revealed the FBI's suspicions*   Athan Theoharis, "How the FBI Gay-baited Stevenson," *Nation*, May 7, 1990.

81 Confidential *laid the accusation to a desire*   Joseph M. Porter, "How That Stevenson Rumor Started," *Confidential*, August 1953.

81 *A story in issue number 4*   Johnson Albright, "The Awful Truth! Willie Sutton, Hoodlum in Lace Lingerie," *Confidential*, November 1953.

82 *automobile heir Walter Chrysler Jr.'s quarters*   Brad Shortell, "How the Navy Ousted Its No. 1 Gay Gob!," *Confidential*, January 1956.

82 *One of the magazine's stranger stories*   John Sears Prime, "When Harvard Was Home Sweet Homo," *Confidential*, September 1956.

83 *"In all the months Peter dated her"*   Lowell Crane, "The Hush-Hush Romance of Christine Jorgensen and a Vanderbilt Stepson," *Confidential*, November 1954.

83 Willson, *gay himself, had learned*   Hofler, 24.

84 *"Once Rory's story was published"*   Ibid., xx.

85 *Otash, one of the magazine's major informants*   Otash, 35.

86 *"Two events during 1955, in particular"*   Val Holley, *Mike Connolly and the Manly Art of Hollywood Gossip* (Jefferson: McFarland & Company, 2003), 30.

88 *Hunter, who had carefully hidden his homosexuality*   Hunter and Muller, 116–118.

89 *Hunter survived the outing*   Ibid., 122.

90 *"By the time* Battle Cry *was released"*   Ehrenstein, 94.

90 *"Do we have a situation here?"*   Davis, *Van Johnson*, 48.

90 *Later there had been rumors that Johnson*   Ibid., 81.

90 *Wynn's father, comic Ed Wynn, reflected*   Tom Vallance, "Obituary: Evie Wynn Johnson," Independent (London), August 28, 2004.

93 *"They needed their 'big star' to be married"*   Ibid.

93 *"For my money, Mayer was the worst of the lot"*   Ibid.

93 *That final act was precipitated*   Davis, *Van Johnson*, 191.

94 *"In his opinion, he is still a conventional New Englander"*   Ibid., 226.

11. "Lizabeth Scott in the Call Girls' Call Book"

96 *One story, about Katharine Hepburn*   Eugene Harte, "Katherine Hepburn, Hollywood's Torrid Tomboy!," *Confidential*, August 1953.

98 *"On one jaunt to Europe she headed"*   Matt Williams, "Lizabeth Scott in the Call Girls' Call Book," *Confidential*, September 1955.

98 *Quillan said Harrison himself asked her*   Unbylined, "Putting the Papers to Bed," *Time*, August 26, 1957.

12. "The Big Lie About Filter Cigarttes"

103 *As Cutter Laboratories was reeling* Ernest Stevens, "The Criminal Record of the Cutter Laboratories," *Confidential*, September 1955.

103 *"We ran stories exposing how children"* Thomas K. Wolfe, "Public Lives: *Confidential* Magazine: Reflections in Tranquility by the Former Owner, Robert Harrison, Who Managed to Get Away with It," *Esquire*, April 1964.

104 *"I heard an argument and saw Weldy"* Unbylined, "Shooting Accident Says *Confidential* Publisher," *Los Angeles Times*, September 7, 1958.

105 *Harrison absolved Weldy, explaining* Unbylined, "Reader Response," *Time*, September 17, 1956.

105 *"Take your wife next time"* Unbylined, "Wounded Publisher Home to Explain Blonde," *Los Angeles Mirror-News*, September 10, 1956.

105 *She described Courtney as an "old bag"* Unbylined, "Singer Mum on Shooting of Publisher," *Los Angeles Mirror-News*, September 17, 1956.

106 *Mike Wallace, who interviewed the publisher* Wolfe, op. cit.

107 *Britton described herself as being his "hostess"* Interview with Sherry Britton, June 13, 2000.

107 *One writer described her as "somewhat possessive"* Richard Gehman, "Confidential File on *Confidential*," *Esquire*, November 1956.

107 *"She was a little nutty"* Albert DeStefano interview, February 24, 2000.

107 *"To be frank," he explained* Gehman, op. cit.

108 *To them, Harrison still was the baby brother* David Gelman and Edward Katcher, "The Man Behind *Confidential*," article 4, *New York Post*, September 6, 1957.

108 *"There's been a death in the family"* Ray Muscarella and Tony Bennett, "The Confidential Story: *Confidential* Backs Down," *New York Post*, September 16, 1953.

108 *"They treat him like a two-year-old,"* Gelman and Katcher, "The Man Behind *Confidential*," article 3, *New York Post*, September 5, 1957.

109 *"There were days when Bob felt"* Ibid.

109 *"The Reader, whatever his name was"* Wolfe, op. cit.

109 *"Harrison dotes on puns"* Alvin Davis, "The *Confidential* Story: Politics and Peek-a-Boo," *New York Post*, September 17, 1953.

109 *"We wouldn't do a final story conference without him"* Conrad, 100.

13. "The Wife Clark Gable Forgot!"

111 *The local telephone company promptly dispatched* Unbylined, "Show Business: Hero's Exit," *Time*, November 28, 1960.

112 *"Clark told me frankly"* http://www.leninimports.com/clark_gable1.html.

112 *"It must have rattled skeletons"* Josephine Dillon, "The Press Said It Wasn't So . . . The Public Was Shocked! Now Here is the Proof from Josephine Dillon Herself!" *Confidential*, March 1956.

114 *The* Wall Street Journal *reported* J. Howard Rutledge, "Sin & Sex: Gossipy Private Peeks At Celebrities' Lives Start Magazine Bonanza," *Wall Street Journal*, July 5, 1955.

116 *For example, the number of feature films released*   Peter Lev, *History of the American Cinema, Volume 7, 1950–1959* (Berkeley, University of California Press, 2003), 303.

116 *Americans spent only 9.4 percent*   Ibid., 304.

116 *Paramount, the first of the major studios*   Ronald L. Davis, *Glamour Factory*, 358.

116 *MGM was beset by turmoil*   Ibid., 197–216.

116 *"For 25 cents each, you can buy Uncensored"*   Jack Olson, "Titans of Trash: *Confidential*'s Copycats," *Chicago Sun-Times*, October 20, 1955.

116 *"Cops are after a new kind of racketeer," wrote one journalist*   Jack Olson, "Titans of Trash: Hollywood Stars Are Targets of *Confidential*," *Chicago Sun-Times*, October 21, 1955.

117 *"You can see the fix they were in"*   Ibid.

118 *"Robert Harrison, career publisher of nudity"*   Ibid.

118 *As* Confidential *investigator Fred Otash put it*   Gladwyn Hill, "Scandal Magazines Face Trouble in the Courts," *New York Times*, May 5, 1957.

118 *In the 1930s, the fan magazines had alarmed*   Goodman, 76–78.

118 *"As a result," wrote Ezra Goodman*   Ibid., 18.

119 *"I have always been of the opinion"*   Ibid., 53.

14. "Robert Mitchum . . . the Nude Who Came to Dinner!"

121 *The novelist James Ellroy was later to tell*   Ehrenstein, 102.

122 *Geisler was known as a fierce advocate*   Geisler, 309.

122 *"Heretofore the circulation of these magazines"*   George Putnam interview with Jerry Geisler, KTTV-TV, Los Angeles, July 27, 1955.

122 *"These magazines are a major threat"*   Jack Olson, "Titans of Trash: Smeared Stars Fight Back," *Chicago Sun-Times*, October 22, 1955.

124 *"Short of being involved in a conspiracy ourselves"*   Ibid.

125 *"I am no devotee of* Confidential*"*   Victor Lasky, letter to Patrick Murphy Malin, August 5, 1955.

125 *Not surprisingly, they quickly discovered*   Goodman, 52.

15. "How Long Can Dick Powell Take It?"

128 *Ginger Rogers described June Allyson*   Unbylined obituary, "June Allyson, 1919–2006: Hollywood's Girl Next Door," *Los Angeles Times*, July 11, 2006.

128 *"June Allyson is to the 1950s"*   Jeanine Basinger, *The Star Machine* (New York: Knopf, 2007), 485.

129 *"What can you do when a pack of lies"*   Unbylined, "The Curious Craze for Confidential Magazines," *Newsweek*, July 11, 1955.

129 *Rushmore said he had become ashamed*   Howard Rushmore, "I Worked for *Confidential*," *Christian Herald*, January 1958.

129 *Harrison bragged that he would pay*   J. Howard Rutledge, "Sin & Sex: Gossipy Private Peeks at Celebrities' Lives Start Magazine Bonanza," *Wall Street Journal*, July 5, 1955.

129 *Rushmore turned up in a hotel in Butte, Montana*   Unbylined, "FBI Helps Hunt Missing Rushmore," *New York Journal American*, July 10, 1955.

130 *Clyde Tolson, associate director of the FBI* Federal Bureau of Investigation Howard Rushmore file No. 100-13058.

131 *Another fight was over Rushmore's plan* Interview with Albert DeStefano, February 24, 2000.

134 *"He has the face of a lordly asthmatic falcon"* Richard Gehman, "Confidential File on *Confidential*," *Esquire*, Nov. 1956.

134 *"Mr. Harrison gave Rushmore $2,000"* Theo Wilson, "Failed in His Biggest Role: Turncoat of Many Colors," *New York Daily News*, January 5, 1958.

16. "The Real Reason for Marilyn Monroe's Divorce"

140 *The story was written by Al Govoni* Steve Govoni, "Now It Can Be Told," *American Film*, February 1990.

140 *Fred Otash called it "the most explosive"* Otash, 73.

17. "What They 'Forgot' to Say About . . . Kim Novak"

143 *"Girls like Kim Novak, Marilyn Monroe, and Jayne Mansfield"* Goodman, 272–273.

144 *"Kim Novak was created not so much by her own talent"* Ibid., 279–280.

144 *For example, the story that Novak was discovered* Ibid.

144 *some women took to using a bumper sticker* http://www.glamourgirlsofthesilverscreen .com/show/272/Ramfis+Trujillo/.

18. "The Left Hook That Unhooked Lana Turner from Bob Topping"

150 *"I didn't know how to make a hotel or airline reservation"* Jeanine Basinger, *The Star Machine* (New York: Knopf, 2007), 217.

19. "Joan Crawford's Back Street Romance with a Bartender"

153 *Howard Rushmore described a dinner party* Howard Rushmore, "I Worked for *Confidential*," *Christian Herald*, January 1958.

154 *He told* Writer's Yearbook *that subscribers* Unbylined interview with Robert Harrison, "Fair Game," *Writer's Yearbook*, 1956.

154 *"Now, most women for the most part"* Ibid., 21.

155 *John Sisk, writing in the June 1956 issue* John P. Sisk, "The Exposé Magazines," *Commonweal*, June 1, 1956.

155 *"Confidential . . . is permanent"* Unbylined interview with Robert Harrison, *Writer's Yearbook*, 1956, 22.

20. "Here's Why Frank Sinatra Is the Tarzan of the Boudoir"

158 *He told the committee that he had sat in a car* James Denyer, "Raid on Apartment Described," *Los Angeles Mirror-News*, February 18, 1957.

158 *"They're a national disgrace"* Associated Press, "Ask US Act on Scandal Magazines," *Los Angeles Mirror-News*, March 5, 1957.

21. "It Was the Hottest Show in Town When Maureen O'Hara Cuddled in Row 35"

160 *"I understood that practically an act of sexual"* Theo Wilson, "Scandal Judge Nixes Telling of 'Rug Party,' " *New York Daily News*, August 20, 1957.

160 *"Word wafts up from Mexico City"* Val Holley, *Mike Connolly and the Manly Art of Hollywood Gossip* (Jefferson: McFarland & Company, 2003), 32.

161 *"On the face of it, the picture"* Unbylined, "The New Pictures," *Time*, February 11, 1957.

22. "Why Liberace's Theme Song Should Be, 'Mad About the Boy!' "

165 *"this deadly, winking, sniggering snuggling"* Darden Asbury Pyron, *Liberace: An American Boy* (Chicago: University of Chicago Press, 2000), 223–229.

23. "Hollywood vs. Confidential"

170 *Judge Walker had, in fact, been an actor* Theo Wilson, *Headline Justice*, 56.

171 *A Sunday-school teacher, Ritzi spent* Unbylined, "Stars Don't Awe This Judge," *Los Angeles Mirror-News*, August 19, 1957.

171 *Harold Conrad, the boxing promoter* Conrad, 109.

171 *George Murphy, MGM's public relations chief* Florabel Muir, "Scandal Suit to Rattle Lots of Film Skeletons," *New York Daily News*, July 30, 1957.

172 *Ronnie Quillan, for example* Art White, "Scandal Magazine Trial Transcript Disclosed," *Los Angeles Mirror-News*, July 30, 1957.

172 *Rushmore . . . told the jury that Harrison* Florabel Muir, "Movie Stars Lose; 100 to Face Scandal," *New York Daily News*, August 10, 1957.

173 *Like Quillan, she had been provided* White, op. cit.

174 *"Judge Walker propped his head up"* Florabel Muir and Theo Wilson, "Stars Shine in Bedtime Stories," *New York Daily News*, August 15, 1957.

175 *Having children and leaving them* Jean Hall, "The Shah Did Her Wrong," *Confidential*, July 1955.

175 *"Scandal Mag's Girl Twice Tries Suicide"* Wire service report, "Scandal Mag's Girl Twice Tries Suicide," *New York Daily News*, May 20, 1957.

175 *"Comb Filmland on Tip Francesca Slipped In"* Florabel Muir, "Comb Filmland on Tip Francesca Slipped In," *New York Daily News*, August 26, 1957.

175 *"Mexican Puzzle: So Where Is Francesca?"* Unbylined, "Mexican Puzzle: So Where Is Francesca?" *New York Daily News*, August 29, 1957.

175 *An already suspicious Hollywood grew more so"* Art White, "Trial Death Threat: Chalky White's Ex-Wife Told to 'Clam-Up,' " *Los Angeles Mirror-News*, August 23, 1957.

175 *Dick Powell and June Allyson hosted a party* Florabel Muir, "Defense Lawyer Backtracks a Step on Maureen," *New York Daily News*, August 19, 1957.

176 *While Rushmore himself had named de Scaffa* Art White, "10 Tattled on Stars, Trial Told," *Los Angeles Mirror-News*, August 24, 1957.

178 *Conrad, Meade said, wrote stories* Henry Machirella and Theo Wilson, "Claims Elvis' Texas Antics Shook a Lot of Dirt Mag's Way," *New York Daily News*, August 27, 1957.

24. *"Believe It or Not, There Are Ten Near-Crashes in the Air Every Day"*

180 *"Why do they pick on me?" he asked*   David Gelman and Edward Katcher, "The Man Behind *Confidential*," article 4, *New York Post*, September 6, 1957.

180 *He was having trouble keeping up alimony payments*   Jim Sterner, letter to Ted Gottfried, December 12, 1985.

181 *Producer Paul Gregory testified*   Art White, "Bribe Story Rocks Trial," *Los Angeles Mirror-News*, August 16, 1957.

181 *"If they took care of their business"*   Art White, "Scandal Case Blackmail Charge Hit," *Los Angeles Mirror-News*, August 27, 1957.

182 *Some, explained the* New York Times, *"would like to see"*   Gladwyn Hill, "Film Colony Fidgits in *Confidential* Case," *New York Times*, August 18, 1957.

182 *"I don't think it will hurt me much"*   Florabel Muir, "Defense Lawyer Backtracks a Step on Maureen," *New York Daily News*, August 19, 1957.

183 *In a step that many saw as too little*   Roger Beck, "Clark Gable's Ex Blames *Confidential* for Woes," *Los Angeles Mirror-News*, August 22, 1957.

183 *Billy Graham also offered Hollywood*   Associated Press, "Graham Mad: Blasts U.S. Taste for Smut Yarns," *Los Angeles Mirror-News*, August 22, 1957.

184 *In one such interview, Corinne Calvet*   Florabel Muir and Theo Wilson, "Gable Never Played with Francesca: Ex," *New York Daily News*, August 23, 1957.

184 *Many of the books and newspaper articles, Ross testified*   Art White, "*Confidential* OK for the Kiddies, Attorney Claims," *Los Angeles Mirror-News*, August 21, 1957.

25. *"Confidential's New Policy"*

186 *After two weeks of deliberation*   Associated Press, "Mistrial Verdict for *Confidential*," *New York Times*, October 2, 1957.

187 *Crowley boarded a plane for New York*   Ted Gottfried, interview with Arthur Crowley, January 8, 1986.

187 *It had cost him an estimated $500,000*   Unbylined, "Retrial in Doubt for *Confidential*," *New York Times*, October 6, 1957.

188 "Confidential *gave the lie to this story"*   Goodman, 79.

188 *"My mother and step-father were both under psychiatric care"*   Unbylined, "Rushmore Rift Blamed for Killings," *New York Journal American*, January 5, 1958.

189 *"Jobless, He Wouldn't Borrow"*   *New York Daily News*, January 5–6, 1958.

189 *"Rushmore was a really mixed-up guy"*   Theo Wilson, "Rushmore Portrayed by Friends and Foes as Jekyll & Hyde," *New York Daily News*, January 6, 1958.

189 *"I did and do regard it as a tragedy"*   Jim Sterner, letter to Ted Gottfried, December 13, 1985.

189 *"Hey, did you hear that?" the cabbie asked*   Thomas K. Wolfe, "Public Lives: *Confidential* Magazine: Reflections in Tranquility by the Former Owner, Robert Harrison, Who Managed to Get Away with It," *Esquire*, April 1964.

Bibliography

I was not a movie fan and knew little about Hollywood before I started this book. I am indebted for my education to the authors of the following books, and most especially to Neal Gabler, whose work put so much of the development of Hollywood into perspective; Ronald L. Davis, for his wonderful examination of the studio system; Thomas Schatz, for his detailed look at the business of filmmaking in the 1940s and 1950s; and Thomas Doherty, for his writing on the development and impact of the Motion Picture Code.

Amende, Coral. *Hollywood Confidential.* New York: Dutton Signet, 1997. Contemporary Hollywood gossip.

Betrock, Alan. *Sleazy Business.* Brooklyn: Shake Books, 1996. Reproductions of covers and pages from exploitation tabloids published 1959–1974.

Bird, S. Elizabeth. *For Enquiring Minds.* Knoxville: University of Tennessee Press, 1992. A cultural study of supermarket tabloids.

Birmingham, Stephen. *The Rest of Us.* Syracuse: Syracuse University Press, 1984. The immigration to America of Eastern European Jews.

Biskind, Peter. *Seeing Is Believing.* New York: Henry Holt, 1983. A look at how Hollywood movies reflected life in the fifties.

Black, Gregory D. *The Catholic Crusade Against the Movies, 1940–1975.* Cambridge: Cambridge University Press. Examination of the impact of the Catholic National Legion of Decency on movie content.

Blumenthal, Ralph. *Stork Club: America's Most Famous Nightspot and the Lost World of Café Society.* Boston: Little, Brown, 2000. The story of one of Robert Harrison's homes away from home.

Boddy, William. *Fifties Television.* Urbana: University of Illinois Press, 1993. A look at the development of the industry in the 1950s, including its impact on the movies.

Bogle, Donald. *Dorothy Dandridge.* New York: Amistad, 1997. The story of the beautiful and tragic actress, who was said to have dated Robert Harrison and who sued his magazine.

Brown, Gene. *Movie Time.* New York: Wiley, 1995. Chronology of the movie business from 1830 to 1994.

Brown, Peter Harry. *Kim Novak: Reluctant Goddess.* New York: St. Martin's Press, 1986. Biography of the star.

Buhle, Paul, and Dave Wagner. *Radical Hollywood: The Untold Story Behind America's Favorite Movies.* New York: New Press, 2002. A detailed look at the Hollywood Left.

Ceplair, Larry, and Steven Englund. *The Inquisition in Hollywood.* Berkeley: University of California Press, 1979. Politics in Hollywood from 1930 to 1960.

Cohen, Lester. *The New York Graphic.* Philadelphia: Chilton Books, 1964. The story of the newspaper that gave Robert Harrison his start.

Conrad, Harold. *Dear Muffo: 35 Years in the Fast Lane.* New York: Stein & Day, 1982. Oddball autobiography of publicist and journalist that includes description of *Confidential*, Robert Harrison, and events surrounding the Mike Todd story.

Davis, Ronald L. *The Glamour Factory.* Dallas: Southern Methodist University Press, 1993. A look at Hollywood's studio system based largely on archives of oral histories collected by SMU researchers.

———. *Van Johnson: MGM's Golden Boy.* Jackson: University Press of Mississippi, 2001. Biography of Van Johnson.

Doherty, Thomas. *Pre-Code Hollywood.* New York: Columbia University Press, 1999. An examination of sex, immorality, and insurrection in American cinema from 1930 to 1934.

———. *Hollywood's Censor: Joseph I. Breen & The Production Code Administration.* New York: Columbia University Press, 2007. Definitive story of the Motion Picture Code.

Drew, Bettina. *Nelson Algren: A Life on the Wild Side.* New York: Putnam. References to Howard Rushmore, a friend of Algren's and of the band of leftists with whom Algren associated in Chicago in the late 1930s.

Ehrenstein, David. *Open Secret.* New York: William Morrow, 1998. Gay Hollywood from 1928 to 1998.

Friedrich, Otto. *City of Nets: A Portrait of Hollywood in the 1940s.* New York: Harper & Row, 1986. Hollywood at its height.

Gabler, Neal. *An Empire of Their Own.* New York: Crown, 1988. The story of the Jewish immigrants who invented Hollywood.

———. *Life: The Movie.* New York: Knopf, 1998. An analysis of how entertainment has overtaken reality in American culture.

———. *Winchell.* New York: Vintage, 1994. Biography of Walter Winchell.

Geisler, Jerry. *Hollywood Lawyer.* New York: Pocket Books, 1962. Hollywood's most famous lawyer recounts his most famous cases.

Goldman, William. *Adventures in the Screen Trade.* New York: Warner Books, 1983. A gossipy inside look at the business of screenwriting.

Goodman, Ezra. *The Fifty-Year Decline and Fall of Hollywood.* New York: Simon and Schuster, 1961. An acerbic account of Hollywood's woes by a former studio publicist and Hollywood journalist.

Green, Abel, and Joe Laurie Jr. *From Vaude to Video.* New York: Henry Holt, 1951. Anecdotes about the development of the entertainment business.

Gruber, Frank. *The Pulp Jungle.* Los Angeles: Sherbourne Press, 1967. An autobiographical look at writing for the pulps.

Halberstam, David. *The Fifties.* New York: Fawcett Columbine, 1993. The history of the fifties in America, told through stories of major personalities of the time.

Harvey, James. *Movie Love in the Fifties.* New York: Knopf, 2001. How Hollywood treated sex and romance.

Herman, Arthur. *Joseph McCarthy.* New York: Free Press, 2000. Biography of America's most famous Communist hunter and Howard Rushmore's onetime employer.

Hofler, Robert. *The Man Who Invented Rock Hudson.* New York: Carroll & Graf, 2005. The story of Hudson's agent, Henry Willson.

Howe, Irving. *World of Our Fathers.* New York: Schocken Books, 1976. Story of the Jewish immigration to the United States.

Hunter, Tab, and Eddie Muller. *Tab Hunter Confidential.* Chapel Hill: Algonquin Books, 2005. The star's autobiography.

Kashner, Sam, and Jennifer MacNair. *The Bad & the Beautiful.* New York: W. W. Norton, 2002. Hollywood in the fifties.

Klehr, Harvey. *The Heyday of American Communism.* New York: Basic Books, 1984. Communism in the Depression era.

Lait, Jack, and Lee Mortimer. *New York Confidential.* New York: Crown, 1948. The book from which *Confidential* is said to have taken its name and some of its inspiration.

Laurents, Arthur. *Original Story By: A Memoir of Broadway and Hollywood.* New York: Knopf, 2000. An autobiographical tale, with a focus on gay life.

Leaming, Barbara. *Marilyn Monroe.* New York: Crown, 1998. The definitive biography of Marilyn Monroe.

Mallen, Frank. *Sauce for the Gander.* White Plains: Baldwin Books, 1954. The story of the *New York Evening Graphic,* newspaper home to Walter Winchell and Robert Harrison.

Mann, William J. *Wisecracker.* New York: Penguin Books, 1998. Biography of William Haines, Hollywood's first openly gay star.

Matusow, Harvey. *False Witness.* New York: Cameron & Kahn, 1955. The story of one of Howard Rushmore's anti-Communist associates and his effort at redemption.

May, Lary. *The Big Tomorrow: Hollywood and the Politics of the American Way.* Chicago: University of Chicago Press, 2000. How politics shaped, and shapes, filmmaking.

——. *Screening Out the Past.* Chicago: University of Chicago Press, 1980. A look at how the motion picture industry contributed to the development of a mass culture in the United States.

McDougal, Dennis. *The Last Mogul.* New York: Crown, 1998. Biography of Lew Wasserman, powerful head of MCA.

McLellan, Diana. *The Girls: Sappho Goes to Hollywood.* New York: St. Martin's, 2000. Lesbian life in Hollywood.

Mordden, Ethan. *Movie Star: A Look at the Women Who Made Hollywood.* New York: St. Martin's, 1983. Theda Bara to Meryl Streep.

Navasky, Victor. *Naming Names.* New York: Viking, 1980. How friends betrayed friends in the hunt for Communists.

Otash, Fred. *Investigation Hollywood!* Chicago: Henry Regnery, 1976. Famed Hollywood private detective tells all.

Reimschneider, Burkhard, ed. *The Best of American Girlie Magazines.* Cologne: Taschen, 1997. A profusely illustrated survey of the genre.

Rosenbaum, Jonathan. *Movie Wars: How Hollywood and the Media Conspire to Limit What Films We Can See.* Chicago: A Capella Books, 2000. An examination of the business of packaging, promoting, and distributing films.

Russo, Vito. *The Celluloid Closet.* New York: Harper & Row, 1987. Homosexuality in the movies.

Sanders, Coyne Steven, and Tom Gilbert. *Desilu: The Story of Lucille Ball and Desi Arnaz.* New York: Harper Collins, 1993. The story behind the story of America's best-known TV couple.

Sanders, Ronald. *The Lower East Side Jews.* Mineola: Dover Publications, 1969. A history of the Harrison family's first neighborhood in New York.

Schatz, Thomas. *Boom and Bust.* Berkeley: University of California Press, 1999. A look at American cinema in the 1940s.

——. *The Genius of the System.* New York: Henry Holt, 1988. Exhaustive look at the business of filmmaking during the studio era.

Server, Lee. *Ava Gardner: "Love is Nothing."* New York: St. Martin's, 2006. Biography of the girl from Grubtown, N.C.

Silvester, Christopher, ed. *The Grove Book of Hollywood.* New York: Grove Press, 1998. An anthology of writing about the movie capital.

Smith, John Chabot. *Alger Hiss: The True Story.* New York: Holt, Rinehart & Winston, 1976. The story of one of America's most famous Communist witch hunts, in which Howard Rushmore participated.

Wallace, David. *Lost Hollywood.* New York: St. Martin's, 2001. The history of the movie business in the last century.

Walls, Jeannette. *Dish: The Inside Story on the World of Gossip.* New York: Avon, 2000. The development of the gossip industry in America.

Wayne, Jane Ellen. *The Golden Girls of MGM.* New York: Carroll & Graf, 2002. Garbo, Crawford, Turner, Garland, Gardner, et al.

Wilson, Theo. *Headline Justice: Inside the Courtroom — The Country's Most Controversial Trials.* New York: Thunder's Mouth Press, 1996. Firsthand account of the *Confidential* trial, by a reporter who was there.

Wixson, Douglas. *Worker-Writer in America.* Chicago: University of Illinois Press, 1994. Biography of Leftist writer Jack Conroy, whom Howard Rushmore idolized in his youth.

Index

Page numbers in *italics* refer to illustrations and captions

abortion, 7, 103, 183
airliner crashes, 179
Aitchison, Johny, 56
Alexander II, Czar of Russia, 27
Alexander III, Czar of Russia, 27
Algiers, 11
Allyson, June
  film career of, 128, *130*
  philandering of, 127–9, *130*, *131*, 176,
    178
  popularity of, 128, *130*
American Civil Liberties Union (ACLU),
  125
American Mercury, 25, 48–9, 53
Anvil, 50
Apollo Theater, 67
Army, U.S., 91–2
Arnaz, Desi, Jr., 54, 57
Arnaz, Desi, Sr., 54–7, *56*, *57*, 173–4
Arnaz, Lucie, 55, 57
Arnold, Dorothy, 3
Arnold, Gertrude, 175
aspirin, 103
Astor, John Jacob, 176
atomic bomb, 44, 46
Atomic Energy Commission (AEC),
  44–5, 47
Ausnit, Edgar, 142, *143*, 144

Baker, Josephine, 19–24
  Stork Club Incident and, 19–22, *21*

white men dated by, 19–20, *21*, 78
  Winchell and, 19–20, *21*, 22
Ball, Lucille
  Arnaz's philandering and, 54–7, *56*, *57*,
    174
  physical appearance of, 54, 56, *56*
Barker, Lex, 68, 147–8, *149*
Basinger, Jeanine, 128
Battle Cry, 87, 90
Baule, Frédérique "Frede," 98
Beauty Parade, 5, 15, 115
Benedict, Michael (Laslo), 142
Bennett, Joan, 63
Bennett, Tony, 40–1
Bermuda Tourist Bureau, 78
Beverly Hills Hotel, 55, 65, 127, 142, 181
Billingsley, Sherman, 22
Binford, Lloyd T., 68
Birth of a Nation, The, 13
blacklisting, 10, 32
blacks, 36–7, 173
  Communist Party and, 23, 50
  discrimination against, 19–22, *21*, 49,
    52, 67–71, *69*, *70*, 73, 78
  and *Gone With the Wind*, 49, 52
  romances between whites and, 7,
    19–20, *21*, 66–78, *69*, *70*, *75*, *77*, 80,
    102, 109, 122, 132, 148, 175–6
Blasgen, Virginia, 158
Bledsoe, Donald, 176
Bogart, Humphrey, 63, 82

boric acid, 103
Bouillon, Jo, 20
Bravo, Jaime, 37, 174
Breen, Jay, 32, 42
Breen, Joseph I., 14
Bridges, Harry, 59
Britton, Sherry, 107
Broadway, 13, 53, 72, 80, 99
  Allyson's career on, 127
  Gable's debut on, 111–12
  Harrison's love life and, 106–7
Browder, Earl, 52, 59
Browder, Raissa, 59
Brown, Edmund G. "Pat," 166
  and grand jury investigation of
    Confidential, 162, 168
  and Hollywood vs. *Confidential*,
    170, 172
Browning, Robert, 53
Burke, Edmund, 125

Cabot, Bruce, 37, 175
Calhoun, Rory, 57, 83–4, *84*, 171
  criminal past of, 77, 84, *85*, 86–7, 173
Calvet, Corinne, 162–3
  and Hollywood vs. *Confidential*, 171,
    175, 182, 184
Calypso Heat Wave, 73
cancer, 101–2, 180
candy manufacturers, 103
Captain John Smith and Pocahontas,
  37, *38*
carbon tetrachloride, 103
Carlton, Ken, 38
Carney, Gloria, 74–7
Carroll, John, 182–4
Casey, Michael Patrick, 160
Catholics, 7, 14, 68, 69
Cavallaro, Gene, 12
Chambers, Dorothy, 31
Chandlee, Esme, 40
Chaplin, Charlie, 59, 122

Chevalier, Haakon and Frank, 46
Chicago Sun-Times, 41, 116–18
Chrysler, Walter, P., Jr., 82, 129
Churchill, Winston, 120
cigarettes, 101–3, 180
Cohn, Harry, 13
  management style of, 32–4
  and publicity for Novak, 143–4, *145*
Cohn, Roy, 53, 189
  Rushmore on, 60, 134, 180
Colony, 12, 25, 107–8
Columbia Pictures
  Harry Cohn's management of, 32–4
  and publicity on Novak, 142, *143*,
    144–5, *145*
Communism, Communists
  in Hollywood, 7, 10, 35–6, 47,
    59, 118
  Oppenheimer story and, 44–7, *46*
  Rushmore and, 25, 36, 41–2, 47–53,
    49, 58–60, 129–31, 133–4, 153, 163,
    180–1, 189
  Stevenson and, 81
  Winchell on, 22–3
Confidential
  accuracy and credibility of, 38–40, 65,
    80, 98, 119, 129, 161, *162*, 165, 185
  audience of, 153–5
  banning of, 161–2, 166, 174
  circulation of, 5–6, 9, 12, 23, 25, 34,
    60, 63, 77–8, 80, 90, 114, 116, *138*,
    140, 153–4, 169–70, 188
  company culture of, 108–9
  cover line of, 40
  demise and closing of, 34, 188–9
  distribution problems of, 187
  finances of, 23, 37, 39, 64–5, 83,
    139–40, 167, 174, 176, 178, 182,
    185, 187
  functions served by, 118–19, 154–5
  grand jury investigation of, 162–3,
    166–8, 171–2, 174, 176

imitators and competition of, 5–6, 63,
115–16, 122, 124, 154–5, 161, 163,
173, 185, 188
launch of, 5, 10, 18, 63, 132, 140, 169
lawsuits against, 40, 78, 99, 122–3, *123*,
124, 125–6, 129, 134, 160–1, *162*,
165–8, *166*, *167*
legacy of, 10, 191
new policy of, 186–7
on politics and politicians, 9, 23, 25,
41–2, 44–7, 59–60, 80–1, 83, 102,
153
promotion of, *9*, *21*, 23–5, *24*, *106*
on race and miscegenation, 19–20, *21*,
66–78, *70*, *75*, 77, 80, 102, 109, 132,
175–6
reporting style of, 6, 8
retraction printed by, 40–1
story conferences of, 109
threat posed by, 63, 116–18, 122–5,
124, 158, 161–2
tipsters and investigators employed
by, 34, 36–40, *38*, *39*, *41*, 55, 58, 63,
65, 80, 85, 98, 112, 118–19, 121,
126, 139–40, 157–8, 171–4, 176–8,
180, 187
writers recruited by, 25, 59–60, 63–4
Congress, U.S., 122
on Communism, 10, 35–6, 47, 53,
58–60
Kefauver crime hearings and, 17
Connolly, Mike, 58, 173
homosexuality of, 64, 86–7
O'Hara story and, 160
recruited by *Confidential*, 63–4
Conrad, Harold, 171, 178
Conroy, Jack, 50, 53, 134
consumer products, 15, 101–3, 180
coonskin caps, 102
Copacabana Club, 73, 80
Courtney, Geene, 104–5
Craig, James, 160, 183

Crane, Cheryl, 148, *149*
Crane, Stephen, *149*
Crawford, Christina, 58, 152
Crawford, Joan
bartender's affair with, 151–2,
153, 176
children of, 58, 152
crime, criminals, criminality, 7, 12,
15–17, 37
of Calhoun, 77, 84, 85, 86–7, 173
Confidential's indictment and, 168–70
Confidential's retraction on, 40–1
homosexuals among, 81–2
Kefauver hearings on, 17
of Mitchum, 120, 122, *123*, 181–2
Crowley, Arthur, 170–1, 173, 182–5, 187
Curley, 68
Cutter Laboratories, 103

Dailey, Dan, *153*, 171, 176
Daily Mirror, 165, *166*
Daily Worker, 49, 50–3, 59
Dale, Alan, 174, 184
D'Amore, Pasquale "Patsy," 139
Dandridge, Dorothy
Confidential sued by, 78, 167, *167*
and Hollywood vs. *Confidential*, 174,
177, 183–4
Daniels, Billy, 36, 68, 147–8, 174, 184
Daniels, Martha Braun, 68
Darcel, Denise, 68
Darrieux, Danielle, 76
Davis, Ronald, 90, 94
Davis, Sammy, Jr.
film career of, 71–2
Gardner's affair with, 66–73, *70*, 78
Hush-Hush sued by, 122
Myles's affair with, 72–3, *75*
Sinatra's relationship with, 34, 71
de Acosta, Mercedes, 96–7
De Carlo, Yvonne, 12
de Havilland, Olivia, 35

de Scaffa, Countess Francesca de
Bourbon y
as *Confidential* tipster, 37, 38, 39, 63,
112, 168, 173, 176
Gable's first wife and, 112, 173, 184
and Hollywood vs. *Confidential*,
173–6, 184
DeStefano, Albert, 73, 107
and Hollywood vs. *Confidential*, 170,
176, 184
Rushmore and, 132, 134
and suits against *Confidential*, 40, 129,
165–7
Diane, 150
Dietrich, Marlene, 96–8, 97
Dillon, Josephine
age of, 111, 113–14, *113*, 117
Gable's marriage to, 75, 110–14, *113*,
115, 116, *117*, 129, 171, 173, 184
impoverishment of, 110–14, *117*
DiMaggio, Joe
Monroe's divorce from, 122, 136,
138, *138*
Monroe's marriage to, 137–8
Monroe's romance with, 3–6, 8, 9, 12
Wrong Door Raid and, *41*, 136–40, 158
Dobbins, Jeannie, 188
Doherty, Thomas, 14
Dominican Republic, 76, 144, 154
Harrison's trip to, 103–6, *106*, 161
Dors, Diana, *153*
Driben, Peter, 16
Drouet, LaGuerre, 187
drugs, 7, 102, 120–2, *123*, 181–2
Duke, Doris
chauffeur's affair with, 74, 77, 122
Confidential sued by, 122, *124*,
134, *167*
Marchand's affair with, 74
Rubirosa's marriage to, 76

Ecstasy, 11
Edge of Hell, 38

Ehrenstein, David, 90, 121
Eisenhower, Dwight, 89, 103
Ekberg, Anita, 37, *41*, 120, 156
Ellroy, James, 121–2
El Morocco, 12, 15, 23, 25, 31, 107–8, 188
Esquire, *133*, 134, 190
Exhibitors Herald, 13
Eyeful, 5, 15–16
Eyewitness, 17–18

Farrell, Edythe, 15–16, 42, 108, 116
Fascism, Fascists, 45, 48
Federal Bureau of Investigation (FBI),
23, 37
Johnson and, 79, 92
Oppenheimer and, 47
Rushmore and, 59, 129–30
Stevenson and, 81
Ferrer, José, *138*
fetishism, fetishes, 16–17
film industry, 10–12, 115–19, 169
blacklisting in, 10, 32
Calhoun's criminal convictions and,
84, *85*, 86–7
competition between television
and, 8, 36, 116, 118
decline of, 115–16
finances in, 36, 116, 118
and Hollywood vs. *Confidential*,
171–2, 174, 182
homosexuals in, 79–80, 83, 84, 85–94,
86, *88*, 89, *91*, 92, 118, 121–2, *123*,
171, 181
lesbians in, 96–100, 97, 99, 122
monopolistic behavior in, 34–5
Motion Picture Production Code and,
7, 13–14, 68
nudity in, 11–12, 120–2, *123*, 144, 182
PR problem of, 118–19
racial issues in, 49, 52, 66–73, 69, 70,
75, 78
studio system in, 6–9, 35, 118, 128,
150, 188

threats to, 63–5, 117–18, 122–5, *124*,
  158, 161–2
white lists in, 118–19
see also Hollywood, Calif.
Flynn, Errol, 109, 122
Forge, 50
Forrestal, James, 130
France, French, 36, 51, 68, 111, 172
  Baker and, 19–20, 23
  and stories on lesbians, 98, 99
Francis, Vera, 176
Frederick Fell and Company, 64
Frew, June, *27*, 105, 107

Gable, Clark, 37, *39*
  film career of, 111–12, *115*
  finances of, 111–14, *115, 117*
  first wife of, *75*, 110–14, *113, 115,* 116,
    117, 129, 171, 173, 184
  philandering of, 110–12
Gabler, Neal, 22
Garceau, Jean, 114
Gardner, Ava, *39*, 176
  black men dated by, 66–73, *69, 70,* 78
  film career of, 67–9, *69*
  Sinatra's marriage to, *68, 69,* 71, 156
Gates, Phyllis, 85–6, *86*
Gehman, Richard, 134
Geisler, Harold Lee "Jerry," 122–4, *124,*
  134, 163
Gerbeau, Roland, 36
Germany, Germans, 45, 51, 96, 176
Gleason, Jackie, 171, 178, 180
Goelet, Robert, 74–7
Gone With the Wind, 35, 49, 51–2
Goodman, Ezra, 63–4, 87
  Confidential's tipsters and, 36–7
  and publicity on Novak, 144
  on value of *Confidential*, 119
  on white lists, 118–19
Gould, Polly, 175
Govoni, A. P. "Al," 42, 103–5, 168
  Dominican Republic trip of, 103–4

Rushmore's alcoholism and, 132
  and shooting of Harrison, 104–5
  and stories on homosexuals, 80
  Wrong Door Raid and, 140
Graham, Billy, 183
Grauman's Chinese Theatre, 40, 159–61,
  162, 183
Gray, Barry, 22
Great Britain, British, 51, 172
  Confidential's investigators in, 39–40
  Liberace story and, 165, *166*
Great Depression, 11, 45, 134
  Communists and, 7, 50, 53
Gregory, Paul, 121, *123,* 181
Griffith, D. W., 13, 34
Gustav V, King of Sweden, 80–1

Haijby, Kurt, 80–1
Harrison, Benjamin, 26, 28–9
Harrison, Paula, 26, 28, 107–8
Harrison, Robert (Max), 5–6, 12–18,
  39–41, 58–60, 64–5
  accuracy as concern of, 38, 40, 129
  ambitions of, 26, *132*
  biographies on, 64
  birth of, 28
  childhood of, 28–9, 107–8, 134
  Confidential's audience and, 154–5
  on *Confidential*'s new policy, 186–7
  Crawford story and, 58
  Davis's relationship with, 73
  death of, 190–1
  as debonair, *133*
  diet of, 108
  Dominican Republic visited by, 103–6,
    106, 161
  education of, 29
  finances of, 14–16, 25–6, 107–8,
    114–15, 125, 129, 154, 187–9
  on functions served by *Confidential*,
    118, 154–5
  girlie magazines of, 5, 15–17, 27, 107,
    115–16, 125

Harrison, Robert (Max) *(continued)*
  heritage of, 25–8, 132–3
  in Hollywood, 14–15, 34–6
  hypochondria of, 108
  and launch of *Confidential*, 18
  legal problems of, 17, 125–6, 165–8,
    170–3, 175–6, *177*, 178, 180, 182,
    184, 187
  love life of, 27, 105–8, 133, 190–1
  management style of, 108–9, 126
  modeling of, 16
  Monroe-DiMaggio romance and, 6,
    9, 12
  O'Hara story and, 160
  Oppenheimer-Tatlock affair and, 45
  opportunism of, 77–8
  physical appearance of, 5, 104, 107,
    133, 134
  on politics, 23, 131, 133
  in promoting *Confidential*, 23–5,
    24, *106*
  puns enjoyed by, 109
  Reader employed by, 109
  respectability sought by, 25, 27, 58, 188
  Rushmore recruited by, 25, 59–60
  Rushmore's conflicts with, 58, 129,
    131–4, *132*, 189
  social life of, 12, 15, 23, 25, 53, 73, 78,
    107–8, 133–4, 188–9
  and stories on consumer products,
    102–3
  and stories on homosexuals, 80, 83,
    84, 96
  and stories on lesbians, 96
  and stories on race and miscegenation,
    67, 73, 77–8
  on story behind the story, 10, 155
  threats to life of, 40, 104–6, *106*, 161
  tipsters and investigators employed by,
    34, 36, 39–40, 80, 157, 172
  Wrong Door Raid and, 161
Harrison Publications Inc., 25, 114–16

Harrison's Weekend Guide, 29
Harvard University, 82–3
Harwyn Club, 23, 107–8, 188
Haymes, Dick, 31–2, *33*
Hays, Will H., 14
Hayworth, Rita, 30–4
  children of, 30–2, *33*
  Haymes's alleged beating of, 32
Hearst, William Randolph, 25, 52, 68
heart disease, 101, 103
Hepburn, Katharine, 96
Hill, Virginia, 17
Hofler, Robert, 83
Holley, Val, 64, 86–7
Hollywood, Calif., 5–8, 12–15, 61–5,
    72–4, 79, 84, 94–5, 102, 108,
    110–13, 125–7, *138*, 151–4, 156
  Arnaz's philandering and, 54–5
  and functions served by *Confidential*,
    154
  Gable's first wife and, 111, 113,
    113, 173
  Golden Age of, 6–7, 34, 94
  and grand jury investigation of
    Confidential, 162–3
  Harrison in, 14–15, 34–6
  Klekner extortion case and, 62
  Mitchum story and, 120–1, *123*
  Monroe-DiMaggio romance and, 6
  mythic view of, 14
  night life in, 34, 147, 187
  O'Hara story and, 159–61
  politics in, 7, 10, 35–6, 47, 59, 118
  Rushmore's visits to, 63–4
  and suits against *Confidential*, *167*, 168
  tipsters and investigators in, 34, 36–8,
    41, 58, 63–5, 112, 121, 126, 173, *177*
  Wrong Door Raid and, 137, 139
  see also film industry
Hollywood Reporter, 6, 58, 64–5, 86, 160
Hollywood Research Inc., 125–6, 182
  closing of, 161, 187

and Hollywood vs. *Confidential*, 171,
  177, 187
Kraft Committee investigation of, 158
and suits against *Confidential*, 167–8
Hollywood Ten, 35–6
Hollywood vs. *Confidential*
  closing arguments in, 184–5
  as First Amendment battle, 172, 187
  hung jury in, 186–7
  reading stories into record in, 174, 183
  subpoenaed witnesses in, 171–2, 175
  tipsters and investigators revealed in,
    171–4, 176–8, 180, 187
  trial in, 170–8, *177*, 180–7
  untimely deaths in, 175
Holtz, Lou, 95
homosexuality, homosexuals, 7, 79–94,
    96, 102, 118, 129
  of Connolly, 64, 86–7
  in film industry, 79–80, 83, 84, 85–94,
    86, 88, 89, 91, 92, 118, 121–2, *123*,
    171, 181
  and Hollywood vs. *Confidential*, 171–2
  of Liberace, 82, 164–5, *166*
  marriages and weddings of, 5, 80, 85–7,
    86, 92–3, *92, 93*
  outing of, 83, *86*, 88–9, 179
  in politics, 81, 83
  restored to heterosexuality, *91, 92*
  of Sutton, 81–2
Hoover, J. Edgar, 23, 130–1
  Oppenheimer and, 47
  Rushmore and, 59, 130
  Stevenson and, 81
Hopper, Hedda, 68
How to Marry a Millionaire, 5–6
Hudson, Rock, 152
  homosexuality of, 83, 84, 85–6
  marriage of, 85–7, *86*
Hughes, Howard, 13, 35, 116
Hughes, Toni, 62–3
Hull, Cordell, 59

Hunter, Tab, *138*
  film career of, 87, 90
  homosexuality of, 83, 87–90, *88, 89*,
    171
Hush-Hush, 116, 122, 188

Ingram, David, 51
In Old California, 34
Investigation Hollywood! (Otash), 85
Irwin, Phil, 137–40, 158
Israel, Sam, 65

Jeffries, Herb, 36–7, 55, 68, 174
Jews
  anti-Semitism and, 52, 73
  in Germany, 45
  Harrison's heritage and, 25–8, 132–3
  in Hollywood, 7, 14
Johnson, Van, 161
  homosexuality of, 79–80, 90–4, *91, 92*
  marriage of, 92–3, *92, 93*
  restored to heterosexuality, *91, 92*
Jorgensen, Christine, 83

Kazan, Elia, 47
Kefauver, Estes, 17
Keller, Helen, 62–3
Khan, Yasmin, 30–2, 33
Klekner, Ben, 62
Knight, Goodwin, 161
Kraft, Fred, 157–8

Ladd, Alan, 128, *131*
Ladies' Home Journal, 114
Lait, George, 144–5
Lamarr, Hedy, 11–12, 32
Lane, Glenn, 62
Langham, Ria, 112, *115*
Larraura, Esteban, 39
Lasky, Jesse, Jr., 32
Lasky, Victor, 125
Laughton, Charles, 121, *123*

Lawson, John Howard, 47, 59
LeRoy, Mervyn, 64–5, 150
lesbianism, lesbians
  in film industry, 96–100, 97, 99, 122
  and Rushmore's proposed story on
    Roosevelt, 131–2
  of Tatlock, 45
Lewis, William, 65
Liberace, 162–5
  Confidential sued by, 165, *166*, *167*
  homosexuality of, 82, 164–5, *166*
Life, 17, *138*
  on Novak, 141–2, *143*, 145
Linn, Clarence, 161, 163, 170–2
Look, 112–14, 180
  on Arnaz and Ball, 55, *57*
  Gable's first wife and, 112–13
  on Novak, 142, *143*, 145
Lord, Daniel A., 14
Los Angeles, Calif., 6–7, 12, 37, *41*, 55,
    58, 62, 95, 164, 191
  and Hollywood vs. *Confidential*, 172,
    177, 180–1
  and homosexuals in film industry,
    87, 92
  Wrong Door Raid and, 136, 139,
    158, 161
Los Angeles Mirror-News, 64, 105
  Gable's first wife and, 112–13
"Lost Leader, The" (Browning), 53
Loving You, 100

Macfadden, Bernarr Adolphus, 13
Machinal (Treadwell), 111–12
Madison, Guy, 75
Madupe Mudge Paris, Prince David, 74,
    77, 122
Mansfield, Jayne, 143–4, 180, 184
Man with the Golden Arm, The, 144
Marchand, Claude, 74
Martin, Dean, 34, 128, *131*, 171
Mayer, Louis B., 11, 13, 37, 91, 93

McCarthy, Joseph R., 23, 131, 189
  Rushmore's work for, 53, 58–60, 134
McDowell, Roddy, 89
McKesson, William B., 158, 161–2
Meade, Fred, 108, 125–6, 161, 168
  and Hollywood vs. *Confidential*, 170,
    176–8, *177*, 181–2, 187
Meade, Marjorie Tobias, 15, 65, 108–9,
    125, 168, 191
  and Hollywood vs. *Confidential*, 170,
    177, 178, 181–2, 187
  Wrong Door Raid and, 158, 161
Merrick, Lynn, 76–7
MGM, 34, 40, 64, 116, 124, 161, 183
  Allyson and, 128, *130*
  Gable and, 112, 114
  Gardner and, 67–9, *69*
  and Hollywood vs. *Confidential*, 171–2
  Johnson and, 90–1, *93*
  Turner and, 149–50, *149*
Mitchum, Robert, 176
  Confidential sued by, 122, *123*, *124*,
    134, *167*
  drugs used by, 120–2, *123*, 181–2
  and Hollywood vs. *Confidential*, 181–4
  nudity and, 120–2, *123*, 182
Mocambo, 34, 147, 187
Mommie Dearest (Crawford), 58
Monroe, Marilyn, 23, 32, 57, 143–4, 173
  DiMaggio's divorce from, 122, 136,
    138, *138*
  DiMaggio's romance with, 3–6, *8*,
    9, 12
  film career of, 5–6, 137–8
  physical appearance of, 3–4, 136–7
  Schenck's relationship with, 4, 6, *8*
  Wrong Door Raid and, *41*, 136–40
Mordaunt-Smith, Michael, 39–40, 160
Morgan, Michèle, 99
Mosby, Aline, 63, 173, 177–8
Motion Picture Association of America
  (MPAA), 14

Motion Picture Production Code, 7,
13–14, 68
Muir, Florabel, 171, 173, 176
Murphy, George, 171–2, 183
Muscarella, Ray, 40–1
Myles, Meg, 72–3, 75

National Association for the
Advancement of Colored People
(NAACP), 19, 22
National Legion of Decency, 14
Navy, U.S., 82, 129–30
New York City, 22, 73–7, 99, 125, 173,
175–6, 187–9
Baker in, 20, 21
Harrison's death and, 191
Harrison's heritage and, 133
Harrison's homes and life in, 5, 12, 15,
17, 25, 28–9, 41, 65, 105, 107–8,
188–9
Hayworth in, 31, 33
and Hollywood vs. *Confidential*, 176,
177, 178, 182, 187
and publicity for Novak, 144
and romances between whites and
blacks, 66–7, 74–7
Rushmore's death and, 189, 190
Rushmore's life in, 50–1, 53, 188
Russian Jews in, 26, 28
and stories on homosexuals, 80
and suits against *Confidential*, 167–8
New York Daily News, 171, 173–6
New York Evening Graphic, 13
New York Journal-American, 25, 52, 58–60
New York Post, 22, 52, 59, 131, 180
New York Times, 52, 165, 182
Niagara, 5–6
Night of the Hunter, 120–2
Nixon, Allan, 176
Novak, Kim, 37, 41, 152
film career of, 141–6
physical appearance of, 141–2, 144

publicity on, 141–6, *143*, *145*
nudity, nudes, 11–13, 63, 118, 144
Harrison and, 12, 15–17
of Lamarr, 11–12
Mitchum and, 120–2, *123*, 182
and stories on lesbians, 96
Tatlock's death and, 43
see also sex, sexuality

O'Hara, Maureen, 159–62
alleged public lovemaking of, 40,
159–61, *162*, 165, 183
Confidential sued by, 160–1, *162*, 167
and Hollywood vs. *Confidential*, 182–4
Olson, Jack, 116–18
On the Riviera, 37, 38
Oppenheimer, J. Robert, 173
security clearance lost by, 44–7
Tatlock's affair with, 44–7, 46
Orton, Peter, 83
Otash, Fred
as *Confidential* informant, 37, 40, 41,
65, 118, 121
and Hollywood vs. *Confidential*, 171,
175, 181
Hudson's homosexuality and, 85
Mitchum story and, 121–2
Wrong Door Raid and, 41, 140

Page, Bettie, 17
Paglia, Camille, 10
Painted Desert, The, 112, 115
Palette, Pilar, 104, 106
Paramount Pictures, 34–5, 116
Parks, Rosa, 67
Parra, Enrique, 160
Parsons, Louella, 68
Payton, Barbara, 75
Pearlman, Edward, 188–9
Peck, Gregory, 77, 171
Phenix City Story, 72–3
Phffft!, 144

Photoplay Awards, 127
Picnic, 144
Pidgeon, Walter, 63, 75, 162–3, 176
police, 43, 95, 105, 116, 135, 189
    as *Confidential* tipsters, 36–7, *41*, 173
    and stories on lesbians, 98, 99
    Wrong Door Raid and, 139, 158, 161
Police Gazette, 15–16, 42, 163
polio vaccine, 103
Powell, Dick, 183–4
    Allyson's philandering and, 127–9,
        131, 176, 178
Presley, Elvis, 100, *153*
private investigators, 62, 65, 74
    as *Confidential* tipsters, 36–7, *41*, 121
    and Hollywood vs. *Confidential*, 174–5
    Wrong Door Raid and, 136–40, 157–8
prostitution, prostitutes, 60–2, 95–6, 104,
        125–6, 179
    Arnaz's philandering and, 55, *56*, 57,
        173
    as *Confidential* tipsters, 36–8, 58, 176
    and Hollywood vs. *Confidential*, 171,
        173–6
    and stories on lesbians, 98, 99
Publishers Distributing Corporation, 10,
        168
Pushover, 144

Quigley, Martin J., 13–15, 34
Quillan, Joseph, 36
Quillan, Veronica "Ronnie," 129
    Arnaz's philandering and, 55, *56*, 173–4
    as *Confidential* tipster, 36–8, 58, 63,
        80, 98, 173–4, 176
    and Hollywood vs. *Confidential*,
        172–4, 176
    and stories on homosexuals, 80

Ray, Johnnie, 80
Ritzi, William (Bill), 170–1, 174, 176,
        182, 184, 187

RKO, 34–5, 116
Roach, Hal, 68
Rogers, Ginger, 128, *130*
Roosevelt, Eleanor, 59, 131–2
Roosevelt, Franklin, 50, 132
Ross, Daniel, 184
Ross, Florence Kotz, 139
Roxy, 20
Rubinstein, Serge, 120
Rubirosa, Porfirio, 76
Ruditsky, Barney, 137–40
Rushmore, Frances McCoy, 53, 135, 163,
        180–1, 188–9, *190*
Rushmore, Howard, 57–60, 81, 98, 108,
        129–35, 152–4, 187–9
    alcoholism of, 132, 163, 180
    on Arnaz's philandering, 55, 57
    childhood of, 48, 134
    Confidential criticized by, 58, 129, 154
    Confidential's audience and, 153–4
    Crawford story and, 58, 152
    death of, 189, *190*
    departure from *Confidential* of, 134–5,
        163
    disappearance of, 129–30
    finances of, 48–51, 53, 60, 134, 180,
        188
    Gone With the Wind reviewed by, 49,
        51–2
    Harrison's conflicts with, 58, 129,
        131–4, *132*, 189
    Harrison's recruitment of, 25, 59–60
    Hollywood visits of, 63–4
    and Hollywood vs. *Confidential*,
        172–4, 176, 180, 187
    love life of, 51, 53, 133, 135, 163,
        180–1, 188–9, *190*
    Oppenheimer story and, *46*, 47, 173
    physical appearance of, *132*, 134, 172
    politics of, 25, 36, 41–2, 47–53, *49*,
        58–60, 129–31, 133–4, 153, 163,
        180–1, 189

proposed story on Roosevelt of,
131–2
Winchell and, 23, 41–2, 47, 53,
59–60, 131
Rushmore, Rose, 135
Rushmore, Ruth Garvin, 51, 53, 180
Russia, 26–8
Ruta, Reggie, 107, 190–1

Sanders, Larry, 16
Satan in High Heels, 73, 75
Schaefer, Hal, 138–9
Schary, Dory, 124–5
Schenck, Joe, 4, 6, 8, 32, 112
Schiff, Dorothy, 59
Scott, Lizabeth, 95–6
    and accuracy of *Confidential*, 129
    Confidential sued by, 99, 122,
    124, 134
    film career of, 99–100
    lesbianism of, 98–100, 99, 122
Sea Chase, The, 87, 150
Selznick, David, 52–3
Seven Year Itch, The, 137–8
sex, sexuality, 3–5, 7, 10–11, 14–17, 67–8,
    77–8, 122, 154, 172–4, 183–4
    of Crawford, 152
    of Gardner, 67
    Harrison's girlie magazines and, 5,
        15–17, 27, 107, 115–16
    kinky desires and, 107
    of Lamarr, 11
    male virility and, 103–4, 156–7, 183
    of Monroe, 3–4, 136–7
    of Novak, 141–2, 144
    of O'Hara, 40, 159–61, 162,
        165, 183
    philandering and, 40, 54–7, 56, 57,
        127–9, 130, 131, 173–4, 176, 178
    see also homosexuality, homosexuals;
        lesbianism, lesbians; nudity, nudes
Shah of Iran, 37, 39, 175

Shouel, Stella, 176
Sieber, Maria Elisabeth, 97
Siegel, Bugsy, 17
Simpson, O. J., 10, 172
Sinatra, Frank, 90, 156–8, 180
    Davis's relationship with, 34, 71
    film career of, 71, 144
    Gardner's marriage to, 68, 69,
        71, 156
    and Hollywood vs. *Confidential*,
        171, 184
    sexual prowess of, 156–7
    Wrong Door Raid and, 137, 139–40,
        157–8
Sisk, John, 155
Skolsky, Sidney, 98
Slander, 161
Smith, Tucker, 90
Snyder, Ruth, 112
Soviet Union, 47–9, 51–2
    Oppenheimer story and, 44, 47
    Rushmore and, 48–9, 52, 59
Star Machine, The (Basinger), 128
Steele, Alfred, 151–2, 153
Sterner, Jim, 48–51, 53, 189
Stevenson, Adlai, 9, 81
Stevenson, Ellen, 81
Stevenson, Venetia, 88
Stewart, Sheila, 136–8
Stork Club, 25, 53, 107–8, 188
Stork Club Incident, 19–23, 21
Strickling, Howard, 114
Studin, Dan, 15, 108, 168
Studin, Helen Harrison, 15, 28, 108–9,
    168, 170, 187–8, 191
suicide, suicides, 135, 175, 180–1
    of Forrestal, 130
    of Rushmore, 189, 190
    of Tatlock, 43, 46
Sullivan, Ed, 13, 22
Supreme Court, U.S., 35, 118
Sutton, Willie, 81–2

Tatlock, Jean S., 43–7, *46*
television, 7–8, 23–4, 36–7, 54, 106, 122, 154, 172
  Calhoun's criminal past and, 84
  competition between film industry and, 8, 36, 116, 118
  Confidential's legacy and, 191
  Winchell's appearances on, 24, *24*
Terry, Dan, 78, 177
Thomas, J. Parnell, 10, 35–6
Time, 44, 63, 87, 118, 161
  Confidential's tipsters and, 36–7
  and publicity on Novak, 144–5
Tipoff, 163, 173
Tobias, Edith Harrison "Ida," 15, 28, 108, 168, 170, 187–8, 191
Todd, Mike, 109, 171, 176
Tolson, Clyde, 130
Topping, Bob, 147–8, *149*
Trujillo, Rafael, 105–6, 144, 154
Trujillo, Ramfis, 144
Turner, Lana, 32, 147–50, 152, 156, 171, 176
  film career of, 149–50, *149*
  hit by Topping, 147–8, *149*
  physical appearance of, 147
Tuton, Robert, 176
TWA, 179
Twentieth Century–Fox, 34, 116, 150
  Gable and, 112
  Monroe and, 3, 5–6, 8

Uncensored, 116, 163, 173, 188
Underwood, Agnes, 64, 173
United Air Lines, 179

Vertigo, 145
Villa Capri, 139

Waldoff, Claire, 96
Walker, Herbert V., 170–1, 174, 183, 187

Wallace, Mike, 106
Wallis, Hal, 99
Wall Street Journal, 114–15
Warner, Jack, 13, 89–90, *89*
Warner Bros., 34–5, 87, 116
Watson, Robert, 83
Wayne, John, 7, 104–5, *106*
Wechsler, James, 22, 59, 131
Weldy, Richard, 104–6, *106*
Welles, Orson, 31, 37, 39, 63
Welles, Rebecca, 30–2, 33
West, Mae, 162–3, 175, 177, 182–4
Whisper, 5, 15, 115–16, 168, 187
White, Chalky, 175, 177, 184
White, Walter, 19
white lists, 118–19
Williams, Edward Bennett, 125
Willson, Henry, 83, *86*, 87
Wilson, Earl, 87, 144
Wilson, Marie, 176
Wilson, Theo, 174
Winchell, Walter, 13, 22–5, 188, 190
  Confidential promoted by, *21*, 23–5, *24*
  Confidential's attacks on enemies of, 24–5, *24*, 47
  Rushmore and, 23, 41–2, 47, 53, 59–60, 131
  Stork Club Incident and, 19–20, *21*, 22–3
Wolfe, Tom, 18, 109, 190
World War II, 8, 10, 32, 35, 51, 79, 142
Writer's Yearbook, 154–5
Wrong Door Raid, *41*, 136–40
  investigations on, 157–8, 161
Wynn, Ed, 90–1
Wynn, Eve, 90–3, *92*, *93*
Wynn, Keenan, 90–3, *91*, *92*, *93*

Yellow Yap, 48

A NOTE ON THE TYPE

The text of this book was set in Electra, a typeface designed by W. A. Dwiggins (1880–1956). This face cannot be classified as either modern or old style. It is not based on any historical model, nor does it echo any particular period or style. It avoids the extreme contrasts between thick and thin elements that mark most modern faces, and it attempts to give a feeling of fluidity, power, and speed.

Composed by North Market Street Graphics
Lancaster, Pennsylvania

Printed and bound by Berryville Graphics
Berryville, Virginia

Designed by Virginia Tan